THE QUEER GOD

There are those who go to gay bars and salsa clubs with rosaries in their pockets, and who make camp chapels of their living rooms. Others enter churches with love letters hidden in their bags, because their need for God and their need for love refuse to fit into different compartments. But what goodness and righteousness can prevail if you are in love with someone whom you are ecclesiastically not supposed to love? Where is God in a salsa bar?

The Queer God introduces a new theology from the margins of sexual deviance and economic exclusion. Its chapters on Bisexual Theology, Sadean holiness, gay worship in Brazil and Queer sainthood mark the search for a different face of God – the Queer God who challenges the oppressive powers of heterosexual orthodoxy, whiteness and global capitalism. Inspired by the transgressive spaces of Latin American spirituality, where the experiences of slum children merge with Queer interpretations of grace and holiness, *The Queer God* seeks to liberate God from the closet of traditional Christian thought, and to embrace God's part in the lives of gays, lesbians and the poor.

Only a theology that dares to be radical can show us the presence of God in our times. *The Queer God* creates a concept of holiness that overcomes sexual and colonial prejudices and shows how Queer Theology is ultimately the search for God's own deliverance. Using Liberation Theology and Queer Theory, it exposes the sexual roots that underlie all theology, and takes the search for God to new depths of social and sexual exclusion.

Marcella Althaus-Reid is Senior Lecturer in Christian Ethics and Practical Theology at the University of Edinburgh. She is the author of *Indecent Theology*, also published by Routledge.

Este libro esta dedicado a todos mis amigos y amores y para todos aquellos que en la vida andan como yo, 'sueltos y sin vacunar', buscando a Dios en medio de amores, amoríos y tántas soledades.

THE QUEER GOD

Marcella Althaus-Reid

Routledge
Taylor & Francis Group

LONDON AND NEW YORK

First published 2003
by Routledge
2 Park Square, Milton Park, Abingdon, Oxon, OX14 4RN

Simultaneously published in the USA and Canada
by Routledge
270 Madison Ave, New York NY 10016

Routledge is an imprint of the Taylor & Francis Group

Transferred to Digital Printing 2007

Typeset in Galliard by
GreenGate Publishing Services, Tonbridge, Kent

British Library Cataloguing in Publication Data
A catalogue record for this book is available from the British Library

Library of Congress Cataloging in Publication Data
A catalog record for this book has been requested

ISBN 0–415–32323–1 (hbk)
ISBN 0–415–32324–X (pbk)

CONTENTS

ACKNOWLEDGEMENTS

Behind every book there is a mixture of struggle and pleasure. There are also discussions with friends, disagreements, coincidences and laughter. It is in this sense that any book becomes sacramental, because in the process of being written it has gathered a community around a common table, where the exchange of ideas and stories shared has been a communion. Behind *The Queer God* there has been such a communion. I would like to express my gratitude to the group of friends and colleagues with whom I have been able to discuss theology, politics and love.

I would like to thank Alistair Kee and Gordon Reid for reading the early drafts and making constructive suggestions. Also Lisa Isherwood, Jeremy Carrette, Graham Ward, Timothy Gorringe, Elizabeth Stuart, Jack Thompson and José Miguez Bonino for their friendship and inspiring discussions on Queer Theory and liberation theology in the times of globalisation.

I would like especially to acknowledge the support and inspiration I received from the people who held the American Academy of Religion Women and Religion Section and Lesbian–Feminist Issues and Religion Group to discuss my previous book *Indecent Theology* in Denver, Colorado in 2001: Kwok Pui-Lan, Robert Goss, Mary Hunt, Lisa Isherwood, Emily Townes and Kathleen Sands.

I also need to mention Roberto González, Tom Hanks and Fabiana Tron from Buenos Aires and Carol Stobie and Lesley Orr Macdonald for being good friends.

Of course, the ideas represented in this book are my sole responsibility.

INTRODUCTION

Theology in Other contexts: on gay bars and a Queer God

The body does not lie, but the truths it tells us may seem strange ...

(Califia and Campbell 1997: 113)

Where are my Latin sisters
Still praying to Virgin Mary
Rosarios, Novenas, Promesas, despojos
¡Ave María purísima!
Forgive me for loving you
The way I do.

(Vega 1994: 240)

Salsa and theology

Where is the salsa in Contextual Theology? Suppose that, as in the poem from Brunilda Vega, someone tells you that Latinas go to the same bar that has been recommended to you. Suppose that you are feeling lonely and think that the world is not a loving place anymore. Then you decide to go to the bar after praying your novena to your saint, or to the Virgin Mary. Perhaps you are asking San Antonio for a lover and you know that at the door of the bar nobody checks for rosaries or religious stamps in your pocket. The same can be said when you are at the door of the church. They don't ask you for that old love letter that you still keep in your bag neither do they realise whose hands your loving hands like to hold. Now suppose that in your mind the church and the Latina bar somehow get mixed up with fragments of memories of the Nicene Creed and of a Christ who died of love for you some time ago contesting the fact that nobody else seems to be dying of love for you anymore. You are thinking about a religion of courage and you go to the salsa bar where a Latina may be friendly with you. But then, torn between love and rosaries, you may wonder what life would be if you were to love her. Remembering the poem from Vega, you know that in the end, you may pray for God's forgiveness: 'Forgive me for loving you the way I do'. But we need also forgiveness for loving God too.

What goodness and righteousness would prevail if you were now in love again, and in love with one whom you are (ecclesiastically) not supposed to love? Where would God be in a salsa bar? Where would the church stand on all this? And where would your Latina sisters be anyway doing their Contextual Theologies? Are they not loving each other on Sunday evenings, between the novenas? Why not?

There are many sexual dissenters whose theological community is made up of the gathering of those who go to gay bars with rosaries in their pockets, or who make camp chapels of their living rooms simply because there is a cry in their lives, and a theological cry, which refuses to fit life into different compartments. The question is *¿Va a haber amor?* (Will love prevail?). The search for love and for truth is a bodily one. Bodies in love add many theological insights to the quest for God and truth, but doing theology from other contexts needs to consider the experiences and reflection of Others too.

Many years ago, Liberation Theologies started to become suspicious of ideologically determined definitions such as what theology is, or who is a theologian. It was the time when liberationists would say that the theologian was a factory worker, or a miner trying to discern the presence of God in a politically and economically oppressed community. It did not occur to them at that time that it was necessary to dismantle the sexual ideology of theology, and for theologians to come out from their closets and ground their theology in a praxis of intellectual, living honesty. God, meanwhile, was also kept hidden in God's own closet. Nobody thought about doing theology in gay bars, although gay bars are full of theologians. Women theologians recorded reflections amongst the poor, heterosexual women of Latin America but never went to salsa bars. The point is that the understanding that arose in Liberation Theology of the possibility of doing a theology for social transformation should also lead us on the journey of re-discovering (or unveiling) the true face of God as part of the Queer theological quest. Far from leading people towards nihilism, Queer Theology has taken Contextual Theologies to new limits and thinking of alternatives which are sexual and political too.

The Queer God

The Queer God is a book about this re-discovery of God outside the heterosexual ideology which has been prevalent in the history of Christianity and theology. In order to do that, it is necessary to facilitate the coming out of the closet of God by a process of theological queering. By theological queering, we mean the deliberate questioning of heterosexual experience and thinking which has shaped our understanding of theology, the role of the theologian and hermeneutics. That process requires from us not only honesty and courage, but also a critical engagement with Queer Theory, non-heterosexual and critical Heterosexual Theology. It also requires us to come clean about our experiences, which in some way or other always seem destined to fall outside the normative sexual ideology of theology. Further than this, it requires us to read *a contramano* (against the grain) issues of heterosexual institutions such as marriage and the subversiveness of popular spirituality in many non-Western cultures. It is from there that not only do we rediscover the face of the Queer God, but also find our relationship with God challenged and see emerging new reflections on holiness and on Christianity.

This book is divided into two parts. The first part, 'Queering theology', is about issues of identity in Queer Theology. It is necessary to reflect on the vocation and also the task of Queer Theology and its sources. This involves exploring what can broadly be called the libertine hermeneutical circle which comes from the Marquis de Sade and Georges Bataille. This libertine hermeneutical circle will help us to understand and unravel a Christian God who comes to us in drag, in the form of the Trinity. It is in the Trinity that gods and people, and also spirits of theologically dubious sexual orientation such as the Holy Spirit (claimed both by men and women), can interrelate meaningfully outside the restrictiveness of the heterosexual parental imaginary.

'Queering Hermeneutics' continues with the use of the libertine hermeneutical circle in an intertextual reading. The proposal is to read the Scriptures together with the work of Pierre Klossowski as well as fiction writers such as Kathy Acker from the United States, Hilda Hilst from Brazil and Alejandra Pizarnick and Federico Andahazi from Argentina. Searching for a way to read the Bible which will displace its heterosexual core in a deconstructionist fashion, the hermeneutical proposal is a libertine one. That is to say, it displaces the reader of the Bible to bedrooms, dungeons and other unusual locations which will enable her to have different and embodied points of view and perspectives. I have been inspired in this by the work of the late Kathy Acker, who in her writing has used displacement techniques which also involve intertextuality. In that way, she has been able to create new meanings through putting into dialogue more than one already existing text – reading, for instance, Charles Dickens and a writer on the Algerian war, or juxtaposing Pier Paolo Passolini's account of his own death with Shakespeare's *Romeo and Juliet* and the works of the Brontë sisters.[1] Therefore, I have been using Acker's approach as a way to read the Bible from the dungeons of Sade's novels, and from the dislocation that writers such as Andahazi (the controversial Argentinian author of *The Anatomist*) and Hilda Hirst, the Queer writer from Brazil, can bring to our perspectives. The question to be pursued in Queer hermeneutics is one of transcendence. Can we displace transcendental heterosexual ways of reading the Scriptures by sexually disconcerting the bodily logic of positioning the reader in the Scriptures?

Part I ends with a chapter reflecting on queering the economy of God's exchange rate mechanism, where through reading Bataille's novel *Madame Edwarda* and Andahazi's *The Anatomist*, we explore issues of God's transcendence and the question of prostitution such as in God the Whore. The biblical text of the story of Rahab (Joshua 2) brings us to a final discussion on queering sexuality, in the context of colonialism, divine transcendence and bisexual identity.

The second part of the book, 'Queer promiscuities', follows the outlined strategy of sexually disconcerting theology by exploring the category of promiscuity by grounding it in the context of Latin American cultures. If God is manifested in history, and more specifically in the events of liberation in human history, then we need to find God's face in loving relationships outside the borders of decent theology, and in the context of the Other as the poor and excluded. Promiscuity as a Queer theological category makes us think about love and also economics. Promiscuities show the strength of love amongst the different patterns of loving relationships in different cultures in Latin America, but also the reality of the excluded. They also help us to understand that popular spiritualities are not only sexually dissenting, but sometimes they elaborate a complex symbology intended to help people to cope with the aberrancies of heterosexual systems. Such is the reality of Moya, a Peruvian 'bisexual town', or the subversive and promiscuous understandings of the Holy Spirit amongst women who have extramarital love affairs in La Puna.

Finally, we reflect on demonologies, as the art of being rebellious loving spirits, and the consequences of such transgressions for the understanding of 'Queer Holiness' in the context of globalisation. The reflection on concrete, Queer experience as the starting point for examining holiness needs to be part of a project of community-based and political holiness. By theologically de-colonising categories such as limbo and hell, and finding their potential subversiveness, spaces of holiness can also be claimed as Queer.

The Queer God will then create a new space for a theological dialogue for and from heterosexual dissenters. Queering theology, the theological task and God is all part of a coming out of the closet for Christianity which is no longer simply one option among others, nor is it a sidetrack outside what has been regarded as the highroad of classical theology. Queering theology is the path of God's own liberation, apart from ours, and as such it constitutes a critique to what Heterosexual Theology has done with God by closeting the divine. In theology, as in love, this quest is a spiritual one, which requires continuing to the Other side of theology, and the Other side of God. That is the side to which I and many of my compatriots have been consigned for centuries, condemned to be permanent aliens for Christianity, for our countries, and for our families.

The Other side is in reality a pervasive space made up of innumerable Queer religious and political diasporas, and a space to be considered when doing contextual Queer Theology. The Good News is that at that edge, still talking about the thousands of symbolic Nicaraguas present in every anti-capitalist demonstration, or the voices of people who stand up to claim the right to live in an alternative economic and spiritual system to the totalitarian globalisation which has pervaded our lives, there is God. Also, claiming against the destruction of nations and individual lives, including the environment, are people still talking about gay or bisexual rights and orgasms and God. The God who has come out, tired perhaps of being pushed to the edge by hegemonic sexual systems in theology, has made God's sanctuary on the Other side. Our task and our joy is to find or simply recognise God sitting amongst us, at any time, in any gay bar or in the home of a camp friend who decorates her living room as a chapel and doesn't leave her rosary at home when going to a salsa bar.

4

Part I

QUEERING THEOLOGY

1

KNEELING

Deviant theologians

I live in constant negotiations
Trying to resolve
The border conflicts raging inside me

(Judit 1994: 218)

By which traditions of impropriety and stubborn tendencies to per/versity (that
Queer, persistent trend to find different versions or alternative interpretations)
does 'queering' as a theological vocation start in us? As Indecent theologians[1] we
do not need to accept a claim to neutrality but maintain a responsible position in
the divine cartography of pleasure and desire. Therefore, the question about who
is a theologian may find an answer in a reflection on issues of relationships, love
and pleasure, in tension or negotiation with the fixed borders of Heterosexual
Theology. An Indecent theologian is a theologian who has learned to survive
with several passports. She is a Christian and a Queer theologian or a minister
and a Queer lover who cannot be shown in public and she is a woman and a
worker: the list of the game of multiple representations extends. A Queer theologian has many passports because she is a theologian in diaspora, that is, a
theologian who explores at the crossroads of Christianity issues of self-identity
and the identity of her community, which are related to sexuality, race, culture
and poverty. In Queer theologies there is, however, a primordial or first diaspora
to acknowledge. It is what we can call the first and most important of the passports she needs to acquire. We are referring here to the diaspora from love or
what Benigno Sánchez-Eppler and Cindy Patton have called the journey 'with a
passport out of Eden' (Patton and Sánchez-Eppler 2000: 1). That journey
becomes a theological space that Patton and Sánchez-Eppler identify as the primordial and complex space of exclusion in the narratives of Genesis. It is
interesting to notice how Genesis has been seen as a text which carries heavy
responsibilities for the subjugation of women and also of nature. The traditional
reading of Genesis has made of mastery and dominion over women and nature a
theological virtue.[2] Even in the more benign readings concerned with the concept of stewardship in relation to the environment, that fundamental colonial
motion of patriarchy persists in a relation which makes of the Other a permanent

minor in need of mastery and control. However, for Patton and Sánchez-Eppler, a deeper sexual reading of Genesis may show us that beyond issues of heterosexual control of men over women, there is a more profound dynamics, a divine dynamics which creates mechanisms of sexual exclusion, one in which homosexuality (represented in this reading by Adam and God's particular loving friendship) is in reality what ends in the exclusion from Eden. That may be the utopian beginning of the Queer diaspora, starting with Other sexualities expelled from the Eden of loving, godly relationships and exiled in lands of heterosexuality. That primordial sexual diaspora, which comes from the displaced love between a man and a God-man, may be the reason why Queer theologies are usually biographical theologies. One needs to follow that diasporic movement which allows us to understand the paths crossed, and the ways in which theological identities are still challenged, transformed, retracted and disguised in Christianity. Queer theologies are tactical theologies, 'using tactical queerness to cruise places occupied by normative straightness' (Patton and Sánchez-Eppler 2000: 14). Queer theologies go into diasporas by using tactics of temporary occupation; disruptive practices which are not necessarily to be repeated, and reflections which aim to be disconcerting.[3] At the bottom line of Queer theologies, there are biographies of sexual migrants, testimonies of real lives in rebellions made of love, pleasure and suffering. On this point, paraphrasing Kosofsky Sedgwick, we may say that Queer theologies are those characterised by an 'I' because the Queer discourse only becomes such when done in the first person (Sedgwick 1994: 11). Queer Theology is, then, a first person theology: diasporic, self-disclosing, autobiographical and responsible for its own words.

Therefore, to reflect on issues of the theologian's identity and ways of doing a Queer Theology, we need to begin a reflection intimately linked to a God-talk on loving and pleasurable relationships. This is one of the most important challenges that Queer theologies bring to theology in the twenty-first century: the challenge of a theology where sexuality and loving relationships are not only important theological issues but experiences which un-shape Totalitarian Theology (T-Theology)[4] while re-shaping the theologians. The point is that in the process of queering theology, this intricate relationship between theology and the theologians cannot be pulled apart without losing something in the process. What queering theologies may lose in the process gives space for new, even if sometimes contingent, formations. For instance, Queer theologies do not disregard church traditions. However, the process of queering may turn them upside down, or submit them to collage-style processes by adding and highlighting from them precisely those elements which did not fit well in the construction of the church tradition and thus were excluded or ignored. Most of the work done around queering church traditions has been related to re-positioning the Queer, Indecent subject in theology and to do that by giving testimonies of other traditions (or the traditions of the Other) concerning love and sexuality.[5]

To queer theological sources in church traditions could simply mean to gather together all the dispersed fragments of love and sexual identity struggles in people's lives, and add to that the struggle for spaces of freedom and social justice which constitute the real Queer traditions of the church, which are characterised by processes of sexual ideological disruption in Christianity, and not by its continuity. Disruption is our diaspora. Disruptive practices of love and sexuality have made of the Queer community a continuum and given us a sense of belonging together with our struggles for identity which are based on difference and processes of transformations.

For bigamy and God: a tradition of sexual theological rebellion

Where can we find such traditions of sexual theological disruption in the church? Everywhere. If I go, for instance, to the history of the church in Latin America, and decide to queer the history of the Jesuitic Missions, I may find that, in many ways, the missions were more sexual than Christian. The point is that Christianity came to my continent more as a sexual project concerned with the praxis of specific heterosexual understandings elevated to a sacred level (as most ideologies are), than to explain Christian theology. However, if Christian theology was difficult to explain to nations of very different cosmological backgrounds, it was more difficult to explain European sexuality to them. In the complex mixture of oppression that the original nations in South America suffered under the missions (Jesuitic or Franciscan, for instance), their theological revolt was also a political and a sexual one.[6] Some Jesuitic missions during the sixteenth century held civil and criminal courts, where sexual disobedience to the Christian European norms was punishable (Wiesner-Hanks 2000: 153). However, the elders called people to rebel against the conquistadors' oppression. Amongst those recorded, there are documents which testify that the religious and political leaders of the *Nahua* nations questioned the sexual understanding of Christian marriage and that in 1680, the revolt of the Pueblo Indians started a call to bigamy and concubinage as a way to return to their own traditions and understanding of sex and society (Wiesner-Hanks 2000: 158). This is an important part of the theological tradition of sexual disruption, for the call to fidelity, to God and bigamy started in Latin America as a result of political and economic oppression. It is interesting to notice that those people understood what today is still not clear, that is, that by disrupting the sexual ideology of Christianity, a whole political project which works against people's lives is also disrupted. Their call was not to ignore the Virgin Mary, because at that point to believe or disbelieve in the Virgin Mary was irrelevant to their struggle, but to call for Other sexual praxis.

This represents a biographical tradition of sexual disruption in the church, because it concerns people's lives, love stories and the suffering of the imposed Christian marriage by the state and the church terrorism of the time. As homosexuality and cross-dressing was also part of many Original Nations' sexualities, one may consider that they were also objects of political subversion at the time, even if specific memories may have been lost. If some nation's peoples stood up for their different understanding of sexuality in relationship to marriage, they may have also stood up for homosexuality and cross-dressing. These rescued memories which become new sources of church traditions from which we would like to reflect in theology may encourage us also to share our own stories of sexual disruption. Queer traditions are made of strange alliances of memories of discontinuity and disorder, shared by communities of people with pride and resistance. The gathering and reflection on church traditions which marks the beginning of disruption is a popular project which redefines the role of the Sexual Theologian, and helps us to discern the future.

The memories of disruption which are going to become our source of contemporary rebellious sexual traditions are not only the Stonewall riots or the memory of the courageous human rights actions by Peter Tatchell or the march in Buenos Aires organised by Lesbianas a la Vista (Lesbians in View) a few years ago, where women walked with their names written on a piece of cardboard to show that they were proud women with nothing to hide. Some even wrote their national identity card numbers under their names, an act that, in view of the recent past of dictatorial regimes in Argentina, displays a kind of political courage which might be difficult to parallel in Great Britain at this time. Apart from these stories of memorable pride marches, we also have our own stories, significant enough for us and our communities to add. That is, stories to relate by means of making alliances between Queer-biographical theology and church traditions. The story I would like to queer is related to the church tradition of kneeling, specifically to kneeling in front of a priest's penis. It was in the city of Rosario, Argentina in the 1960s, as part of the liturgy of confession and first communion, that I knelt down in what was part of a normative thing to do for Catholics. And yet it was transgressive in its own way, because a mistake I committed on kneeling generated a flow of gender and sexuality, linking them to issues of identity; that is, the identity of women kneeling in front of priests, and of priests, and God. I was going to take my first communion and therefore I was instructed to confess to the priest who was in charge of the catechesis in his parish to which my grandmother belonged at that time. For ritualistic purposes, boys were expected to kneel in front of the priest, who used to sit on a low chair for the purpose of children's confession. Girls were expected to kneel also, but at the right side of the priest. Children did not use the confession box. In retrospect, one could see the liturgical symbolic geography relating to gender and sexual positions in the church's structures starting to be organised, precociously, amongst that group of eight-year-old children, gathering around the position of the priest's penis. That was also part of the catechesis, a recognition of positions concerning the ubiquitous divine phallus. As I recall it now, insecure about what I was expected to do, I decided to follow what my (male) cousins did and instead of kneeling at the right side of the priest's chair I assumed the position straight opposite to the priest's genitalia. I refused to move from there, and that earned me a rebuke first by the priest himself, and then by God Almighty as I needed to add that rebellious incident to my confession. I ended by confessing my act of kneeling at the priest's penis to the same priest but also, without knowing it, I somehow became by default a confessor in myself.

The ritual of kneeling has several interesting elements for us to consider. First, the dialectics present at the liturgy of the confessor/confessant or the 'who is who' of the church order; second, the sexual geography of the ritual, which may be considered at the base of heterosexual relationships and marriage. For instance, in the history of sexual rebellions in Latin America, confessional kneelings were important to disorganise the extensive practice of sodomy amongst homosexual and heterosexual people alike. However, in a way, we may say that the confessant also transgresses what she confesses, and what she confesses is the reconfiguration of space, sex, gender and politics in the church. Kneeling is troublesome and it has a theological referent in the church's also troubled waters of sexuality and power. A whole symbolic sexual order is obviously manifested in kneelings as positions of subordination and sites of possible homo- and hetero- seductions, because these are theologically distributed around the axis of the priesthood's male genitalia. The priest's penis carries the sacred connotations of the phallus as a transcendental signifier of the theological discourses to everyday Christianity, and kneeling is a liturgical positing designed to centralise and highlight this.[7] Queering theology and the theologian is closely related to queering love and God. Doing a theological reflection which takes as a point of departure the genital axis of T-Theology, confronts us with a geography in which we need to make the distinction between events and the ordering of knowledge. Following Elspeth Probyn in her distinction between 'locale and location' we may distinguish here between the locale as a place (for instance the marital home or the theologically adjudicated places of women in liturgical acts) and the location (the ordering of knowledge; its logical sequence from, for instance, Western heterosexuality) (Probyn 1990: 178). Through a process of Queer localising – not globalising – of our reflections we are confronted with both elements and their complex set of relationships. The locale is the event of kneeling and the special configuration of it; it is also the affectivity model (or lack of it) presented in the church. The location is theology as a type of knowledge which orders these spaces of determination for the theologian and for her love life. Probyn's proposal here is useful for us. She asks for more work to be done in the area of the knowledge which fixes and makes subaltern units of the locale (Probyn 1990: 186).

I have said elsewhere that theology is a sexual act, and therefore to reflect on the theologian, her vocation, role and risks means to take seriously the changing geographies of Christian kneelings, and confessionary movements, and how they relate to positions of affection in Christian theology. In this way, queering who the theologian is, and what is her role and vocation is a reflection on locations, closely linked to the locale's events and spaces made of our concrete and sensual actions. As an illustration of this, it would be useful to remember that when the then Cardinal Archbishop of Santo Domingo met a group of priests and theologians of liberation to discuss issues of marriage and celibacy in the church, he commented afterward:

11

These are frustrated men; they are embittered and full of stupidity ... Let them leave [the church] as soon as possible. In my personal opinion, I believe that once they get married and their women ill treat them, they will become tame men.

(Pérez Aguirre 1994: 40)

Jon Sobrino commented on this as a 'sad anecdote', in which women (absent in the church discourse) are represented in the context of marriage as abusive of men (Sobrino 1992: 752). In this, the locale and the location of women in the church and in their heterosexually adjudicated roles become almost indistinguishable and sinister.

But the theologian is, after all, a material girl and lives in a material world. Those sensual actions we referred to are sexual and political ones, and they imply sensuous, material positions around hierarchical church models constructed from the axis of priests' penises. They are economic and political and organisational models which organise love, finances, God and theology based on their historical positional understandings. The materiality of this reflection extends beyond the flow of desire analysed in Feminist Theology, which does not consider pleasure as the site of theological reflection. Pleasure is locale; desire is a location. Desire, as an abstract concept, matches the kneeling at the priest's penis in the sense that, following Butler, we are here in the terrain of separating penises from phalluses, even if the penis is the prototype of transcendence and divine transcendence (Butler 1993: 103). As Lacan has already said, the Father is more present when he is more absent (Marini 1992: 172). That absence is transcendental, but only in dependence with its penis's model.

The point for us to consider is that if we are going to take a position in the small circuit of dualistic and heavily hierarchical understandings of the behaviour of sacramental bodies and souls, then we could start by asking how the theologian should be located, that is, by considering how a theologian is positioned and also, how we can consider the theologian as an event, independently of her doing theology. As theology has been developed as a (closeted) heterosexual art, it works quite naturally in secretive spaces which tend to be violent and dyadic. For instance, the kneelings occur in the liturgical sites of the dyads of God and humanity; Father God and Son God; Creator and created. Even the Trinity has become a (dyad,) independently of mathematics, in this short-circuiting of amorous relational patterns of heterosexual ideologies in theology. In that short-circuit, violence occurs by death, by abortions. Life is prevented and excluded.

Troubling dyads in confessionaries

Have you obeyed? Have you scandalised anybody? ... Have you been in bad company? Have you read indecent novels or magazines? Have you dressed in an indecent way? Do you keep *dangerous liaisons* (*relaciones peligrosas*), especially with people of the opposite sex? ... If you are married: Have you been faithful? ... If you are a worker: Do you create problems by encouraging fellow workers to complain?

(Azcarate 1960: 139–40; my italics)

Hello my name is Father Tim ...

(Sheryl Crow, 'Sweet Rosalyn', song)

Even if the locale is clear, it is the theologian herself who needs to be considered as an event, that is, the theologian represents a certain kind of relationship related to her particular position in relation to the church and to Christianity. The event is a coming out of a significative anarchism against dyads. It must be said that nobody should consider heterosexuality as a particular type of demonic sexuality, but its hegemonic construction is. As an ideology, heterosexuality is defined by its own secretiveness between twos; this is the logic of husband and mistress; or husband and boyfriend; or wife with her beloved: their secret cannot be shared with the spouse. That quality of secretiveness has been passed to theological reflections when theology has functioned as a mere sexual ideology based on dyads. Has the theologian as a confessor and confessant the ability to disturb this? She has if we consider that confession may be considered positively, as a Queer thing both in the sense of, following Kosofsky Sedgwick, being a transitive experience or a *troublant* declaration (Sedgwick 1994: xii) cutting across communication with elements of sexual difference and restless positions. The Queer theologian, like any other person whose reflections come transitively (in the Freirean sense of a potentially transgressive and creative process) from some closet of her soul, is also wanted for confession. This happens because the theological art, like any other sexual art, is dependent on the persuasive power of sexual re-representations, achieved in positional confessions which are acts also of re/membering for dis/membering purposes when we realise that the past we confess is disqualifying what we are. Is the Queer theologian amongst the absolvers or the absolved of the sins of theology as ideology? Is she sitting inside the confessionary or does she prefer to kneel down on the cold church tiles? Opposite to what? Arguing with the phallus, or glancing at it from a safe distance? We can start by asking Queer things, for instance, related to what the church wants the theologian to confess and what God needs for her to say openly: Does she keep dangerous relations? Did she ever go on strike? What has she not confessed yet? In theology, complicated questions usually require far more complicated answers. In this case, any answers we attempt to give would, apparently, depend merely on a discourse on morality and ethics from a chosen Christian perspective. By that we mean the theological disquisition on responsibility, linked to confession in the discourse of Christian ethics. The theologian is a confessor because she gives an account of a Christian belief which can be located in the combination of some theological *episteme*, providing some challenges and some continuation through different epochs. The theologian confesses the past by discerning the transmission of beliefs while expecting two things to happen. The first is that a continuation of the re-representation of a theological praxis will happen again. This is a belief in resurrections, and needs to be understood in the sense that every theological community deals with and elaborates on the memory of significative events which provide encouragement for new Christian action and reflection, and also forgiveness for the oppressive theological past. Second, and in relation to this last point, is that the theologian expects this encounter of communities from past and present to create a new understanding by the act of resignifying the past in a sharing of memories of belief in itself. However, those memories may need to be resignified to be forgiven in the act of confession, as the sharing of memories in the confessionary is a forceful act, not anymore spontaneous but responsive, in the sense of responding according to a provided theological expectation. Elspeth Probyn, in her analysis of Jeanette Winterson's novel *Oranges are not the Only Fruit* (Winterson 1990), shows how disabling memories can be for a person whose identity is precisely in struggle with a past and whose whole process of identity formation is made by disruptions and not continuations (Probyn 1996: 112). The past may just be saying what we are not, while having a role in disauthorising the process that we have become.

This confessional link between communities of Christian praxis basically constitutes the role of the theologian, for it is in the dynamics of 'retroaction' – in which Levinas saw the role of forgiveness – that the confession act is rooted (Gibbs 2000: 350). Obviously there is a sexual genealogy and epistemic construction of the Christian ethics of confession. Foucault has already unveiled, in his hermeneutics of desire, issues related to the sexual ethical embodiment of confession in relation to docility and other mechanisms of oppression internalised by the act of representing the story and the identity of the Other in historical Christian confession. That unveils for us a crucial point, related to what Butler calls the localisation of the heterosexual matrix (Butler 1990: 12), localised in our understanding of confession and in the role of the theologian as confessor. This matters because Christian ethics is a discourse concerned with the positioning of bodies and the re-configurations of the individual and collective praxis of bodies dealing with bodies, and with the body of the sacred itself. Remembering that our task is the Queering of theology, we should now be able to embark on the road of per/versions to start to think about the theologian and her praxis outside dyadic constructions, and to reflect on her vocation, role and risks, in transit from closeted theology.

Every theologian is bisexual

> Let us return to the sign 'queer' in an effort to demonstrate the political potential of this model.
>
> (Namaste 1996: 83)

The confessor/confessant dynamic represents, as we have already said, a theological dyad. Queer theologians are called to be suspicious of them and to come out in an almost sacrificial way, for theological (and especially Queer) confessions are costly and demanding, and cannot be taken lightly. Why? Because even if we understand the role of the theologian as a complementary mixture of confessor and confessant we still struggle for limited choices. This happens because we declare the past for forgiveness but also absolve it because theologians belong to the same community of Christians which re-presents the theological discourse. These are the choices and reconciliations offered to us by Heterosexual Theology as ideology, which conform the web of location of theology. One per/version of this is to do a theology choosing a pink (feminist) or blue (masculinist) theological standpoint, without disabling the heterosexual dyad. There have been instances when gay or lesbian theologies also did not discuss the instability of non-heterosexual identities, then producing a 'blue with touches of pink theology'. What happens then if the theologian does not refuse to produce an unstable theology, even if she is under the current threats of metaphysical and material (academic or church based) electrocutions? The Queer theologian who keeps involved in the hard problematising of her role and vocation, finds the way forward lies in her commitment to pervert Christian theology, by the disrobing of what underwear is left in the standing of the theologian. That way is also a way of electrocutions sometimes, and electrocutions become a part of life. It has happened and still does, in many forms of Liberation Theologies where the risks of theological honesty are heavy. One way to electrocution is to say, clearly and frankly, that although churches and theology have been ignoring this at their peril, the theologian's flow of desire, in its purest form, is a critical bisexual desire. This is obviously not a question of an individual sexual identity, but of an epistemological identity which considers bisexuality critically, that is, not assuming that bisexuality *per se* is a liberative force unless there is a critical reflection of its relation to other sexualities. What we are trying to say here is that independently of the sexual identity of the theologian as an individual, theology is the art of a critical bisexual action and reflection on God and humanity. The interesting thing about this is that a bisexual critical epistemology could be considered one of the main challenges for any theologian in the way that we are not including 'the bisexual theologian' in the discussion (as a new and interesting perspective to add to what is already done), but more important than this, we are saying that it is only bisexuality which displaces and causes tension to the established heterosexual dyad implicit in the theologian's identity and task. For example in theology the dyad of the heterosexual family is not so different from the one of confessor and confessant before subversion. That should not surprise us because the theologian as a heterosexual species is in itself a reminder of the provisional status of any confession of faith, or declaration of fidelity to sexual positions in Christianity. The bisexual theologian (or the theologian who thinks critically bi- or polyamorously) is in the unique position of acting and reflecting in a theological praxis based on two basic elements: first, the relation to the closet, and second, the way of transcendence via the instability of God, sexual identity and humanity.

We are now saying that irrespective of her chosen sexual identity, in the act of doing theology the theologian's vocation is towards what we have called a critical bisexuality. Moreover, we may be able to speculate that the liturgical location of confession should have made of theologians bisexual practitioners. Let us consider this last point in detail. Theologians are only able to confess their faith (or discernments of belief) in their communities by publicly declaring faith in certain relationships: for instance, a belief in certain patterns of relationships, such as the case of the Trinity. By believing in the Trinity, we mean that there is an acceptance that theology is not a symmetrical art (a dyadic, one-to-one relationship with issues of dogma and tradition) but is a twisted one, following a path of reflections marked by disruptions of dyads or scandals. For we are not saying that God is one, manifested in a father–son relationship, but that God is a relationship of three. This is a disruption of *scandalous* or little stones on the pavements of theology (to use a biblical metaphor) which are an important part of the presence of the 'third' in theology as a process. Apart from that, Queer relationships provide the encounter of the third type in theology *par excellence*. For instance, the confessionary scene is made by an encounter of the third, or the encounter with the Queer, because the dyad is disrupted by someone else who confesses a difference, or non-alignment with herself. 'There is no Other of the Other', says Lacan (Marini 1992: 178) referring to the symbolic Father, but if we use this concept for God, we could say that Queer Theology has restored the Other in the Other; that is, it has proved that God has a back. It is God who confesses God's primordial non-alignment with Godself, that is, God's back is made of difference.

Because critical bisexuality means here to think in a triadic way, it is not complementary but permutative, thus providing a location of non-rigid exchanges amongst people's actions and reflections, as a base for a theology rooted in more genuine (and diverse) dialogues. The point is that because bisexual desires do not relate indiscriminately to any form of sexual identities, but only to some form of sexual identities which heterosexuality cannot necessarily grasp, and in a fluctuating basis, theology as a critical bisexual art can still be thematic and particular. Perhaps the point in Bisexual Theology is that the instability of the sexual construction of Christian ethics, the reading of the Scriptures and systematic theology becomes more obvious in their contextual and transitive processes of desire. That is the nature of the subversiveness in theology which lies at the core of a critical bisexual praxis. It is because bisexual desires cannot be pinned down in a stable or fixed way that the theological process differs. For a start, it may resemble minor earthquakes or tremors occurring through a life story at the points of reflection where the bisexual theologian introduces a metaphorical third person into the discourse. However, to think three is to think an exchange system, not a role-model system (as happens for instance in the heterosexual understanding of the Trinity). That is where Royce's idea of the 'social infinite' is useful to recall. In a triadic heterosexual relationship the three terms in relation are not meant to be interchangeable but specific to certain tasks (Gibbs 2000: 250). In this sense, the understanding which may go beyond the family model of two does not necessarily obliterate traces of discrepancy. Critical bisexual thinking may be closer to a way of thinking which could leave behind the complicity (and, we will add, secretiveness) of rigid dyads. The point is that theology is not a private matter and involves more than a domestic contractual act of two people.

A triadic Bisexual Theology has a third, undisclosed sexual component in the confessor/confessant model then. As a process, this may almost be represented as a body of knowledge, the body of the Queer Other in transit from closets while relating with other bodies in their own transits. Triads are more than three only if this flux exists. Using a Trinitarian example we can say that every Trinitarian divine person is related to other bodies who share their own particular closets while interchanging affections and economies with any other bodies of the Trinity, and in a location made up of different circumstantial contexts. The Queer theologian develops a Bisexual Theology by understanding this fluidity of thinking and by permanently introducing 'unsuitable' new partners in theology, which makes it difficult to fix – but this is precisely what allows changes of position and numbers in her confessor/confessant vocation.

By going critically bisexual, the theologian as confessor and confessant of faith needs to go beyond the theologically positioned dyadic family who historically represent the subjects of doing a theology, who take explicit bodily positions in relation to others and understand themselves according to these (Diprose 1994: 19). The two parts of this dyad need to become more than two, and also need to be contrasted with non-straight relations in order to provide theological acts with different practices of dialoguing and reflecting in communities. That may also involve the theological dialogue of different communities reflecting plurality more than homogeneity, for example leather S/M people with gay leather men who are not SMers; lesbian women of the sexual radicals inspired by people such as Pat Califia, Susie Bright and Tamsin Wilton with lesbians against pornography; or the work of the Roman Catholic liberationist Mary Grey with the Body Theology of Lisa Isherwood and the radical Sexual Theology of Jeremy Carrette. That may provide a more honest base for a new ecumenical movement of a radical type.

The ritual of confession is in itself significative theologically in this: it signifies positions of power but sexual positions too. For instance, the fact that there was a girl's way and a boy's way to confess in Argentina during the 1960s was part of the symbolics not only of kneeling in relation to the priest's genitalia in the church, but of the position of women in Argentinian society. The angle your body was positioned in relation to the priest's penis was also the angle you took in relation to the church's phallus and its authority. This was the distance which ruled your life in the Roman Catholic Church in Argentina, quite apart from the setting of the rules at an early stage concerning the alienation of bodies in their close encounter with priests. It was the distance and location of women in relation to authority too, and also of abuse. The epistemological underpinning of that theology of confession was located around two genitally defined and theologically threatening bodies of desire.

17

Docility: images of hetero-hell

What is closest to the image of hell in theology? According to the late Uruguayan theologian Juan Luis Segundo, it may be docility, although the answer he gave is somewhat more complex than that (Segundo 1997). It may be either a lack of choice, or on the contrary, it may be considered that one reaches hell by making a real option against God as a given. The mere fact that hell signifies a theological location for those who did have an option, as for instance a different sexual one, and the courage to take it up, is paradoxical. This paradox brings us to discuss issues of docility in theology.

According to Foucault's analysis, different societies need different bodies performing different things (Foucault 1980) and a whole Lacanian analysis could be elaborated on why boys in my country had to kneel in front of the priest's penis while girls didn't. However, hell was the lack of options which could fulfil the role of destabilising the whole theological basis of arguments by re-positioning bodies in different kneeling exercises. From another perspective, an option outside kneeling (or for the priest positioning his penis in another direction) was a path towards hell.

This tight body practice of kneeling gave way to different modes of docility and acceptance of the orders of society and church in my country. The Argentinian Misal that we quoted earlier homologated a body which read indecent magazines with one which went on strike; the bodies of those who did not contribute economically to the church, or were deaf during mass, were equal in this mathematics of grace to having more than one sexual partner at the same time (or in the case of Argentinian women, more than one sexual partner during her whole life). However, Foucault's theory of the effects of dominant moral codes goes far beyond the effects of creating docility amongst bodies. Dominant moral codes are far more subtle and dangerous because they constitute the embodied ethos (and ethics) of the people who follow them. This is an ethics that is a hermeneutics, because its goal and objectives move around the re-interpretation of bodies. A medical theological ethics, it performs a kind of cosmetic surgery to dissimilate bodies, in order to train and push them through selective performative praxis towards a confessed agreement. Such agreement has been based on the sexual action and reflections of a disciplined Christian body. The hermeneutics which are responsible for the self-induced formation of the body come, according to Foucault, from a dialectics of punishment and confession (Foucault 1977). Punishment is the violence to which bodies are subjected when contravening orders. Punishment is hell by indocility, or by an option when opting is not accepted, but confession is, following Paulo Freire, the art of internalised oppression not only by rejecting actions but also by disavowing the attitude of opting. That is in essence the concept of prescriptive behaviour in Freire's *Pedagogía del Oprimido* ['Pedagogy of the Oppressed'] (Freire 1979: 37). This is Foucault's ethical hermeneutics in a nutshell: by confessing, the subject allows itself to be re-presented and interpreted by an Other who has followed a similar pattern before. Confession is, therefore, the closest image we may have of hell. It is the true effect of sacred power; a colonial practice to observe mismatches in the symmetrical organisation of power in societies but also to measure the consequences of options. Is that what the theologian is supposed to confess, her desire for hell as an alternative and a right against a Sexual Theology behaving as an authoritarian ideology? Or an escape from prescriptive hetero-hells of love? In doing that, she can become a Queer confessant by queering the ongoing processes of representation by becoming suspicious and unfaithful. In that case, the Queer confessor starts doing theology by acknowledging her first longing, that is, the exile of her body. In the Bisexual theologian, the exile is infinite although not alienating. Critical Bisexual theologians produce a shift in the disciplinary systematisation of theological labour and domesticity by simply displacing what we can call the politics of mono-loving. How can we even envisage the role of the theologian if it is going to remain mono-faithful to one heterosexual, or lesbian or gay, or uncritically bi way of understanding? How can we start the task of interpretation (fundamental in the confessor/confessant role of the theologian) if it is not going to depart from the dyadic references, fatally bound to family formation based on two opposite sexes and desires? Moreover, desire in Queer Theology needs to give a place to located desire, that is, pleasure. Queer Theology is a materialist theology that takes bodies seriously.

Queer tango

Why am I a stranger in my own life?

(Sheryl Crow, 'Everyday is a Winding Road', song)

I have never ... been to bed with a gentleman. Never. Look what purity! I don't have anything to be ashamed of. My gods have made me this way. There must be a reason for that ... This is the truth when you are a pure and honest homosexual.

(Vargas 2000: 20)

If we wanted to continue reflecting on the theologian as confessor and confessant by looking at popular sources for a critical Bisexual theological tradition, we should not need to go very far from Latin America. These theological bisexual sources need to be found not only in bisexual stories, but in ways of thinking. Popular songs in Latin America can provide good examples of this. Chavela Vargas, the Mexican singer who was the lover of Frida Kahlo, confessed her Queer purity as a lesbian woman, and she passed this on as her message to the youth in Mexico and in Spain: do not feel discouraged but give yourself to the world instead as a pure and honest homosexual, because there is dignity and beauty to share here. She also speaks of exile, and the desires she had many times in her life to say to someone loved 'let us go somewhere else where we can love each other in peace' (Vargas 2000: 20). Chavela is a beautiful lesbian woman in her eighties who in more than one way destabilises what she stabilises by claiming her lesbian identity and yet speaking about love in whichever form it may come. That is somehow critical bi/thinking. By assuming the purity of her lesbian life, she destabilises the purity of the moral assumptions of heterosexuality, by displacing the category of contamination and moral illness associated in Latin America with homosexuality by the so-called straight people. Meanwhile, she stabilises this displacement by finding a divine origin to her lesbianism, what she calls the 'gift of her gods' (Vargas is a very spiritual woman and a practising *Chamán*). That destabilises the heterosexual spiritual claims of many Latin American Christian religious discourses. Chavela sings songs queering the displacement of love in the lives of displaced people. In Latin America, sentimental songs are another chapter to add to the gathering of Queer church traditions which we were referring to at the beginning of this chapter, as many of them speak about love and the (church's) legal cartographies of opposition beyond patriarchal heterosexual marriages.

In Argentina we sing tangos, which are also hard stories of perpetual displacement worth considering in this gathering of new sources of theology. Tangos and Mexican songs are heterosexual on the surface, but they have their closets too. In tangos we find the displacement of desire (loving one who does not love us, or cannot love us in public) and the displacement of social locations (as in processes of impoverishment, for instance). Generally in tangos both displacements are mixed with each other, and poverty and misery meet loneliness and the loss of love, which represents the ultimate suffering of the poor, and the crux of Queer social exclusion. People working in the pastoral care of the elderly, such as in the Metropolitan Community Church in Argentina, know how fear, poverty and isolation are the only companions of many old sexual dissenters.

Can tangos be another source for a Queer Latina Theology, or at least for an Argentinian Queer Theology? Tangos are songs about different forms of being 'exiled' and, as such, represent the experience of exile abroad or in a more general term, in the 'internal exile experience' of one's own country (Savigliano 1995: xiv). This is the reason why tangos are Queer, because they represent a longing, a melancholia of displacements. They may represent the result of permanent disencounter with the meaning of love (Savigliano 1995: xv), or social outcasting processes in Argentina or abroad. The theologian as a Queer confessor listens to stories of exiles, of wandering lust or excessive dreams and actions which go beyond the ideal frontiers. As a critical bisexual confessant, the theologian also knows in herself these practices of the struggle for representation which violate spaces, shorten distances and anticipate the unknowing of desires at the margins of pervasive mono-loving representation. Savigliano's idea of tangoing as a way of thinking ('a poking' and practice of immobilisation of the logics of academic discourse) (Savigliano 1995: 16) may be showing us the way that we need to approach any attempt to go deeper into the issue of who is the theologian, or to be more precise, who is the Queer (or Indecent) theologian. We can say that a Queer theologian is a theologian in/of exiles; she is the hidden address in the notebook, or the lover who does not phone at weekends, or cannot hold hands with her in church: she is the one who knows her closet, but also the complexities of it. Bisexuals may have more than one closet in their lives. She is the theologian who confesses to being away from home not even knowing where home is, while refusing to allow representations of herself or her own representations of others, if these deny the reality of exile not as a category lacking (settlement, or a going back home, for instance) but as a place to be in itself. A theologian who can only participate in the contingent processes of representation of people in transit, nomadic subjects who follow their longing for different forms of purity and holiness and especially find their grace in the lands of the sexually exiled.

The confession becomes then an intimate act amongst the exiled,[8] a positioning in relation to sexuality and in relation to the colonial lists of escapades or wanderings outside the established territory of a dis-embodied Christian ethics. It is a Christian ethics which needs to represent other bodies and their desires according to a particular constitution of the habitat and the habitual – remembering here that ethical thinking is related to a 'dwelling' or a practice of dwelling (Diprose 1994: 19), as configured in the bodily acts of Christian people. According to Diprose, the problem is that universalist contractarian ethics cannot deal with sexual differences (Diprose 1994: 20), as they construct the categories of the habitat and the habitual in uniform ways, basically the ways of the (heterosexualised) idealised white and middle class man. But if ethics, following Foucault, is understood instead as a hermeneutics of self-formation (Carrette 2000: 23) then the dilemmas of the Queer theologian are also related to disrupted processes of self-formation, to the point that self-representation processes which are at the core of the confessant theologies can allow themselves to be subsumed at the end, whatever queerness appears. That is to say, the art of the confessionary is an art of listening without consolidating (Jagose 1996: 131), or to follow an argument from Butler (1990: 32), the Queer theologian may confess and receive confessions on the intentions and effects of the theo/political discourse, its resistance points and its attempts to recover the Queer subject by the existing network of power. This may be an act of 'tangoing' in itself. There is poking and playing footsie here as theological *agent provocateurs*, and it may even follow some rhythmic dynamics from *Tango Argentino*: a sadness, a longing, but also a resilience in its capacity to 'hit and run' as in some kind of guerrilla tactic. Tangoing may provide us with a dishonourable way to do theology by allowing the confessant theology to become a spectacular confession, as tango does in its 'public display of intimate miseries, shameful behaviours and unjustifiable attitudes' (Savigliano 1995: 18; 61).

Obviously, this requires a study of the scene of confession, and the Queer scene to be precise. Tangoing may be a way to get into the rhythm of a theology in movement which does not care for sitting even if offered a chair. It may disclose the fundamental differences between the critical Bisexual theologian and the mono-loving one. Basically, the call to do theology is different, because it disrupts certainty. The eschatology is different, as bisexuality disconfirms in the future what the present verifies. We may remember here that it was Deleuze who argued that God is not the bender of time anymore. So the French philosopher concluded that 'Time has stopped being curved by God ...' (Deleuze 2001: 4). In philosophy, this means that neither temporalities nor notions of movement need to refer to God like kneeling in relation to a priest's penis during confession. Therefore theologically speaking, notions of the tradition of the church are yet to be discussed; eschatologies may be in the past, while traditions, for Queers, are always in the future. Critical bisexual epistemologies in theology delay and confirm this gathering of traditions in their own context, because that God who was the theological arbiter moving in an axis of time and space has been displaced by a more dis-articulating God of fences and exiles.

In the next chapter, we shall begin to reflect theologically on libertine traditions and hermeneutics, as a way to facilitate the crossing of the ideological heterosexual fence of God while reflecting in a critical bisexual way of acting and reflecting, that is, of doing a critical Bisexual Theology.

2

QUEERING HERMENEUTICS

Oh ... that I might be scourged with ... iron burning rods ...

(St Augustine: 44)

'Oh, Monsieur,' I said to him, 'to what limits you do carry your villainy!' 'To the ultimate periods,' Roland answered; 'there is not a single extravagance in the world in which I have not indulged, not a crime I have not committed ...'

(Sade 1991: 679)

God can no longer guarantee any identity! This is the great 'pornography,' the revenge taken by spirits on both God and bodies.

(Deleuze 2001: 293)

Libertine evocations

Let us consider these obscene images: the Queer theologian can be seen in the confessionary, strategically and sexually located in relation to the phallus of the church, but in a departing mode. Her theological engagement exposes her own longings and stories of exile to the third parties of the confession. Or this other one: the Queer theologian can be seen as putting her hands under the skirt of God, in a scene of almost Augustinian spirituality. Why Augustinian? Because it is a corporeal and intimate spirituality in which the theologian's desires for the flesh (manifested in metaphors such as those quoted above, suggestive of S/M libidinal force) get mixed with other ultimately transcendental desires such as that for God. But in Queer Theology, that transcendental desire is a located desire, that is, a site of specific pleasure. Queer theologians are the ones who consider to what excesses God takes God's love for humans, that is, which are God's transgressive desires and how we have sadly tamed or limited these villainies, as Sade's text calls them. Let us explain this. 'Villainy' is an interesting moral category which puts together an action considered criminal with a class connotation. A villain was a rustic villager, an evil and at the same time a poor person, and as such, is the old representation of what we could call today the dangerous stranger at our gates. By taming the villainous vocation in theology, we have made of poverty and sexuality strangers, evil strangers. What we need to recover, paraphrasing Klossowski on 'Sade, the Philosopher-villain', is the theologian-villain, who can be 'villain to the core' (Klossowski 1995: 36), thus making political and sexual transgressions a presupposition of doing theology. For instance, as Klossowski says, prostitution only transgresses because there is a meaningful construction of the moral property of an individual body (Klossowski 1995: 39). In the same way, we could say that the the- ologian-villain only transgresses because there is a need to recover the possible, since our present theological order has eliminated different forms of existence in its praxis. The theologian-villain gathers her sources of theology through sexual story- telling,[1] traditions of sexual (and not just gender) rebelliousness in the church and also Queer literature and even films. There is an Augustinian heart in them, in the sense that we find the presence of strange, almost Queer bodies of desire is disturb- ing (and disturbed) because of the way God's presence seems to move around the stories of films from, for instance, Eliseo Subiela or Pedro Almodovar.

In Queer literature there is in itself a libertine's evocation, an evocation of the Queer condition (and vocation) of *libertinaje*. *Libertinaje* is the Spanish term for the condition of being a libertine but also in common speech of acting 'beyond freedom', or taking advantage of freedom for illicit acts, which is also theological in its memory of the libertine's body, made up as it is of transcendental enigmas and transgressions of the freedom of the flesh. For people of my generation in Argentina, the libertine memory is also a political memory, which became focussed over a period of centuries in a dualistic split of freedom. For that was the *libertad* versus *libertinaje* (freedom versus libertinism) debate that arbitrarily delimited and ordered not only sexual behaviour but also issues of a much longed-for democratic life. To campaign for a democratic vote was, at one moment during the 1970s, a clear libertine act (*acto de libertinaje*). People's campaigns abused the boundaries of the freedom granted by the Junta's coup d'état. To have a gathering of more than three people in your house was also a libertine act punishable by law. How do we differentiate freedom from excessive freedom (*libertinaje*) in that discourse? What is wrong with excessive freedom (if it is freedom)? When does a *Carnaval* start to behave like an intimate reunion? In Latin America, politically and theologically speaking, the churches, like dicta- torial regimes, tend to give the name 'libertine' to their fears. They fear the freedom manifested in the praxis of bodies gathering together in rebellious ways, outside the signposts of their opaque and limited discourses. They fear the bod- ies determined to proceed by interrelating and combining themselves in the small hours, but also the recreation and discovery of new ways of relating to each other as in an act of sabotage, which destabilises the relationship between God and humanity by questioning human relationships and, by default, God's rela- tionships too. In our example, other fears were related to the combination of the popular votes and voices shouting in political disagreement. They were also fears of bodies cuddling together to become more bodies as in times of persecution of love and justice.

24

To evoke that political body of *libertinaje* in the context of a search for God or in a symbolic of redemption is suggestive of having a theological and political common ground of transgression. That transgression moves beyond a cultural setting of socially accepted sexual covenants, and takes us into political spaces. These spaces also define theological praxis. Sade did theology in the private space of the intimate reunions which mirrored (even if in a convex way) his experience of the public realm. The 'scene' is the locale site but the location is a web of knowledge which converges and reinforces or authorises the locale. We need, however, to do a contextual analysis of locations. Consider for instance that most of the libertine literature of the eighteenth century was organised around a feudal worldview made up of masters and slaves and relationships of pleasure in extreme servitude which, strange and even repulsive as it may look to us, was at the time a social and economic reality blessed by church and princes alike. In contemporary Argentina, Alejandra Pizarnik has written *La Condesa Sangrienta* [The Bloody Countess], a story based on the life of a sixteenth-century Hungarian noblewoman, Erzébet Báthory, who was accused as a torturer (Pizarnik 1971). Pizarnik's book was written during the time of the construction of concentration camps in Argentina, when the reality of torture pervaded Argentinian society. She also wrote poems about God, in the context of madness and the presence of something sinister in her life that was not only her personal context, but her social and political context during the time of dictatorship in Argentina. In that way Pizarnik confessed her location in her transgressive writings, as a young lesbian Jewish poet, suffering from schizophrenia under one of the most sinister and bloody political regimes Latin America has ever seen.

Contexual Sadean theology

It is interesting to follow the configurations and entanglement of local theological models such as the Trinitarian model. At a surface level, it may never occur to us that the Trinitarian model confesses an economic location which can converse with Sade's work. This happens because the ruling of economic orders, those of divinity, and the ruling of intimate relationships, go strangely well together. The Marquis de Sade's texts on imagined orgies can be read from a contesting hermeneutical perspective and in strict accordance with a debasement of class and social order made of bodies stretching themselves inside and outside the constraints of totality and hegemony. Such could be for instance a Trinitarian Theology of exceeding the borders of the divine three. Or we could use Sadean texts hermeneutically, showing through excess how totalitarian interpellations (as obedience to the worldview of masters and servants) can be subverted by that same excess. That may be part of the task of the role of irony in Queer Theology, as an excess of dis-authorisation in T-Theology. In a time when Third World theologians have made contextuality a hermeneutical key, it is sad to notice how contextuality has remained linked to the geographical more than the epistemological. By epistemological contexts we mean the fact that ways of knowing relate to each other. That was, by the way, one of the key factors in the work of the Zapatistas, who, using the Internet, were able to connect people belonging to the same epistemological context no matter what their geographical situation. A glance at an epistemological libertine landscape, such as the Sadean one, may connect to our epistemological context too, by giving us hints of difference in questioning theology and thinking critically about relationships. From there we may broaden our theological imagination and perceptions and be able to move to a Queer Theology of alternative reflections and actions.

What interests us now is to consider what we may call the libertine theological landscape. Technically, the libertine's speech is to be found not in theology but amongst the studies done in the field of literary studies. Today and in everyday life, we may not speak of libertines any more, or if we do, we may use the term in a broader, even ironic sense. T-Theology may never mention the deeds of libertines except in a few moral discourses because theology does not 'speak' of what it considers unspeakable (that is, outside the category of the productive in sexuality). Who are the libertines? Suppose we say that libertines are sexual free-souls. However, with the coming out of some heterosexual historical practices such as serial monogamous relationships, or simultaneous poly-loving (including adultery) relationships that could conceivably have been seen in the past as libertine practices, such things are seen today in another light since they have lost their secrecy and status as oddities. In theology, the libertine is amongst us and is buried in us. The theological subjects cross all the sexual constraints of ideal heterosexuality. Queer Theology has welcomed the SMers, the 24/7s, leather folk, genderfuckers and *Travas* (the Argentinian nickname for transvestites) into the midst of its hermeneutical circle and theological enquiries. We could be referring here to the libertines as sexually and politically transgressive people, who participate in that epistemological Sadean matrix which was present at the construction of the libertine body in some Queer ways, but not necessarily in any one specific way or in all of these ways. What we should like to organise here theologically is the libertine body as presented in Sadean literature as a hermeneutical circle. Following Marcel Hénaff's study on Sade (Hénaff 1999) we discover which are the hermeneutical keys of interpretation that combine to construct the Sadean libertine body and can be important for a queering of theology.

Sadean hermeneutics

The following are hermeneutical points of reference that come from the Sadean construction of the libertine body.

Bodies transgressing limits, that is the assumptions of heterosexuality

The resistance to normal relationships, and to the normalisation of sexuality, requires in Sade the necessity to move out of the limits of heterosexuality. The politics of sexual representation in Sade do not reflect any heterosexual norm;

26

people's affective contexts are homosexual, bisexual, lesbian relations, and generally incestuous. In the libertine narrative, and in the libertine body, binarism does not exist (this is what Hénaff has called 'the ruin of the law') (Hénaff 1999: 40). In Sade, heterosexuality seems to have been perceived as a solid category, thus immovable. He may have thought that no transgression could exist if heterosexuality was going to remain as a sexual expression. However, heterosexuality is not a stable category, not even theological systems considered as heterosexual. To disengage ourselves theologically from binarism, there are more options than simply lesbian and gay theology. Queer Theology is a broader category whose permanent intent is instability and as libertine in a Sadean scene, its aim is not to reflect any normative project while allowing a creative process made of the interactions of different orders to happen.

Programmed scenes

There is an absolute absence of romanticism in the libertine narrative. There is no spontaneity, no chivalry or amorous scenes of love's supplication. No gentleman gathers flowers for his lady. No lady stands by her man (or her woman). This happens mainly because the scene in which the libertine acts is programmed carefully, to the last detail. There is no space for spontaneity. Covenants are pacted and agreements are made amongst people on the sole basis of what is going to be acted. This covenanting in itself is a pleasurable praxis, in the way that it chooses and combines the flow of desires and then fixes them. Interestingly, we are confronted here with the circle of inner contradictions present in covenantal theology, or the Christian reflection on original pacts. As in Sade, covenantal theology may be lacking in love due to the need to fix grace and the love of God in preconceived positions. However, in the libertine epistemology, we need to ask ourselves who is pacting what, that is, whose is the political power constructing non-consensual covenants and what sort of mechanisms are found to tell us of an attempt at consensuality. Is Genesis a scene of homosexuality lost in the paradise scenes between Adam and his He-God, and Eve and her She-Serpent? Has YHWH God worked through consensus when fixing the scenes of female submission and men's pains in history? We cannot consider the narratives of the Christian covenant as consensual, but we could find the points of its submission and mastery.

An abundance of artful combinations and an obsessive pursuit of variety in the scenes

> I recount all that transpired, I conceal no detail; but have a little patience, Sire, and we will gradually reach more entertaining circumstances.
>
> (Sade 1990: 369)

Such is the human imagination, Thérèse; the same object is represented to it under as many forms as that imagination has various facets and moods ...

(Sade 1991: 600)

The limitations of any narrative programme of the order of the excessive are given by the limitations of the possible articulation of the amorous relations present in the same narrative. Excess also has its frontiers or frame of self-reference. Therefore, it is no surprise to notice how Sade needs to return to small points of scandals or surprises which change the combinatory possibilities by small degrees of variety. The scenes are carefully planned. Nothing is hazardous. There is a principle of order organising them which ensures a high degree of control, and to which this adds a 'non romantic' almost impersonal sense to the amorous relationships, except for the variations. The variations in the narrative usually come as little contraventions or slight twists to what has been pacted and is expected. As a result of these multiple and infinitely small series of variations, the amorous narratives tend to work as mini-mirrors for different people to keep seeing and re-creating themselves in their relationships (Sade 1991: 601). However, the same reality of the limitation of the excess, and the need to counteract that with variation, can be detected in Christianity. Human history, for instance, traditionally limits the excessiveness of God. Is not Jesus (and the prophetic tradition) the variation in the scene of a limited God? The Pauline condemnation of the 'letter that kills' may be a clear indication of the limits of the pacts and a call to look for variations in our relational way of understanding God. Paraphrasing Derrida, we may add that without deconstructing the covenant (the law), justice cannot be done (Derrida 2002: 43).

Violence of desire counterbalanced with time delay: expectations

One instant, my fine boy, one instant ...

(Sade 1991: 293)

I need a few days to make my preparations

(Sade 1991: 417)

The urgency of the passions is consistently contrasted with the delay mechanisms of the narratives which build expectation in the reader. An ethics of passion and urgency is systematically contradicted and played against an ethics of delay. Such delays or acts of patience work by intensifying desires while somehow magnifying the value of the expected in the narrative of the pacted scene. That is also a mechanism of building utopias. The whole project of the Kingdom relies on the articulation of these two ethics of passion and restraint which may also function as assuring the continuation of the project of the Kingdom for different generations of Christians.

Combinative reduction

Hénaff calls the play of narrative condensation in the libertine's narrative 'combinative reduction', consisting of the following steps:

1   Through multiple combinations of amorous relations a corporeal system of meaning is reached.
2   Once a certain meaning has been reached, that is the narrative has been 'saturated' (nothing different or 'more exciting' can be expected), the scene, as in certain dreams, is simply dissolved.
3   Finally, the dissolution of the scene usually gives way to another scene, subject to the laws considered before, that is, counteracting excessive limits with minor variations, and delaying the sense of urgency.

'Combinative reduction' is the name of this hermeneutical circle of interpretation. It bears a resemblance to the resurrection narrative, as if that narrative could have set out to create a model of interpretation itself. The scenes of the gathering of the friends of Jesus, his betrayal, the path to crucifixion and finally to death can be read from the multiple combination of bodies present in them: kisses (as in Judas), people escaping nude, civilians and soldiers pushing each other, threatening each other's bodies, culminating finally in a dissolution scene. Crucifixion is actually dissolution with Christ dying as a dissolute Messiah. The Messiah's epic has been saturated in the Gospel narrative and now has been dissolved in the ultimate limitation of God's excessive power. It may, however, be continued with a new scene. New embraces, new bodies touching other bodies and all kind of sensous interactions may occur again. Recognising the saturation points in theological reflection may be an important clue for analysis to start a queering or new process of theological praxis.

Another important element of this libertine epistemology mentioned by Hénaff is the transgression of the traditional, approved sites of philosophical discourse which we find constantly in Sade. For instance, philosophy happens in the boudoir. Suddenly theology does not take place in the university or seminary but in the bedroom. The dislocation of the theological discourse from its naturalised locus produces several other dislocations. In a way, this is nothing else but the typical strategy of delinking theology and ideology, as done in Christian Base Communities, factories or conscientisation groups in the 1970s. Sometimes the delays (the ethics of patience) between the saturation of one scene, its dissolution and the mounting of the following scene, come from long philosophical debates about theology, the question of the citizens' identities, and the mystery of evil and suffering in human life.

The point for us now, doing a heavy sexual theology outside the normal conventions, is how to insert some of these perceptions into our reflections, which come from this absolute construct which we call T-Theology. Of course, we cannot find today our contemporary reflections alongside the feudal economic ethos of Sade, but we can think theologically at the intersection of postmodernism, the expansion of capitalism in globalisation processes and in the critical stand of the construction of the sexual body which comes from post-colonial and Queer Theology. There is something lurking in our globalised world, which has something in common with the libertine theological rebellion of Sade, his anticlericalism and the desire to sideline the hegemonic worldview of Christianity as a sexual ideology. What we find here is the presence of systems made up of a combination of different kinds of exchanges and transgressions, which do not need to be equivalent amongst themselves while forming a topography of eros. For instance, the work of Sade and the erotology of the Brazilian writer Hilda Hilst occupy different sites and locations of erotic exchanges. However, what they may have in common is that these texts of subversion of bodies, as present in Sade and Hilst, succeed by creating different sorts of indexes of relationship between a subject and its objects. Using a concept from Peter Hitchcock, we can say that they create theological prostheses, by showing the presence of mutations in the theological images of the body and the body of God and knowledge (Hitchcock 1999: 87).

On theological prostheses

Yes, my mother tongue has lost me.

(Khatibi in Derrida 1998: 36)

This libertine body then creates a process of theological mutations or prostheses simply because it has its own built-in hermeneutics, a sexual hermeneutics which provides us with body-maps, with a cartography of wild dreams, of transgressive movements in search of radical breakthroughs in our ways of thinking. Church dogmatics, heavily relying on the organisation of bodies and political and sexual relations, have made of the libertine an alien not only in its reflections on, for instance, God and the Trinity, or the politics of grace and redemption, but in its ecclesiology. Ecclesiologies are hermeneutical exercises on organisational structures. It is the church's ecclesiological hermeneutics which constructs the lives of moderators and bishops. Church committee decisions and organisation are contained in a closed circuit of signifiers in which the main signifier is a sexual name, the name of the Father (Sedgwick 1994: 72). However, the powerful theological praxis of transformation usually comes from the direction of aliens working through these systems. It is only from the body of aliens in the history of theology (for instance, women, natives, people outside the heterosexual order or racial hegemony) that hermeneutical avenues bring us new promises to old theological practices.

Theological prostheses form a restless body in movement challenging the contextual limitations of political and divine character, while at the same time surpassing them. They also form the unbeliever's body, that is, a body which has stopped believing in divine sexual grand narratives, or the atheists of heterosexually based theologies. They bring impatience, irony, and a capacity to destroy by imitation. That is part, as we remarked before, of the role of covenants or pacts, to provide us with a heuristic device which teaches us how to subvert the law. It is also to be seen in the uneasiness shown by the apostle Paul in relation to the law. The law depends on the minuscule twisted ways which in the end allow its continuation only by welcoming scandals or disruption in order to facilitate new beginnings and permanent growth. Hermeneutically speaking these new beginnings work as some kind of fictional mirrors which function with a logic of permutations. This logic of permutations can be seen in Sade. In Sade's novels, once everything has been shown and said (as in the biblical account of Genesis), the texts reach a saturation point and a new scene begins as a fresh account of a new sexual genesis. Permutations usually give us material for the beginning of anti-genesis, by creating prosthetic processes where bodies 'embody praxis' by embodying the scandalous in their hermeneutical circle (Hitchcock 1999: 87). Theological prostheses are the attempt to recover what has been lost in theological language, which is also a language of origin, written in a dynamics of transplantation, a critical bi theological language dealing with the incommunicable (Derrida 1998: 8).

What are the scandals of theological prostheses in Queer hermeneutics? The answer is: the theological language of the Queer Other. This alien language can lead sexual theologies towards new leaps of indecency by taking the road (of methodologies) which is more alien to Christian hermeneutical options. This is the *via rupta* (road without repetitions or returns) which Queer Theology may take in order to be able, paraphrasing Derrida, to 'reinvent without an itinerary' (Derrida 1998: 58).

Let us reflect on orgies as hermeneutical reinventions, that is, using the structure of Sadean descriptions of orgies, for instance from the perspective of epistemological organisation. First of all, let us consider how communication happens in theology. As T-Theology is still colonially based, its covenants are still similar to the covenants of colonial industrial landscapes. Yet the referent of this economic discourse tends to have one main direction, for example towards the ports of export and import. The British built the railways of Argentina to the port city of Buenos Aires, from which leather, tannin and other raw materials were exported to be processed abroad and later imported back to the country by the same empire which took them in the first place. In the memory of Argentinian people the real processes of internal communication (like the guerrilla paths of liberation criss-crossing the country) always relied on paths cut out of the sides of mountains, or tracks cut through jungles, constructing new routes outside the logic of capital profit. Colonial T-Theology employs the high road to the city and the centre of the empire. But for post-colonial theologies there are paths which turn off towards Others. However, the Other bodies have succeeded in adding the *vias ruptas* of new economic webs, sometimes avoiding exploitation and providing the empire with that quality of infinitely minuscule variations in the native's economic and affective transactions which led the colonial empires to call the natives unreliable and disconcerting. Primitive forms of what today are

31

called 'workers' unions' can be seen in these disruptive routes of interpretation against pervasive ideologies, producing alliances of the poor and disenfranchised. In the colonial and neo-colonial empires of Latin America these alliances can be perceived as forms of orgiastic communications at the margin of the legalised forms. We could call them perhaps, the orgies of the poor.

Therefore any sort of disorderly gatherings (the meetings of disorderly communications from subversive bodies) were from time to time banned. In the 1970s Bible study groups of Jehovah's Witnesses in my neighbourhood led to the appearance of Black Marias and imprisonment for whole families. But the reasoning behind such actions, which produced the sad spectacle of grandmothers and grandchildren arrested in the middle of the afternoon at gunpoint, was a moral one. These meetings were transgressive, not because of their specific activity of reading the Bible or other religious texts, but because they transgressed the Junta rules on the number of people who could gather in one house. From that perspective, their meetings had the quality of an orgy in the sense that an undesirable number of bodies were present in the same place under suspicion of producing unlawful exchanges. Their morals were doubted and they were portrayed in a framework of excessive communication. Jehovah's Witnesses were depicted as excessively religious people, *pasados de revoluciones* (literally, 'beyond revolutions', that is, 'beyond normality'). The love stories of the Other (their love for their countries, for their communities or religious faith) always contain recollections of confrontations with the law when they transgress the borders of justice. Many years earlier, the *descamisados* (shirtless people) of Eva Perón were depicted as the primitive 'bestial hordes' (*aluviones zoológicos*) of the poor. Eva Perón herself went from being the political leader of social reforms to being portrayed as a prostitute in the fictional narratives of the hegemonic theology of Argentina during the 1950s. She became a 'woman with an excessive past', whose public speeches gathered too many bodies in Plaza de Mayo. The bodies of indigenous people and the despised multitudes of the poor and exploited were mixed in excess in public rallies. And that was also an orgiastic characteristic of Perón's popular movement.

The hermeneutical circle of the libertine orgy tends to be in working order as it travels through the unknown of difficult political times. As in Sade, it was not the bodies gathered without clear beginnings or ends, or even along known roads of communication of the flesh which was exciting, but the fact that something new was still to come, announced by the merging of bodies of ideas in alternative ways (Deleuze 2001: 291). The excesses and transgressions of political and religious systems were named as *libertinaje*, a category which in Argentina could take us nearer the concept of orgy as a political metaphor.

Those libertine paths, linking poverty and sexuality and homologising or at least combining some of the hermeneutics of excessive sex with excessive justice, still exist in theology. Many hermeneutical lessons can be drawn from the metaphor of the orgy. In moments when countries need liberation instead of development and theology needs a substantial departure from sexual ideologies which support political backwardness, we may turn back to swimming and even build unexpected, scandalous new bridges in the memory of all those who found themselves on the other side from T-Theology and its colonial sense of property. It is true that during the past 30 years Liberation Theologies have denounced that mixture of theology, ideology and culture which still takes us to the ports and from there to imperial theology. A project of a sexual and political theology may now find that in any of these uncomfortable paths for imperial thinking in theology, a new theological epistemological break can happen. This can in turn guide us to dis-center T-Theology (the theology of the empires) but obviously at a cost. Such a cost comes from the dream of breaking the knot of affective and political investment that we have with imperial Christianity and its interpellative power in our lives. But people who spend their lives travelling theological *caminatas* (walks) along alien paths know that main roads, unfortunately, cannot depart from their goals. The main road of T-Theology sooner or later always leads us to the same (forced) agreements, to similar exchanges and values of pre-understood laws of capital profit. It seldom lets us perceive the historical presence of God in different, unfamiliar surroundings. Only a theological methodology of resistance may end integration and adaptation.

Find God in dark alleys

Why then do a theology from the libertine body? Why should we wish to re-read the Bible or even re-engage with Augustine from a Queer perspective or find in the Trinitarian model a divinised orgy? The answer is simple. We need to walk in these different paths at a time when Sexual theologies have left behind the male/female naturalised discussions within Christianity in order to focus on the particular construction of masculinity and femininity of which the discourse on God not only has something to say but, as we shall argue, on which it might depend. Obviously, the voices coming from Queer theologies have added even more strange alleys to our quest. There has been a shaking of the foundations of the politics of sexual identities, the abandonment of the homogenous search for identities and the politics of the centre/marginal geographies. The point to consider now is how we can ever know theology from different centres, such as the centre of a Queer nation. This may not be called a theology from the margins any more, but a theology from recognisable, legitimised (if not approved) and visible centres which have been rendered invisible. We need to reflect in the area of different sexual ways of knowing which could be considered foundational (even if always provisory, as in a process of theological praxis) for a new way of reflecting on God and on us. In a way, what we need is to recover the memory of the scandal in theology, and with a vengeance. This is the scandal of what T-Theology has carefully avoided: God amongst the Queer, and the Queer God present in Godself; God, as found in the complexity of the unruly sexualities and relationships of people; God, as present in the *via rupta* of previously unrecognised paths of praxis, that is, paths carved with machetes in jungles, as the paths of experience

33

(and of people at the margins) usually are. The theological scandal is that bodies speak, and God speaks through them. What Jean-Yves Lacoste has called a kenotic existence (Lacoste 1994), that is the realisation that human beings need to accept that they exist only in the image of God, could also mean to realise that Queerness is something that belongs to God, and that people are divinely Queer by grace.[2]

It is interesting how, according to Marcel Hénaff, the libertine body (as inscribed in Sadean literature) is precisely a site of memory of scandal (Hénaff 1999: 1). Sade himself is the site of the scandalous and of what can only be whispered, the place of the truth of rumours. Marie-Christine Lala, in her article 'The Hatred of Poetry in Georges Bataille's Writing and Thought', has considered how Bataille focusses his attention on 'that *part maudite* – that doomed part – of exchange, whose use value he generalizes through the concept of the impossible...in terms of logic, economics and religion' (Lala 1995: 105). That *part maudite* is an Otherness which cannot even be mentioned. We may go as far as to say that doing Queer Theology is the site of the *part maudite* in theology, to which a sexual, Indecent Theology needs to turn in order to find the Other way of knowing God at the margins of T-Theology. It is not the site of individualism in theology that we are pursuing here, but the site of the intimate reunion, of community gatherings, of interrelationships, the dynamics of which 'don't go to the ports' (using our previous metaphor of imperial road building) but where complex processes of exchange (physical, emotional, and as in the case of Sade, intellectual) occur. Our search is for theological interchanges of intimacy, sexual identities and politics in the dark alleys behind our churches; the search for God in dark alleys. However, how far can we go? Is a libertine based hermeneutics too outrageous or illegal to consider? And since when has God been a host of law and legality, instead of justice? New hermeneutical circles need to be imagined, and new hermeneutical sources (excluded *parts maudites*) provide a way to find God in dark alleys.

The sources for what we may call a libertine epistemology in theology come from other canons. They may come from literature, from Sade to Califia and Tee Corinne to Hilda Hilst and Federico Andahazi; from rituals of pleasure and fundamentally, from people's critical reality of love lives. In them lies the possibility of liberating God from God's current hostage status to Heterosexual Theology thus challenging us to a theology from loving relationships at the margins. The libertine literature may give us many clues into a different way of knowing sexually, but obviously also brings with it its own horrors. That is the reason why the theologian wanting to reflect on Sade needs to justify herself for committing herself to stories of such an excessive nature. There is the excess of sex, but all kind of other excesses too present in Sade as in Bataille and Klossowski, or even Alejandra Pizarnik. It is true that there is no Christian ethics morality present in any of these stories, but it is also true they are only that, stories which work as an accumulation of spectacles in a restricted economic exchange where the exchange values differ. At least we can say that Sade's stories do not have a sacralised character such as in the case of the Biblical pornology. Whether believing in the historicity behind the Bible or not, horrific stories of gang rape, torture and murder have been part of our Sunday school teaching and bear more responsibility for sexual crimes in their many dimensions than Anais Nin's *Delta of Venus*. Many years ago theologians such as Drora Settel and Phyllis Trible amongst others reflected on the pornography and violence towards women (and the poor Canaanite populations in general) in the Bible. Did these things written in the Bible really happen? Did Sade spend 120 days in the castle of Silling? Was Masoch in the taxi when the Venus in Furs kissed him? Did Bataille really meet God in God's second coming, in the dark alley where God was the madam of a brothel? These are stories; weird stories, but stories. There is an anecdote related to this to be found in Sybil Holiday's *Consensual Sadomasochism* (Henkin and Holiday: 1996). Holiday, who works in sex education, recalls how she had recommended a friend of hers to read Samoi's *Coming to Power*. Her friend read the book but made the following remark to her: 'I find this all fascinating ... but tell me – please, you don't really hit each other with *cats*, do you?' (Henkin and Holiday 1996: 49). Of course, in S/M vocabulary, cats are not cats. There is no need to phone the Royal Society for the Prevention of Cruelty to Animals since 'cats' are metaphors for playful whips (or the cat-o'-nine-tails). In a similar way, reflecting on a Sexual Theology done from a libertine epistemological perspective, we must be aware that sometimes cats are not cats. We are dealing here with what Hénaff, in his seminal book on the construction of the libertine's body, made very clear: reading stories/texts/dogmas for what they are – 'linguistic creatures' trying to express the inexpressible of transgressive acts, by a poetical and economic reading (Hénaff 1999: 9). As Barthes has put it, all the game of the erotic combinations in Sade, its order and sanction *'sont d'ordre rhétorique'* that is, belong to a rhetorical order (Barthes 1971: 37). The poetic is the point of rupture and creation as it occurs in the body of the libertine transgressors, the programmes of disruptions, re-combinations and new castings of intimacy and sexuality, and the hermeneutical circle they summon. In the economy of the text, processes of symbolic value and representations of the world (and the divine) come forward bringing new light (and darkness) to our understanding of Sexual theological reflections (Hénaff 1999: 12).

An epistemology from the *libertinaje* of bodies needs to allow different areas of Queer intersections to come out, and needs theological 'cats' in order to continue with the task of Indecenting, that is, of doing a materialist, concrete theology which has departed from idealist grounds of understanding in a scandalous way. In the biblical sense, a theology which aims (as only Queer Theology can) to scandalise, that is, to be a stone on the road to force theologians to stop, fall down, while pausing in their pain and thinking during the pause. Queer Theology forces us to pause and see the intersections on the theological road which are provided by a superimposed post-colonial and Indecent reading in theology, together with materialist analysis. This is a reading which should be excessive and yet, made up of pacts often transgressed by multiple variations and combinations. A reading of passion and impatience, producing permutations and unexpected novel combinations, as in the libertine way, with new bodies (of action and experience) added and counted.

That will constitute and define the damned part of theology: a space of sexuality, race and class lies. The ones that theology has classified and numbered as the Alien Nation of God do theology in their bedrooms and can teach us a couple of things about God, love and justice.

(God) in the name of vulgarity, horror and impurity

God is nothing if He is not, in every sense the surpassing of God: in the sense of common everyday being, in the sense of dread, horror and impurity ...

(Bataille 1995: 142)

Did Shadow know that Shadow was dead? Without any doubt. Shadow and herself were associated for many years ... Sometimes the clients called Shadow, Shadow; but Shadow replied to both names, as if Shadow was, effectively, Shadow, the one who was dead.

(Pizarnik 1985: 58)

There are three elements which either alone, or combined with others, summon images of the uncivilised, the savage, and the sexual deviant body alike. These elements are vulgarity, horror and impurity. To reflect on them is to reflect on the constitution of exclusion in theology, in the double sense of formation by exclusion and of the legal body of moral allowances allocated to people in a particular historical setting. By vulgarity, horror and impurity the Other of Colonial theologies has been defined as constitutive of the dirty (dark) body of the native. In theology, the dark body is God read in retrospect.[3] This reading in retrospect of God and the body of the Other is done by the non-dyadic discovery of the licentiousness of God. God became a relationship and an unnatural one, because sexuality is not a given.

The attributes of vulgarity, horror and impurity in God are to be seen as in Bataille, as rendering a sacrificial type of wound in the death of the transcendental God, and the beginning of the unravelling of a Shadow-God. This is a God who might remind us of something from the above quoted poem from Pizarnik: a God who does not know that God is a dissolute (in the dissolution of the cross), or a God who does not know about our own entombment of identity struggle, that is, our dissolutions. But it is also a God of horror replying to our horror by redistributing frontiers and allocations, in an exercise of an economy of horror where God's self needs to be sacrificed in order to continue existing. That is the necessity of the category of excess in theology too. Vulgarity is what qualifies the location of God outside the non-civilised sites of theology, and in the space of the dirty. It is interesting that the horror of the orgy in theology may represent here the supplement of the mono-loving God, that is, the non-relational God which does not survive well outside its ideological sites. As a shadow of Godself, God also has the potential of replacing God in the Trinitarian combination when introducing non-monogamous and sexually unstable structures of loving relationships for a change. Meanwhile, the category of impurity has always functioned as a theological force fulfilling its role as the canvass of redemption. In Colonial Theology, it also gives an affirmation of purity by default, or white-glaze, to Christianity in its role as spectator at the native orgy. In that sense, the Trinity lost its orgiastic quality and became a mystery. However, the real mystery is how it has been possible theologically speaking to merge the God-Father's self referential monogamous love (the discourses of the jealous God) with the polyamorous love of God in community which is the Trinity. Impurity may work here as an unveiling of sexual ideology in the construction of God. The fact is that the *part maudite* in theology has no language except the language of the orgiastic, where alternative dynamics are presented and new body configurations found. When the missionary novella, that genre favoured by imperial churches, flourished theology was very aware of the need of eliminating the possibility of a Shadow-God, that is, condemning theology to damn God by a sudden closure of sex and race. The civilisation of God is a subject that a Third World Queer Theology such as Indecent Theology needs to take very seriously, in order to facilitate our encounter with God in dark alleys, which are not the alleys of danger, but on the contrary, of home. However, the good thing is that Colonial Theology can come from its closet at any time, because God is Queer.

Colonial Theology displaced horror, vulgarity and impurity by disrupting any possibility of an economy of horror in the discourse of Christianity. The theology of the master crossed much more than geographical frontiers, but interrupted any possibility of allowing a process of the coming out of God (that is, God beyond the boundary of Western ideology) by creating specific confines for theology. If God was ever going to come out of God's confinement, that was the moment of confrontation in the encounter between God and the Other's God. However, this never happened and God became the master of the orgy of the Trinity. There is a need to understand the possibility of a kenotic act coming from Godself as theologically liberative, even for the divinity. We will now explore this from a libertine hermeneutical standpoint.

It is worth thinking that the act of kenosis of God in Jesus (that self-emptiness of God's power, amongst other divine attributes, in order to become human) needs to go beyond the God-Father in Jesus in order to become a vulnerable, unpowerful God figure. The feminist discourse on the positive theology which may surge from the vulnerability of God in Jesus needs not to be denied but transgressed. I have already reflected elsewhere about the placing of Jesus-bottom in a dialectic of tops and bottoms which come from sadomasochism (Althaus-Reid: 2000), and how this perspective confronts us with a more strange and less biologically constructed account on the dialectics of God and Jesus' own vulnerability. Let us start to argue here in a more traditional style of thinking kenosis from Feminist Theology. Let us consider that somehow in Jesus God loses Godself, and perhaps some elements of patriarchy go into a process of abasement giving space to a different, out-of-this (patriarchal)-order new God/man (Radford Ruether 1983: 137–8). However, such kenosis could theoretically still pay at least some of the bills left in theology by the colonial orders, by producing an effectual relocation of assumed landmarks. This kenosis we are talking about now requires the assuming of the margins of the Other, of the *part maudite* of God. How could that kenosis of the non-threatening, civilised and pure God have occurred if it was not by displacing the Other-God? This is the God whose site is outside horror and vulgarity. When will the 'savage God' then make an appearance, with the full dressing of the Queer God, reclaiming the place of transgression in theology? In Liberation Theologies, it has been accepted that little can be known of God, except in what is perceived as the revelation of God in history. However, the point that has been missed is that such revelation of God in history is also a revelation made through the history of human relationships, and intimate relations. What the horror at the native's orgy, and the perceived tainted vulgarity of the Other's intimate loving exchanges have failed to perceive is that of God's revelation in them. This is the point that I have argued in my previous work with that Queer, political thinking which informs the project of an Indecent Theology. The revelation that occurs in intimate acts, in the perceived chaotic history of intimate human relationships in history, has been systematically marginalised and silenced by a highly idealistic sexually hegemonic theological project, heavily dependent on a colonial model.

However, the kenotic Queer model can even go beyond the finding of God's revelation in the complex world of human sexuality, and using a dialogic model imply that God's divinity depends on God's own presence amidst the sexual turbulences of human beings' intimate relationships, whose knowledge is the knowledge of the excluded queerness in Christianity. In the words of Bataille, 'Only a shameless, indecent saintliness can lead to a happy *loss of self*' (Bataille in Gill 1995: 40). In kenotic divine processes, this will be God's loss of Godself, or the loss of the proper God giving way to the Indecent or Queer God.

Indecent saintliness, or the Queer kenosis of God incarnate, needs to participate of a different theological sense of knowing. It requires strategies of critical bisexual interpretation, the encounter with Queer traditions and the libertine body as sources of theology, and new theological metaphors such as for instance, orgies. These are all strategies of disaffiliation and of the identification of the Queer nomadic subject of theology. What sort of discoveries can be expected from these new paths, or *via rupta*, of this Queer kenosis of God? We can expect a God in dialogue with amorous relationships, but from other sexually transgressive epistemologies. For instance, we can expect the kenosis of a libertine God, and we are going to explore this in different forms in this book. One kenosis which may occur, is that of the Voyeur God.

Sexual salvation: the Voyeur God

The mirrors wherewith the room's walls ... cast multiple reflections of
an animal coupling, but at each least movement, our bursting hearts
would strain wide-open to welcome 'the emptiness of heaven.'

(Bataille 1995: 151)

If we are going to use the libertine's constructions of the voyeur as a theological
resource, we must realise that there are different options here. In Bataille, for
instance, the construction of the voyeur is different from that of Sade. In Sade,
the only voyeur is in reality, the reader, since in the corporeal system of the
Sadean libertine novels, 'to see is to be seen' (Hénaff 1999: 111). The libertine
body of Sade is a multiple body, or a body in transit as it is usually constituted by
the scenes of the orgy. As there is little for the eyes to see that has not already
been shown, in Sade God is present as part of the voice of desire, always in transit and in expectation. Theology is spoken in bedrooms, and God's speech comes
in the middle of orgies (Hénaff 1999· 53).

However, for Bataille, the quest of the voyeur is different because it is of a
more mystical nature. In *Madame Edwarda* (Bataille 1995) Bataille presents the
woman prostitute as God, but the theophany only comes into effect as a specific
effect of looking, and more specifically, of looking at her pubis. In the story its
protagonist, Pierre Angelique is presented as a tormented man, struggling with
his own anguish. Pierre Angelique speaks about suffering a deconstruction
process in which his self is involved. So he says 'a foul dizzying anguish got its
nails into me' (Bataille 1995: 148). This is a translation from the French '*l'an-
goisse...me décomposa*' (Bataille 1971: 19) – anguish deconstructs me. The scene
is one of deep existential loss. Pierre Angelique goes to a brothel to find God in
a prostitute called Madame Edwarda, in a text where a sexual need is also a spiritual one. Moreover, this search for God is explicit in its corporeality. He
recognises God (he 'sees God') only when Madame Edwarda asks him to see
her pubis (and to kiss it in public – thus adding a sexual theophany to a public
confession of his faith). Bataille's scenes, although intimate and therefore limited in their construction, are not theatrical like Sade's. The libertine in Bataille
is not the sexual quasi-automaton of Sade, but a wanderer of the experience of
inner spaces (*l'expérience intérieure*), as contrasted with the external sense of
dilapidation and trespass of the scenes. It is as if Bataille has a vocation or a call
to voyeurism, which is an engaged, mystical one. It is a vocation in tension with
the desire to engage with a de-composition (anguished deconstruction?) of religion which correlates with that sense of loss in Christianity. In Bataille, and
specifically in Madame Edwarda, it is as if God demands the voyeur. God manifests herself only to the voyeur and God relates to the one who searches for the
divine as a voyeur too. Through voyeurism, the protagonists understand and
God speaks because, demanding the voyeur, God also shows God's voyeuristic
vocation. What does God the Voyeur offer? Sexual salvation from an all-seeing

God and a self-exposing God. In Queer Theology, sexual salvation is part of a sexed theophany.

If voyeurism is to be used by us as a Queer hermeneutics it is simply because in theology it is always possible to acknowledge a different location, much closer to the unnameable understanding of the communities of the sexual Other than to a legally prescribed theology. For instance, a theology whose concreteness comes from the sensual appropriation of some of the subcultures which negotiate their identity from some subversive standpoint or antagonism with the centre whilst maintaining at the same time the integrity of the theo/logics of fetishism.

Let us consider sexual salvation. Let us consider that without rupture there is no salvation, for restoration, like salvation, obeys the theological compromises of a different order, the field of engagements, not of new beginnings. Let us suppose that the Christian message of salvation is related to the presence of God that we discern in the codes of human relationships. Therefore a salvation discourse would require a transcoding exercise of intimacy and the liturgical exchanges of desire happening amongst people. These are economic and political liturgies but also sexual liturgies. Sexual salvation could be defined then as an act of mapping God in sexual relationships, a kind of recognition of the dislocation of the sexual subject in Christian theology which has also produced our estrangement from God – it has defamiliarised us with God. This defamiliarisation with God accompanies the habit of our souls – that is the souls accustomed to conform to market theologies and their current political and sexual ideologies. These include a theological aestheticism and a fear of breaking from old modes of religious production. After all, even the prophets of Israel owed their unpopularity to their failed attempt to redirect conforming souls towards liturgical ruptures in search of critical realism. However, the problem is how do we distinguish ideological interpolations from the real desires of our souls? Might it be that we can do this by recognising that people's complex webs of relationships are not transparent, but opaque and oblique, like an attempt to gasp for fresh air outside the stifling texts of (hetero)sexual ideologies? The concept of Christian salvation has served totalitarian theological synthesis well, whenever controlling, defining and organising people's sexuality was the objective of dogmatics. Truth, manifested in a desire for harmonious and orderly forms, denied the chaos of sexuality, and the chaotic God which emerged from it. However, there is a sexual supplement in salvation which may show us that the road to untidiness and indecency is worth the effort. This supplement of sexual salvation is a dangerous surplus within Christianity. Its power is the power of the per/verted[4] options that bring the possibility of alternative imaginaires to current versions of power in order to produce rupture as a counter-discourse to the symbolic violence of totality. The symbolic violence we are talking about here is linguistic violence. In order to produce a praxis of peace, such violence needs to be opposed not just by reflecting theologically on the themes of the Other, but also on the use of the grammar of the Other. That includes the use of paradigms, allegories, modes, accentuation and conjugations of the subculture from where relevant themes emerge. Such is for instance, the enterprise of Queer theologies, which include socio-semiotics with theological reflections, using the grammar of Queerness. If sexual salvation is the per/version, the alternative version of grace and redemption coming from sexual subcultures which represent the radical praxis of sexual politics, it is their episte-mology which counts, not just their practices.

Let us be more specific still in considering the supplement of salvation present in fetish subcultures. Some forms of fetish subcultures may exist amongst the diverse forms of civil religions and there are theological issues concerning the liturgical and mythical aspects of the ceremonial and metaphysical order of the communities concerned. A fetish theology may be in itself a kind of confessional act, for confession is the act of confronting truths of unequal legitimisation orders; the act of presenting theologically marginalised subcultures and their condemned truths to the authorised truth of dogma. The theologian of sexual salvation, grounding her discourse in fetishism, assumes then the role of becoming a confessing subject and a confessor herself, professing her vocation of reflecting from the margins of sexual orthodoxy.

We will attempt to decode one element from fetishism, the voyeur's gaze, in order to identify another aesthetical body (or the aesthetical body of the Other), this time made of theological codes which may be present there. Following Foucault's studies on the gaze from his book *The Birth of the Clinic* (Foucault 1973), we may start by asking how do we see or understand the work of salva-tion in our lives. It is interesting to notice here that I associate the concept of 'salvation' in the European context much more clinically than I would do so in my own country, where 'Salvation' is close to the concept of escape as in 'a nar-row escape' (*escapada*). Effectively, 'I am saved' or 'I have been saved' (*me salvé* or *estoy salvada*) is almost an economic metaphor for poor people suddenly find-ing a source of income. *Escapada*, in the slang from Buenos Aires, has also the sexual connotations of hidden love affairs or loving encounters, thus making of salvation, in a popular sense, a truly sexual salvation. In Western theology, it seems that the clinical aspect of this concept is linked to illness, victimhood and deviance, and with it there is the implicit call to normalcy, or salvation as the 'disruption of disruption'. Salvation may be associated in some circles as a refer-ral from a diagnosis of the human condition. Such diagnosis, of course, is done with vested interests and in dependency on how much a person can join nor-malcy after the disruption of salvation. There are compartmentalised ways in which a whole hierarchic system based on sex, gender roles, class and race inter-relates to bring to each of us the particularity of our salvation. Obviously here salvation is a metaphor for accustomed souls, not for the disruption of perni-cious religious common sense. It is as if salvation cannot overcome the reification religious process accumulated by centuries of sexual ideology in Christianity. It was Lukács who in 1921, talking not about Christianity but about issues concerning the organisation of the Communist Party, claimed that the problems they were encountering were of a 'spiritual type' (Lukács 1972: 116). The point he was making was that capitalist processes of reification were

to be challenged in people's own way of thinking already domesticised by impe-
rialist hegemonic thought. In the same vein, we can say that sexual ideologies
have reified Christianity, but thinking salvation has sadly sometimes produced
more attachments than revolutions. Salvation has lost agency when it becomes
dependent on the masculinist look, thus helping to reify patriarchal structures
based on heterosexual thought. But there are different and more spiritual ways
to look at salvation. Theology (and theologians) may be hiding in the shadow of
their hetero-orthodoxy, but there are ambivalences or subversive aspects to be
rescued and encouraged even in heterosexual systematic theologies. This point
of subversiveness can be found also as a denouncing prophetism, if we consider
the voyeuristic gaze and decide to do theology in a sort of 'I saw you' attitude.
In that case, we could claim that any theologian may be accountable for arous-
ing theological needs, guilt structures and flows of desire from the persistent
and condemnatory theological look at the intimate lives of other people which
is what Christianity has been. This may also be part of a form of doing a surro-
gate theology to which Western theology is, sadly, accustomed. However, the
voyeur's gaze can carry the intention to dislocate power. Suppose we want to
consider here the voyeur's gaze in the framework of erotic photography and the
power implications of the look. If we locate our understanding of power in the
context of influencing people's spiritual decisions and social understanding of
relationships, we may ask first of all, who legitimises theological power?
Dogmatics or ecclesiology aside, the first challenge that the voyeur's gaze presents to us is that its power is outside the order of legitimation. Theologically,
this is the area of dialogic understanding. If the voyeur exercises a power, it is a
fluid kind of power, or power on the move, in the blink of an eye, outside the
sphere of ideological jurisdiction. There we find that the lack of legitimacy in
the voyeur's gaze is the path to transient desire, but also to guilt. The so-called
passivity of voyeurs needs to be re-examined. Although we need more discussion on issues of sexuality and passivity before condemning the latter, the act of
the voyeur far from being passive is an act of active dislocation of sites of pleasure and control of power, specifically present in the power of images to arouse
feelings and emotions, including sexual emotions. Voyeurism and fetishism have
in common this dislocation of power and of identity. The voyeur looks and sees
in the other what the other cannot look at. The voyeur masters the surroundings, contexts, and materiality of the body in location. From what perspective
does the voyeur understand? From all the perspectives of watching with
impunity, adding the pleasure of new angles, of all the angles and non-autho-
rised points of view to what is seen.

Any theological praxis which seeks to save us from fixity, the obsession with
coinciding with the eternal sexual ideology and the limited choice of angles, may
be inspired by that. If fetishism may be considered a civil religion, it is only
because heterosexuality is a belief system, therefore, it is a trust in a model of
relationships, or a trust in an ideology invested with the eternity emitted from
God's own presupposed hetrosexuality. However, Bakhtin reminds us that the

organising forms of art are people's bodies (Morris 1994: 18). Belief systems are organised around people's bodies, and people's bodies in relationships, and in sexual relationships. People's intimacy has historically been a space for localising belief systems. But people's identities allow us here a belief in a spirituality in diaspora, of a grace in movement. The voyeur's knowledge becomes then part of a form of migration or diaspora of gazed identities. The reconfiguration of identities is part of the voyeur's project, although the main activity lies in the voyeur while the passivity is in the performer(s). However, who defines us re-defines herself too, and the identity construction of the voyeur's gaze has a mutuality. That reminds me of an image from my infancy in Argentina. In the children's Catechism the 'eye of God' was a triangle with a pupil in the midst from which came streaming rays. Does God's identity depend on our relationships, befriending, loving acts? If God is a seer, that semblance to the image of God's likeness that we may carry with us according to Genesis 1 is not related to individuality as much as to what I call the ceremonial of intimate relationships as seen and understood from all angles at the same time. Thinking about and discerning God from a voyeur's epistemology favours mutuality in the construction of God's identity. God is then here not the big eye which follows us like an Orwellian policeman, but a dialogic God, whose identity is dependent somehow on people's own loving relationships.

Filiations

The fact is that doing theology from a libertine perspective may suddenly confront us with the ultimate hermeneutical perversion of the excessive sites of transgression of horror, vulgarity and impurity, that is, the filiative disruption or the transgression of a filiation taboo in theology. The Voyeur God may confront us with this. Disrupting the work of filiation in theology has already been done, mainly by women theologians. Just to mention a few examples: Mary Daly turned her back on God the Father; Daphne Hampson rejected the ghost of Christ; James Cone departed from the White Jesus; and I, in my previous work on Indecent Theology, have turned away from the Virgin Mary of Latin America. These are gross acts of disaffiliation and although not everyone will agree with them, it should be recognised that they require courage: disaffiliations of this order are not undertaken lightly. Disaffiliation has something to do with taking the familiar into unfamiliar contexts. Thus, taking Christian theology into the house of feminism makes women abandon and even deny any link with the Christian fathers. However, it is a fetishist strategy. For example, bondage has been approved in the familiar images of crucifixion, artistically reproduced and found throughout the world, to be contemplated in the broad light of day. However, what of a red crucifix hanging from high, corsetlaced boots, in a room dimly illuminated by a candle? Bondage is not to be seen in the theologian's bed, in the sense that bondage cannot inform a serious Christian reflection without tainting it, because bondage belongs to a different landscape, and to use the category theologically is, metaphorically speaking, 'a crucifix hanging above a bed with black satin sheets'. That is the scandalous position of what I have previously called Indecent Theology: a theology of liberation which, while exceeding the ideas of colonial liberation, surpasses the discourse of the correct God while searching for a more equivocal theological reflection. However, to mix a theological discourse based on a Latin American theology of liberation in dialogue with Queer Theory, could prove to be not just scandalous but deeply unfilial. Many referents which stand in paternal relationship in a kind of affective investment are discovered and reflected upon beyond the bonds of the habitual and the loved. Obviously this may leave us with the sensation that to be a theologian is to respond to urges of parental divine ingratitude, and in a way, nothing could be more true; sexual ideology in theology should be betrayed. Moreover, when Bataille confronts us with the possibility of the unique encounter that is the encounter with God face to face (or face to pubis) he resorts to suggesting an experience of overflowing, of letting go, as the ultimate transgression and metaphor of God. In fact, to put it simply, this represents a betrayal of God by Godself. The rupture or transgression of the theological path requires us somehow to assume God's own determination to be led astray. The transgression of family bonds in the writing of the libertine's narrative may well represent the sense of outrage that colonial and sexual affiliations have created, and the narrative of violence which is necessary to break with them. But disaffiliations are not necessarily individualistic, out of context relationships. Disaffiliations imply critically re-working the context of loving relationships.

This encounter in filial transgressions does not imply fixity, as in the case of a static God, fixed paradoxically in an idealist heterosexual transcendental position which implies God's encounter with a similarly static subject. The Queer subject is nomadic, unsettled and does not have a sedentary vocation. Her boundaries of affiliations are constantly on the move, thus destabilising the settling ideals of Christian ethics.

Using the theological memory of unsettling loving experiences, we should be able to think about an experience of God in movement as expressed by the rhetoric of an erotic overflowing of the divine. Curiously, in that erotic movement suggested by Bataille, we are suddenly confronted with a mixture of eschatology (utopia) and revelation. Eschatology is the utopian horizon of our reflections but revelation brings to us the inevitability of the past, and the past of God in history. Revelation as the re-imagining of the historical sexual and political discourse of God is always, from a Queer and post-colonial perspective, a project recast in the filial past. For instance, we need to go back to what has not been said because it was not inscribed in the filial code of proper and improper affections; to the ethics of loyalty to the master's decisions; to the primal heterosexual covenants. But if faith, and especially a Christian one, does not necessarily need to be considered as a subjective correlate of revelation (and therefore revelation is not a fait accompli), disloyalty and disaffiliation to the master's theology is necessary and desirable. A revelation which allows faith to reach its goal, or find what was lost, that is, a revelation in search of its own people, needs other patterns of relationships. If not, we shall have an example of revelation without that erotic overflowing of Madame Edwarda, because in such a case, we shall be falling into nothing more than a mediation, a typical product of a Christian ethics of patience. Eschatology would then be the science of postponement, because in theology, the filial always looks at the past in search of traditions of authority. However, there is no eschatology, no possible reflection on the alternative project of the Kingdom of God, unless the capitalist dictum 'there is no alternative' is also overthrown. That, however, would also require a process of disaffected investment in what we have grown to believe without questioning. We are talking here of the place of turbulences, of disaffiliations in revelation because the superimposition of a Queer experience of the world with a nativisation discourse in theology has made Christianity a site of violence. We are talking here about the violence of dogma; the slaughtering of grace and redemption, where economic processes have been fashioned in a bartering mould, like in a medieval economy exchanging a financially costly grace for sins. Can a second coming of theology, this time a Queer one, the most unfilial of all theologies, facilitate the final coming out of God? In the next chapter, we shall reflect on how a kenosis of the Trinity, which is a God-community in loving relationships, can help us through this path of thinking God and love from a different sexual perspective. The coming out of God will not be done without company though. The queering of human loving relationships and the love amongst Others always need to come together.

3

QUEERING GOD IN RELATIONSHIPS
Trinitarians and God the Orgy

> Is life so fragile that it can withstand no tampering? Does the sacred brook no improvement?
>
> Chairman Sheng-Ji Yang, 'Dynamics of Mind'
> (Sid Meier – *Alpha Centauri*)

Leading God by a dog-collar

If we wanted to reflect on a second coming of Christ, we should need to start by acknowledging that the second coming of the divinity is a sexual coming and a sexual kenosis. Theology has conceived God in history as a relationship (a community, for instance) expressed in the Trinitarian metaphor. That relationship has been politicised, culturalised, and made a centre of gender reflections in Feminist Theologies.

However, more reflection is needed to sexualise the Trinity,[1] in order to understand our kenotic existence not only as a sexual one but as a dissident one. The task of Queer Theology is precisely to deepen this reflection on the sexual relationship manifested in the Trinity and to consider how God in the Trinity may come out in a relationship outside heterosexualism. The queering of the Trinity is simply the following: How might the Trinity lead us into the kenosis of heterosexual practices, within justice but outside the law? Therefore, the questions we may want to ask would need to be related to the queering of God as processual. Using an image from the S/M scene we may ask, for instance, how can we lead God astray (consensually), and how could a theologian facilitate this God-in-relationship towards a kenotic self-betrayal? How to complete the Queer kenosis of the divine which is so close to the heart of the Other theologian, that is, the ultimate coming out or the complete, unabridged confession of God? After all, we should like to consider theology as a dialogic art or a communication process which involves multiple directions, and all of them reconfiguring multiple identities in theology. How can we reflect, following our discussions in the last chapter, in an unfilial theological way, that is, in a grace not indebted to historical subjugation processes and without criminalisation? That grace which works by dis-gracing the native and therefore organising the Christian universe of colonisers by default should no longer be considered a pertinent category.[2] What we need is the memory and menace of what has not been said yet in grace, that 'false memory' of the undecidable in theology which, as Laclau might suggest to us, will make of theology the political act of what should be said or revealed one day (Mouffe 1996: 9). The point for theology is that these memories of the 'excesses of excess' which Bataille calls 'turbulences' (Bataille 1967: 96) can only grow and abound inside the limits of the intimate. As Geoffrey Bennington says in his article 'Introduction to Economy I', growth and excess rely on the economics of intimate encounters (Bennington 1995: 48), like the encounters of lovers or the intimate reunions of Sade's scenes. The question for us now is to consider how the transgression of the borders of the discourse on God can occur in that intimate theatre of passions. This would constitute what we can call an intolerant act of theology, meaning by that the resolution of the tension between leaving the closet theologically while still internalising its oppressive memory, a theology which does not tolerate the intolerable. This would be in itself an act of courageous faith and for that we should need an epistemology which will not faint when we most need it. Mysticism may be unable to speak because it faints at the crucial moments of militancy, but eroticism seems to be of a stronger and unashamed nature (Bataille 1995: 141–2). If theology has its own cowardice and fears, the horror of uncontrolled bodies and especially of the orgy made up of unrestricted bodies may be the stronger. There are bodies whose fluids overflow the metaphorical discourse of theology, but they have lost materiality and sensuousness. Theology can see blood in wine but not blood in blood. The Vatican can see tears in the eyes of the statues of the Virgin Mary, or sweat on her robes when considering the legitimacy of a claimed apparition, but cannot see a trace of semen on her skirts.

In part these difficulties in the process of facilitating a coming out of the closet kenosis for God are due to ethical conflicts of a pedagogical nature. Opposing the pedagogy of passion (in the sense of a Christian ethics of passion) as suggested by the texts of Bataille, there has been proposed a Christian ethics of patience. Somehow a Christian ethics of passion could understand a theological reflection done by the love of immediacy, velocity and the urge to give a voice to the cry of the people which comes from the flow of the desire for justice and love. Liberation theologies, having been born in the matrix of the urgency of revolutions, frequently breached the decency, the decorum and the serenity of the expected theological discourses by introducing turbulent bodies in their reflection and by doing so with passion and impatience. The hungered body, the emaciated body, the lonely body of the Other (tortured, ill, accosted, the oppressed sexual body), came into theology with the characteristics of a passional ethics. However, the traditional North Atlantic Christian ethics of patience still prevails in that delaying of desire which characterises its thought. This happens because the body in love is postponed and the resurrected Christ needs to be sent to heaven almost too soon.

According to Hénaff, an ethics of patience has the advantage of producing a waiting game with an expectation of mediations. Mediations delay desires and extend the time of their demands. This is a virtuous process in itself, in the sense of seeing merit in virtuality, that is, an ethics of mediated – delayed – justice. The Christian ethics of patience delays desire (Hénaff 1999: 122), but unfortunately does not make it pleasurable because traditionally, theological patience has been one of the subaltern virtues, a collaborator with empires and a nurturer of filiation processes in theology.

Instead of this, it is the ethics of impatience which leads us to find in a libertine hermeneutics the facilitation of the kenosis of God. The subject of our Queer Theology, in conversation with God, is not to be seen as a hegemonic, unique subject. On the contrary, the Queer subject has given space to the dissonant and the multiple in theology. The first thing to consider when doing Queer Theology is to search for the lost referent of the dissonant lovers in theology. What happens to the lovers in theology? Where are the amorous impatient relations in theology? We need to reflect on this, because God's kenosis is a kenosis of love which does not need to be subjected to delays.

It was Deleuze and Guattari who, reflecting on the nature of philosophy, considered how it is philosophers who have introduced the concept of friendship in what we can call the discourse of the pursuit of wisdom (Deleuze and Guattari: 1994). Interestingly, this has been done by the naming of the reflections on knowledge 'philo-sophia' that is, the friend of wisdom. Deleuze and Guattari traced a path of creation from friendship in philosophy, which makes us wonder why churches got accustomed to doing theology outside close friendships, unable to trace the intimate reunion in the historiography of theology. That friendship pattern of philosophy introduces the concept of the philosopher as a friend of her creations, and a companion of her reflections, that is her conceptual world and praxis of action. There are elements of conviviality and distanciation mixed together here; in turn, they may combine the intimacy of a friendship with the disdain of love, or the obliteration of filiations, that sense of love towards the master's narrative which is so difficult to avoid and creates so many broken hearts amongst women philosophers. However, as Deleuze and Guattari suggest, more than a friendship as a generative creation in philosophy, we may be talking here about something closer to a lover's relationship. Are Queer theologians then the scandalous 'lovers of God', the ones who belong to the discourse of interrogations and re-readings while disaffiliating, that is negating their promised love at any time and at any moment?

The Queer theologians, as we have already said, introduced the body into theology, bodies in love, bodies entangled in ethics of passion – and transgressive bodies at that. These bodies are not the usual ones: they are libertine bodies. But these bodies are unsettled and also produce tentative, unsettled reflection. We may call them nomadic bodies. What sort of theologian ('knower of God') is it that we can call with Sedgwick the melancholic subject (Sedgwick 1994: 80), the mourner of all the early closures of meaning in Christianity? Following Sedgwick's lucid analysis of the silencing of Queer discourses and their subjects, we may well consider the fact that we live in a theological world where God is known by gossip – by elite gossip. This is the area of the 'everybody knows' discourse. 'Everybody knows God' carries a certain complacency and complicity with it, perhaps the complacency of the original pact of the monogamic, monoloving heterosexual *telos* (Sedgwick 1994: 74). What can dismantle or remove this ethos if not the theologian's nomadic desire for crossing frontiers made of theological condemnatory gossip? And how can God leave God's own closet if we do not engage in this nomadic movement of theology?

The kenosis of the theologians: Queer wanderlust

Perhaps Queer people receive a special sense of divine vocation or a wanderlust that makes of them un-institutionalised, restless nomads. Are these bodies to be compared to nomadic theologians permanently searching for the warm lips of the Other, as voyaging vaginas stretching themselves into strange and loving borderlands? Has Christian theology ever considered the desire for travel with backpacks and temporarily habiting with strangers that some people experience in their lives? It might well be that Christian theology has presumed redemption for such a long time that it has forgotten to look at what travels in its midst. Redemption has, after all, been made the ultimate prison for the desires of nomadic bodies. Redemption fixes our souls, but the two different economic orders present in nomadism and in redemption exchanges make them exclusive and incompatible at the same time. Redemption, in New Testament business terms, buys, pays the highest price (in classical theology, with another body, the body of Christ) for the opportunity to close the restless weeping wound of the nomad. The objective is to reduce the longing that moves the Queer nomadic theologian to search for God. Christian redemption aims to construct the body in quietude, in a steadfast, equilibrated, and unexcitable manner. This is the economy of the gift, which requires an exchange (the basic exchange system on which Christianity is based) and a settlement from it. However, nomadic bodies are unequilibrated, excitable and incorrigible. Their search for themselves always draws them on, reaching out for other warm lips, other bodies, like exiles unable to be satisfied with their first country of adoption. The interesting thing here is that in theology, the desire for exile is also a desire for revelation. That is the desire which started the historic exodus of women from the church in the 1970s under the symbolic leadership of Mary Daly: the exodus of militant people from politically conservative churches in Latin America during the infamous decades of Pinochet and the Argentinian Junta. The nomadic condition of our bodies is therefore the starting point of Queer theologians in search of a reflection on the love which crosses borders. Nomadic Queers are searching for God's nipples and soft lips and trying to bite them in oblique ways in order to achieve some oblique transcendence in their lives. Félix Guattari uses a concept which may be useful for us here, that is the concept of transversality.

Transversality is the flow of ideas and experiences, like a drunk walking in zig-zag patterns, while bringing together odd, dispersed elements, not necessarily in harmony. The nomadic body is the unsatisfied body in transit which carries with it oddities from the journey. But for Guattari, transversality as a corporeal, body-concept works not only by extending its borders but also by remembering. Thus Guattari says: 'When I was a child, I was, so to speak, in pieces ... I spent years trying to pull myself back together again. Only my thing was, I would pull along different pieces of realities in doing it' (Guattari 1995: 7). It means that a Queer Theology whose subject is the nomadic sexual subject of theology, needs to come to terms first of all with the forgotten body parts and dismembering ceremonies to which persons or communities have been subjected in the past. That is in part the historical task of Queer Theology. In doing that a person or community may be able to reposition herself, with her broken identity and conflictive sexual reality becoming/getting closer to another body. From that we can assume that theological originality, so necessary for the kenosis of God, may begin: not the originality of 'the new', but the originality of visibility. Finally, we can put nomadic Queer theologising on the screen when forgotten, suppressed, unvalued or underprivileged fragments of our lives get access to public theological discussion. As nomadic Queer theologians, our praxis can travel in open daylight, positioning ourselves in regard to new loving and political referents, divine and mundane. Queer Theology does theology with impunity. Borders of thinking are crossed. Borders of prayer are crossed. Body-borders. God may cross God's own borders too.

The nomadic Queer is the image of the unstable or irredeemable body of a theological subject who lives amidst insecurity and risk. The question in theology is about how Queer lovers do theology: they wander into each other's spaces, digress at points of desire, position and reposition themselves amongst themselves and amongst others and, eventually, participate in some creation of new (partial) conceptualisations of love and God. That is the material from which Queer, Indecent Theologies (and their theologians) are made. Queer theologies are a refusal to normalisation, to the recycling of old borders and limits of any theological praxis, while resisting current practices of historical formation that make us forget the love which is different. The love of different social systems, or different bodies. The love of different and unpredictable desires. A Queer theological project is not only a theology from and of the body: it is a theology of the travelling body which crosses borders between unnameable countries, and it is given away by transversal kisses and re-configurations of desire. And nomadic subjects transverse people, economic universes and also God. Queer theologies are to be found at the point of production of more creative epistemologies of the divine and a sense of twisted transcendence.

The Christian hope of any Queer kenosis of God comes basically from daring to start analysis and reflection on the sexual production of God in the heterosexual ideology which has pervaded theology. It was Péguy who defined Christian hope as 'essentially a counter-habit' (Péguy 1961: 1406), or an in-habitable site of the heart. Péguy was elaborating on the theme of grace, and how a dynamic of freedom versus habit is sometimes established in Christian theology. Habits, including the rubber ones, give a person a sense of normativity, which may be found in dissent, but the theological task of reflecting on the co-production of

God requires breaking points. Here we find some elements that characterise the historical task of a Queer theological project of leading God astray. First, never repeat and second, keep decency at bay (in order to fight the theological vocation of normalising discourses about God). In theology, to repeat can be associated with many modern habitual trappings, such as those into which 'theologies at the margins' may fall when they become simply attempts to induce oppressed multitudes to invest their identities in the centre-defined theological exercise by a simple economy of inclusion. Some gender-based theologies fall especially into that trap: they end reconciling themselves with androcentrism by getting re-absorbed into the system via heterosexual ideals of equality. This is, by the way, the old capitalist trick of making workers believe that they should behave as if they owned the firm, so that the welfare that their masters enjoy should be considered as if it was their own. This is why one can see that discourses of equality which do not break with a system of decency end up behaving as if they were the IMF of theology. Their ethical actions consist in giving credits for short-term survival projects by regulating the theological pertinence of themes and motives while prescribing an epistemological order (the labour reform policies which introduce exclusion as logical acts) and creating 'external debts' amongst theologians. These are for instance the debts of theological affiliation. Decency in theology keeps us not only in debt forever but also guarantees that there is heavy accumulated interest to pay. However, a search for Queer epistemologies would make us realise that precisely our counter-hope might only come by making theology in the image of our own Queer bodies. Focussing on nomadic Queer subjects we should be able to produce an uneducable and incorrigible theology, an un-habituated grace. While for many to have been able to start a theological project informed by sexuality may have been reduced in the past to introducing sexuality as a theological theme, a Queer theologian would like to go further. It is not enough to open, for instance, a theological reflection on masturbation, using masturbation as the motive of an ecclesiastical or eschatological concern (are masturbators going to be amongst the elect?), but rather to think Christian eschatology from an epistemology derived from masturbation. That would be part of the project of reflecting on the production of God, not just God's edibility as in the case of a theology done only for consumption purposes. However, the search for a Queer God is a theological *caminata*, which implies walking into different neighbourhoods, leading to different and sometimes obscure alleys. It is not always possible to bargain logics or identities as was the case in a sort of old-fashioned cultural-theology, a name replacement exercise of the type that began when in Latin America people were forced to hide their faith and gods under Christian names and rituals.

This was done for reasons of survival, but in more recent discourses of the gospel and culture type it tends to become simply a theology of dictionaries, that is, of the explanation of a centre-based theology in the native's terms. That sense of omnipresence of God in history and in culture is the essence of the colonial master. But then, we may doubt how realistic it is to ask a Queer Theology to produce a post-colonial dislocation of God's (heterosexual) omnipresence. Perhaps Hitchcock's oscillatory metaphor (Hitchcock 1999) may give us a clue of what is the path of Queer Theology: it is a pendulum or to use an Argentinian expression, *una pulseada*. *Pulseada* means wrestling, but with the extra connotation of 'pulse' as in to be able to feel the pulse of the other. In theology there will always be *pulseadas* with the God of the Centre but inertia is a powerful option to remain there. After all, even the God at the margins of many radical theologies has become only a lateral shadow or God-mirror. But the aim of the corruption of the ideology of normativity by sexual contamination, which informs our Queer theological path, is to move objects and subjects of theology around, turning points of reference and re-positioning bodies of knowledge and revelation in sometimes unsuitable ways. Consider the theological text as a libertine theatre of desires. Consider how a libertine epistemology could inform our present reflections by confronting us with other ways of knowing, of confronting different bodies in unusual terms and how these ways of understanding may lead us into a Queer theological praxis for our times. The point is that we cannot think a Queer God without understanding different sexual ways of knowing. Today sexual subcultures, and specifically fetish communities, not only know sexually differently but have that capacity for nomadic knowledge which we require in theology. That is to say the place of embraces and amorous gestures in theology fulfils a hermeneutical function.

The body of the libertine, that nomadic body par excellence, has never been considered in a theological dialogue. Without doing that, God may also be condemned to never come out of the confessionary closet. The fear that Christian theologians may feel is understandable. The back street alleys that we need to take in order to begin our search for a Queer God (or God of the Queers) are not necessarily the heavens above. Alas! Little do we realise that as Deleuze and Guattari have said, 'there is no heaven for [theological] concepts' (Deleuze and Guattari 1994: 5). The mistake of believing in some sort of neutrality and/or the intrinsic goodness of theology has taken apologetics a long way, which, paradoxically, usually causes it to fall short. The fact is that Queer Theology is a form of dark theology too, where we may encounter more than one hell awaiting us. The good news is that we need to rethink the hell-spaces of theology to which Queers have been condemned throughout history. Hell may always remain as an option for totalitarianism from a liberationist perspective, but according to Segundo, as we have seen, there is also a hell which 'is deserved' or merited by those who opt to leave the dominion of theo/ideological centres of power (Segundo 1997: 88). Hell-spaces are spaces of ideological rebellions in Heterosexual Theology.

Aberrancies: the kenosis of sexuality

If the theological subject is the nomad, the theologian may be thought of as constituted by a nomadic Queer community, dismantling and re-arranging liturgies made of other bodies' borders. The Queer God is not only non-habitual but also omnisexual. This we have in classical theology: an omnipotent/ommipresent God. This we have been consuming: a theology made of multitudinal categories for God. Let us go back to Guattari's work on transversal thinking here, as we consider the importance of the identification of functional theological articulations or 'components of passage' (Guattari 1995: 10). Components of passage are those elements which may allow other ones – invisible until now or excluded – to enter into the reflection of God's omnitude. In Queer Theology, they work as conceptual facilitators. These 'libertine facilitators' could be relevant for our Queer theological intention to focus on lapses, deviations, per/versions or aberrancies which have been excluded or undervalued in previous theological analysis. A Queer proposal then is to modify God's master file with a new list of aberrancies (vagaries; things that go astray or became deviated as if they were nomadic dissenters).

When theology has tried to convey a sense of God, it has done so with anthropological and hetero/androcentric fervour. Also with a straight fervour, manifested in theological terms. The most interesting of the list of divine attributes, mingling as they do with terms which seem to come from Viagra adverts such as *potentia inordinata* and *actus purus*, presents a list of 'omni' attributes for God, which succeed in representing divine qualities in relation to people. The 'omni' attributes are related to mastery and potency in the use of power: all knowing, simultaneous presence, complete goodness and freedom. In the 'omni' list however, there is an aberrancy lurking under the surface of God's omnipotence, but invisible. The identification of a component of passage, like sexuality, may give us a clue to the relation between the omnipotency of God and his never flaccid phallus. God is the masculine (heterosexual) powerful: never tired or without impetus, God's power is unlimited and procreative and linked to God's omnipresence. However, the aberrancy is not there: this is the sexuality of the powerful God pro/creator. The deviancy component lies in an attribute of divine non-procreative sexuality: in the omnisexuality of God.

Suppose that we wanted to consider this libertine trend of God as omnisexual, that God is in every way sexual and in all things, sexual. God's omnisexuality may be considered then the aberrant referent of God's omnitude which might be able to return the lost presence of the polyamorous body to its theological discourse. Turning again to our previous reflection on doing a production-theology rather than a consumerist-theology, we might find that reflecting on the omnisexuality of God could radically challenge our understanding of our relationship to God. This is because of the different epistemologies presented by dialogic and critical bisexual approaches (or triadic approaches) to theology, and because in this dynamic God depends heavily on our intimate relationships to configure Godself. The Voyeur God, for instance, may depend for God's own kenosis on what God sees and learns from our bedrooms or closets, for affective and sexual habits inform identity and inform God's own identity too.

If Queer Theology is a body-grounded theology, that is, a theology based on the incorrigible, uneducated, libertine body, we may start by building a hermeneutical circle precisely from there, from that libertine, licentious and problematic body which refuses the Christian fixed exchange rate and makes of the redistribution of its own frontiers a precious thing. God may be a divine identity in transit, fixed transitorily in the complexities and amplitudes of human love, freedom and in the libertine's ways. Does freedom need to end where libertine desires start? The cartography of frontiers between freedom and its excesses is a contentious, high theo-political issue.

Graham Ward has elaborated an *Allegoria Amoris* to consider a different cartography of knowing, based in a different Trinitarian loving (Ward 1998: 252). In this article, Ward is reflecting that meaning is not fixed, and names (as in the case of the names of God), more than fixing or designating specifically a God's definition, act as performatives. That is to suggest that the Trinitarian formula acts, more than says. As Ward explains, the kenotic narrative 'narrates a story of coming to know through coming to love' (Ward 1998: 253). Considering the Trinity as an allegory of love, by finding that love which is different in the Trinity, we can find a different epistemological ground for our reflection, while grounding our kenotic existence in a Queer experience of being as divine and transcendental although oblique and not having a vertical axis (Ward 1998: 253).

Following this reflection from Ward, we could start to embody the *Allegoria Amoris* as a Queer *Amoris*. For instance if, in a libertine and Sadean fashion, I was going to take pleasure in the act of counting and combining the numbers of sacred personae intimately and divinely related in Christian theology, I should start by saying that it takes two to tango, but three to be a divinity. Or that two may dance with pleasure but only three can make it divine. Why am I saying this? Because we are talking here about identity and, specifically, about divine identity. The point is that Christian theology shows, fortunately, a good understanding of the non-coincident identity of people even if in its historical development it may have been contradicted many times. That is to say, the Trinitarian formula expresses the material reality of the intimate reunion where God is not expected to coincide with Godself. In a time when theology has become preoccupied with issues of diversity and plurality in its discourse, as opposed to the more essentialist assumptions about the so called 'nature' of humanity, God has also been the object of theological de-essentialisation processes. One can briefly mention here the Feminist theological project in its original enquiry into Christ's masculinity, the quest for the Black Christ, the Gay Christ and more recently the reflections done by theologians seeking the face of a post-colonial Christ. However, although the theological subject has been and still is queried and rightly destabilised from a prefixed Christian horizon, there have been few if any theological attempts to de-stabilise God, that is the other partner of the theological dialogical process. We may suspect that the difficulties of bringing a more plural and diverse vision into theology are related precisely to the homogeneity of the concept of God. How can we even start to introduce the concept of a diverse subject in theology, that is, a woman, a de-centralised subject from the colonial space, a person reconsidering heterosexuality from a bisexual or even an heterosexual out-of-the closet theology if God remains essential, stable, fixed and therefore non-diverse and unique? We are not only confronted here with an issue of monotheism, but deeper than that or more relevant to our quest, we are facing here the extension of the conceptualisation of mono-loving relationships in Christian theology.

Mono-loving

Stand by your man.

Tammy Wynette

Should the country song 'Stand by your man' become the twenty-first century classic hymn to be sung at Sunday worship? The repetitive, monotonous lines express in such a simple yet powerful way the reality of repetitive, monotonous relations from the heterosexual matrix of sexual imagination. Mono-loving lives and mono-loving gods sooner or later may face short-circuits in their systems, expressed by lack of creativity and nurture. It is at this moment that we need to queer God as if God was to be found in a mono-loving situation of the worst kind or in a different, polyamorous Trinity. For instance by locating God in the intimate reunion of poly-loving bodies which may be intrinsic to the Trinitarian image. To do that, we need to revisit the Christian concept of kenosis as it has been developed from the New Testament base, in order to explain unusual relationships, for instance, the way God relates to Godself, that is, God's own identity questioning (symbolised by the relationship between God and Christ) and the amorous dealings between God and people.

Kenosis is a concept that has been historically used to develop an understanding of the relationship between God and humanity via Jesus Christ. Based on the text of Philippians 2:7, where the Greek verb *kenoo* (literally, 'I empty') appears to have been interpreted around the images of God's voluntary letting go of Godself in Christ, this phrase from the text of Philippians has become important simply because in Christianity, the problematic of having a credible God/man is deep and complex. We can find a rich kenotic discussion running through centuries of Christian theology, raising basic questions concerning how God could have 'let go', that is, become non-God or human. From there, the main arguments have been aligned, as Sarah Coakley carefully explains in her article 'Kenosis: A Subversion', on details such as the proportion of humanity and divinity expected in Christ, as in the discussions of Cyril of Alexandria in the fifth century (Coakley 1996: 90) or what sort of human did God become and what happened to God's divine attributes when becoming a man, as in the argument of Thomasius in the nineteenth century (Coakley 1996: 95). As Coakley clearly points out, there are issues of communication present here because the difficulties arise from trying to reflect on the way the two natures of the divine and the human can interrelate with each other. This theological interest in communication reflects in reality a long history of theological struggle with issues of power and how to find a dynamic of disempowering which does not disempower so much, but on the contrary, can give a twist to the concept of God's omnipotence and in the end make God even more powerful than before. The kenotic debate has been based on a tension between 'The Power' of God (absolute, imperial) and the power of Jesus (fragile, vulnerable, flickering between Jesus' outbursts of his 'I AM' identity and his failed praxis). In reality, this has been a 'power to power' kenotic understanding, that is, how to find in Jesus the imperial power of God which is not self-evident, and make of it a grandiose theological speech of power. This last point has been crucial not only in theology generally but also amongst liberationist and Feminist Theologies, which have striven to redefine power from the margins. 'Empowering' the poor has been a difficult process of replacements, re-conceptualisations and other devices which could pragmatically deal with the reality of empowering without giving any real power to anybody (in church or in society). The issue of the power of the vulnerable has been important in Liberation Theology, and also in Feminist Theology. In the latter case the emphasis on 'power in vulnerability' has been stressed as positive not only for women but also for men (however men or women are defined here). Radford Ruether's reflections on the kenosis of patriarchy, as produced in Christ (a kind of letting go of patriarchal frames of thinking/acting presented in Christ) has been a much used and sometimes abused concept, which, although it can lead to easy triumphalism, is still worth considering. Coakley, in her article which aims to unveil the oversimplification of kenotic understandings in Christian theology, has warned us that there is a somehow naïve alignment of genders (Coakley 1996: 106) in the distribution of power attributes to God and to Christ, which perhaps also needs to be queried (or *queeried*).

However, the historical discussion on the kenotic or 'letting go' process of God in Christ is basically in debt to a grammatical approach to theological reflection which has only recently been questioned. In theology learning about God has sometimes been a grammatical art and in the particular case we are discussing now, a study of style in power, the dynamics of punctuation of persona (divine and human) in the theological reflection and the approved conjugation of actions or divine verbs. Recent modern work in the study of languages has demonstrated the difficulties and sometimes even the futility of the grammatical school of teaching foreign languages, but theology has yet to learn this truth. Instead of emphasising a grammatical approach in the process of teaching and learning foreign languages, ethnographic methods (which, by the way, were pioneered by Freire in his education for liberation programmes) have been considered more effective. Instead of learning punctuation, students begin their learning processes by active observation of people interrelating amongst themselves in everyday life. Could this be also a Queer way to re-discover God, by active observation of God's polyamorous relationships as in the figure of the Trinity? Could a Freirean conscientisation process be a crucial factor in the process of the kenosis of God?[3]

A Queer kenosis may then consist in engaging with God as part of a theological project which aims to lead God astray, that is, facilitating God's own disempowering act but without presuming to know what original power is there

56

to let go. As the whole complicated history of the kenotic debate in Christianity seems to have been concerned exclusively with different struggles of the historically perceived dynamics of human power, based on a biologising process of God's ethos, the Queer perspective needs to depart from this radically. For instance, reflections on kenosis may inform the construction of a hermeneutical circle which may help us to recognise clues about God's own suicidal attempts. It was Paulo Freire who, as part of his dialogical method of education, first suggested the idea of the master allowing himself or herself to be assassinated. According to Freire, in any process of education for liberation, one of the most important aspects to recognise is that dynamic of self-effacing which the teacher needs to practise in order to let go (in favour of the students' own empowering process), as part of what we may recognise as a kenotic moment in the life of a dialogical style of education (Freire and Shor 1987: 89). Interestingly, this process is not very different from a divine kenosis where somehow we may assume that some form of God being or power is self-empty and devolved. The entry point for our nomadic subjects will be to recognise that precise point, the moment when the Master God commits suicide. However, it is important to recognise that the moment of precisely timed suicide in the divine kenotic process may be made up of different elements. That will make of God's death a suicide with many names. For instance, we may ask ourselves how God can commit a heterosexual suicide? That will lead God to commit larger and more fruitful suicidal acts such as those leading God to omnisexuality.

An omnisexual kenosis is a melancholic art, well fitted for theological subjects such as Queer nomads, because it represents a continuous attempt to understand sexual identities as a process consisting of the movement of emptiness not only of heterosexuality and heterosexual constructions, but of any other constructions of sexuality. For there are many longings of the heart amongst the nomadic people of God which go frustrated or even unacknowledged: but could the same be said about God's own heart? We may ask ourselves in this moment what is that which dies in a kenotic omnisexual process? What privileged point(s) of suicide needs be highlighted here? Just now we may say that in an omnisexual kenosis what dies is the mental (or rational) stability of God as a concept. It is not just the point of a power-measuring exercise in kenosis that we are talking about here, as in the more grammatical discussions of Christ's kenosis as a transmutation from omnipotence to less (but not ineffectual) power. What is at the stake here is not just God devolving itself in Christ but in the Trinity, and in the Trinity understood as an orgy, that is, a festival of the encounter of the intemperate in two key elements. The first is the theological presentation of God as an immoderate, polyamorous God, whose self is composed in relation to multiple embraces and sexual indefinitions beyond oneness, and beyond dual models of loving relationships. The second is the commitment of an omnisexual kenosis to destabilise sexual constructions of heterosexual readings of heterosexuality itself, bisexuality, gay and lesbian sexual identities and transvestite identities. The kenosis of omnisexuality in God is a truly genderfucking process worthy of being explored.

By reflecting on that, we will not only be able to find a hermeneutical circle of kenosis to re-discover the sexual relationship core of God, but also in ourselves as the community of God's people.

The closeted Trinity

Let us start with a libertine arithmetical queering. What is three? Two plus one (as in the heterosexual scene of husband, wife and lover)? Or is it one plus one plus one (as in detached loving encounters of affectively independent people)? How do we define faith here? Faith is a pluri-fidelity, as in a contained reunion in a time of religious exchanges. Different ways of combining ones to make three have different theological and amorous connotations and therefore different faithful results. The Trinity may be pointing us to a case of restricted polyfidelity, that is, in this divine triad three persons who enjoy a kinship close relationship are faithful amongst themselves. The lines of exchanges between the three could be multiple and yet they might remain in a faithful situation. We should be even more suspicious than that in considering the Trinity as an expression of polyfidelity. We may ask if there are more than three in this triad because as in real life and relationships many other friends and lovers may be hidden in the closets of each person of the Trinity. To presume otherwise would force us to fall into gender (and sexual) divine stability; the Godman–father who only relates to the Godman–son and the God–spirit. Precisely the figure of the Spirit here is reminiscent of the hidden third man in many heterosexual marriages, where the husband practises rough trade, or the lesbian lover of the wife (or any other combination), making us suspicious of what clusters of forbidden desires are hidden under God. Therefore, one of the first 'deaths' occurring in this kenotic process of omnisexuality is the death of the illusion of limited relationships. That is, the death of the mono-lover, which signifies the end of the hidden, silenced persons of our lives. Our beloveds are sometimes like holy ghosts. But the point is to ask whether by opening up the hidden relationships of each person of the Trinity we might not destabilise power through desire and knowledge. For instance, we cannot presume to know the identities of this extensive polyfaithful group of sacred friends. At one point we could exercise theological imagination and say that the son lies besides his Magdalene and his Lazarus. Has God the Father maintained his conflictive emotional relationship with someone else? Is there any third party, of non-heterosexual inclination, or a woman heterosexual but out of the closet, still part of this otherwise mixed masculine circle? A woman lover amongst male lovers? Can we reflect on say, the relation between God the Father, Jesus and Lazarus? How do these three exchange affection with each other? Are they *amigovios*[4]? Why not? At this point, we should start speaking about *Trinitarians*, a term which combines another two terms: the triad (as the persons who belong to the Trinity) and the historical or economic Trinity. Some theologians like to speak about an immanent and a historical (or external) Trinity (for instance Leonardo Boff (1988)) but the division of the public and the private represented in this kind of thought does not resist much theological queering. The point is that unless we fall into dualistic thinking in theology, the historical (public) acts of the Trinitarians cannot differ too much from their private ones.

As we search for examples of possible affective and sexual exchanges amongst the Trinitarians, the most important thing for us is obviously not to find personalities but sexual identities, even if they are badly shaped by the time spent in their closets. The Trinitarians do not need to have heterosexual relations, nor so-called 'same-sex relations' since no same-sex relations in reality ever exist. The invention of the concept of 'same-sex' relationship is heterosexual, since it is based on the notion of a limited number of sexualities and also their equivalences. The fact that two women may have a sexual relationship does not imply that they belong to the 'same-sex' at all, even if generically they may be called lesbians or bi. The difficulty for heterosexuality is to grasp the fact that not all sex has a name or a date or place of discovery.

We are searching here for clues, such as the point of a patent leather shoe appearing through a door that is slightly ajar, or even the tiny corner of a frilly blouse caught in the locked door of a church wardrobe. A definitive blouse left outside of the closet of theology is the Anti-Christ, not as a different persona representing the antithesis of what Christ was and stood for, but as a sexual identity. Or to be more specific, as an Anti-Christ(ian) sexual identity which may be the denial of any given and permanent sexual identity, beyond the dyads of T-Theology. This Anti-Christ represents a truly Trinitarian sexual identity which is basically bisexual in the sense of disjunctive, unstable and engaged in a process of permanent creation and self-destruction. It is not 'anti' in the heterosexual sense of oppositional, reversed and thus, a sexual complement but 'anti' in the sense of acting against Christ or any fixed sexual identity attributed to Christ. This Anti-Christ dissolves whatever Christ(ian) desires are there, for other men and for other women, reminding us also that men and women are not dyadic sexual identities: they are multitudes.

In the next chapter we shall continue our reflections on God's kenosis as the act of leading God astray by reflecting on the work of Pierre Klossowski as presented in his books *Roberte ce soir* and *The Revocation of the Edict of Nantes* (Klossowski 1989). Our intention is to see how much we can get defamiliarised with the hetero-normative God, and how to recognise God as 'the stranger at our gates' of Klossowski's theological novel, *Roberte ce soir*. For that, we shall keep walking in the path of a hermeneutics of defamiliarisation while making new links and alliances between theology and Queer thinking.

59

4

LIBERTINE DISCLOSURES

The master of the house ... waits anxiously at the gate for the stranger
he will see appear like a liberator upon the horizon.

(Klossowski 1989: 12)

The Gospel and inculturation: God the Sodomite

Whenever we reflect on the Other we always need to think too about God as the
ultimate Other, but also as a concrete, articulated other.[1] Queer theologies reflect
on the strangers at the gate of Christianity, that is the people whose life and experiences do not fit with T-Theology. However, theology works in a dialectical way,
and to reflect on Queer lives always implies reflecting on a Queer God too. In this
chapter we will reflect theologically on God as the sexual stranger at the gates of
theology. In order to do that, we need to consider further tactics of defamiliarisation and connections: the Deleuzian concepts of deterritorialisation and
reterritorialisation could also be important (Deleuze and Guattari 1990: 164).
Deterritorialisation is a useful concept which helps us to perceive hints of what has
been left outside the theological heterosexual spaces and moreover, what unusual
ideas we can find in God and in the Trinity when we bring bisexual thinking to
bear on them. This concept applies to the notion of abstracting from an original
context, as for instance in moving out of an original context which has impeded
not only the formation of new understandings but the creation of new links or
connections amongst ideas. Reterritorialisation is then precisely that act of making
new connections or re-codings of reality once an original context has been superseded (although not necessarily obliterated). These concepts can be used in a
positive and subversive way. Thus God, by being free from the obligation to partake of the theological compound of heterosexuality, deterritorialised Godself by
being free to walk 'without using its hands', or with hands free for the first time,
to use a Deleuze and Guattari metaphor from *A Thousand Plateaus: Capitalism
and Schizophrenia* (1987). What can a God who suddenly may refuse to use God's
hands become? What we are asking here is how the deterritorialisation of God's
body may proceed. In this we realise that there is a task of accompaniment, or the
fulfilment of an escort vocation in the Queer theologian who witnesses to the

liberated territories of being God that have suddenly been made available by an act of Contextual Theological independence, in a sort of agrarian reform, redistributing and determining new free land of Christian praxis to be given away. And God can become then a multiplicity, not an anonymous or vague multiplicity but rather an organisational principle which does not need oppositional or complementary combinations (as in heterosexual thought). That multiplicity is part of God's change of God's own context of behaviour but also part of God's own becoming as an 'affective, intensive, anarchist body that consists of poles, zones, thresholds ...' (Deleuze 1997: 131). That is, an unpredictable and random system where the Trinity may not remain as such, including its statistics (or logic of three). We are left with a God who does not belong anymore to those genealogical lists of the Scriptures, because suddenly God does not belong to the context of the procreative and therefore may be able, as Klossowski could put it, to overcome the need for recording an original model. That means also leaving behind God's own fear of copies (Deleuze 1997: 66). God does not need anymore to be 'the God of our fathers' to have a bond with the people; bonds do not need to be procreatively, genitally defined and dyadic (Sedgwick 1994: 71). God can be free to experience transitions and oscillations and to become multiple may mean only one thing: to disown the name of the Father, or the name of the heterosexual dyadic family. That name of the Father installed at the centre of our divine cultural system (Sedgwick 1994: 72) needs to be recognised by Christians as a hidden presence of limitation in our hearts. This is the limitation produced by the internalisation of oppression or the affective investment we make in ideology and Heterosexual Theology alike.

We are talking here about a tactic of deterritorialisation of God which may be part of a gay, ironic art of God's own becoming. It is interesting to notice that Deleuze mentions 'irony' as 'the art of multiplicities' (Deleuze 1997: 182). An ironic God is not only a multiplicity, but it also means that God belongs to that gay genre par excellence, the irony, which can define and redefine the art of being divine and gay. Divinely gay, the non-heterosexual people of God have much to share and say about God, outside the boundaries of heterosexual ideology.

Reinterpreting differences in deterritorialising and reterritorialising theological tactics needs to avoid the nuisance of authoritarian prophetism. Without authoritarianism, prophetism is usually something else, because the prophet is never dialogic but certain. The problem is that authoritarian prophetism may centralise marginal concerns too and produce a consistent although exclusive message. As Spivak suggests:

> It is ... not only the structure of marginalization centralization that assures the stability of cultural explanations in general. The fence of the consistency loop, as I argue, also helps ... in order to make my behaviour as a female consistent with the rest ... I would have to be defined as a sexless (in effect, male) humanist – and the rest of me would be fenced out of the consistency loop. The strongest brand of centralization is to

allow in only the terms that would be consistent anyway or could be accommodated within an argument based on consistency.

(Spivak 1996: 43)

In Christianity the prophetic task has been seen many times as one of denouncing inconsistencies or multiple combinations of meaning arising from 'possibilities ... out of context' (Spivak 1996: 43). It is precisely the necessity for bifurcations, or disrupting possibilities, which may create the need in the Same God to become a Different God. Following Foucault, we can say that the medical discourse on God, which is based on a triple articulation between the visible, the expressible and a 'stable' God may end only when its hidden structure may be unveiled (Carrette 2000: 13). And what is the visible and the expressible of the Trinitarian God? The dyadic family structure. In each God and each Jesus of theological discourses (including many discourses of difference) there are dyadic identities giving unity and coherence to divinities. Therefore, the so-called stability of God is no more stable than heterosexuality in itself, and theology needs to become anti-prophetic, that is, allowing the dialogue with discontinuity to happen.

In order to explore this Trinitarian episteme and open a random system in which God has declared Godself liberated from the closet, we can consider grounding our discussion at this point on a different hermeneutical framework, such as the libertine circle of interpretation which we may find in one of Pierre Klossowski's theological novels, *Roberte ce soir* (Klossowski 1989). We will later use a structure of interpretation provided by Georges Bataille and the Marquis de Sade. These three writers present us with different understandings of divinity and give us unique enlightenment from their starting point which is one of affective and sexual relationships. Klossowski, in *Roberte ce soir*, 'thinks God' from the creation of almost canonical laws of hospitality and an angry attempt to make God manifest Godself through a frame provided by a kind of 'libertine atheism' (Dean quoted by Carrette 2000: 70).

This angry libertine atheism of Klossowski forces God as a divine traveller to reach the end of God's own coming out process. The text on which we will reflect is *Roberte ce soir* which belongs to the trilogy of Klossowski's novels included in *La Loi de L'Hospitalité* [The Law of Hospitality]: *Le Souffleur, Roberte ce soir,* and *La Révocation de l'Édit de Nantes.* It is, with the exception of *Le Baphomet,* the most theological of his novels. From Bataille, we are going to consider in detail a text already anticipated, *Madame Edwarda* or the text of the 'Whore-God', that is, a God that is revealed through the abjections of prostitution but also poverty, presenting a reflection on the mature prostitute as the revelation of God manifested as an 'indecent exposure of God' (Althaus-Reid 2000: 208). Finally from Sade, we will reflect on his *Philosophy in the Bedroom* and the act of submission as a challenge to the Western Christian paradigm (Carrette 2000: 83) which is the context of the process of the deterritorialisation of God. At the end, we should be able to conclude with a different understanding of the kenotic trajectory of the Trinitarians (that is, the divine people in the Trinity) outside the system of the sacralisation of the ideology of heterosexuality.

Sharing the theologian's wife

You must realize from the start that once [questions] are asked you are going to be less free, even if you refuse to answer.

(Klossowski 1989: 21)

What will happen to God?

(Carrette 2000: 18)

I came across *Roberte ce soir* some years ago due to my interest in Klossowski as a libertine atheist theologian. The basic story of the novel is one with which many theologians may have points in common, if not in the suggested actions of the novel, in the theological anguish and questioning of the protagonist. For a start, the protagonist, Octave, is presented as a 'Professor of Scholastics at Y***' (Klossowski 1989: 9). Octave is a theologian living with his wife Roberte and a nephew who is a theology student. For any theologian reading through the grain of this complex and enigmatic text, the patterns of alienation and anxious reflections which belong to the affective mood of Heterosexual Theology are clear. The conjugal unhappiness of Octave and his belief that he needs to make this unhappiness contagious may reflect a prosaic aspect of monogamy but also presents the theologian as a disseminator of reflections on divine intimacy and alienation, as between God and people but also amongst Godself.

In fact, it is surprising that not many theological reflections have originated in *Roberte ce soir*, since Klossowski touches on many relevant issues such as the vocation of the theologian, the relationship between the theologian and God, claustrophobia and the existential basis of God as the Trinity. The story line is deceptively simple and difficult to recount. Octave, unhappy in his relation to Roberte (who is described as rigid and hostile towards Octave's theology, while enigmatic and deceptive in her sobriety) has devised what Deleuze has called a process of deterritorialisation (a way to abstract the relationship from its context) and reterritorialisation (a new codification from the breakthrough of former impediments) to challenge the situation. In this process, Octave wants to introduce Roberte to a sharing, expressed as a meeting with the 'rule of hospitality which our traditions condemn as shameful' (Klossowski 1989: 9). That tradition which is about to be challenged is the mono-tradition of Christianity: the mono-loving mono-gamy rule of the dyadic family. Octave, the theologian, wants to share Roberte – his wife – with *strangeness*. Klossowski describes this as waiting at the gate for a stranger to appear (Klossowski 1989: 12) in order to be able to perpetrate a confusion of identities between the master of the house (himself, the theologian), the host (as the stranger at the gate) and the hostess (Roberte, his wife). *Roberte ce soir* is therefore a story about theological traditions disrupted by the bifurcation strategies of hospitality and a search for a kenosis of God through a sexual encounter with strangers. This is a tale of sharing and giving away gifts with an almost theological condition of grace (or gratuity) in a hospitable economy of sexuality. The interesting point is that in the story, the divine identities are hesitant about the encounter; the kenosis of God does not seem to be natural. Klossowski was interested in how bodies talk of God, in a way that in his writing we may see traces of a powerful and destabilising body theology which, by default, destabilises God too.

The law of hospitality to which Octave wants to introduce Roberte is expressed by a stranger at the gate. That stranger is the Count della Santa-Sede (literally, 'Count of the Holy See') thus making *Roberte ce soir* a story about a theologian who wants to share his wife with the Vatican. The Vatican is, somehow, the stranger at the gate. Roberte, the theologian's wife, is the hostess who receives and at the same time is given to strangeness, but not without fierce struggles, in an atmosphere of contradictions of an almost sacramental nature. A theologian does not need to be Queer to identify with the desperate attempt of Klossowski in *Roberte ce soir* to make a rupture of the discourse on God from which God can come out in a different way. As Roberte says of Octave in *L'Édit de Nantes*, a theologian is a 'Professor of an anachronistic science, canon law ... [a survivor] of a bygone period which *the disorder of our own has restored to fashion*' (Klossowski 1989: 114; my italics).

What is the sharing (or merging) act of hospitality that Octave the theologian is trying to achieve when he declares that the master will become one with the stranger (Klossowski 1989: 13)? Maybe here we shall be able to find the problem of accidental communications in theology finally exposed. By accidental communications we refer to the permanent dislocation of intimacy in the theological discourse which the messianic construction of theology does not resolve but aggravates by highlighting it. This happens because the accidental incommunication between God the Father and Jesus may be resumed in the induced confusion of Octave's theological strategies in sharing (and merging) his wife with a stranger. And that is the Queer quest: that the master of the house should no longer be the master of the house; that the guest who seems to be so far away from his home should be thought of as if he is not. That the host may be translated into a guest and a guest into a host (Klossowski 1989: 12–13). It is in this (sacramental) sense of merged identities that the existential basis of Roberte, as the mistress of the house, needs to be encouraged to pursue a Foucaldian infidelity of origins, or a disavowal of the dyadic rituals which accompany religious discourses, such as the 'spurious symmetry' denounced by Sedgwick in her article 'Is the Rectum Straight?' (Sedgwick 1994: 73). The symmetry which needs to be betrayed in the theological discourse is that which is present in social, political and religious inter-implications, as when they deny that different sexual universes may, after all, exist. In this we may recognise the dream of intimacy with God by kenosis. The dream which gave birth to Jesus was primarily a desire to make of the master a host, and of the host, a master. In

64

a way, it was a theological vision of finding God through a heterosexual system of exchange, using for its own purpose dual communication and the politics of sacred dispossession. However, in this system of hospitability, was it possible to have a God which did not resemble its own production?

This argument comes from Deleuze and Guattari, the idea of God the Lobster: a God whose identity lies in processes of sedimentation (through the location of substance and form) and a 'folding' consisting in God finding new linkages and emergent properties (Protevi 2001: 39). God the Lobster is the result then of a differential process which adjudicates God's partiality and a lack of resemblance with for instance, sexual productions. As the Christian incarnation is an act of sexual production, contained and located in a restrictive economy, that concept is not novel in Christianity in relation to the God-host of Jesus. Still, a lack of resemblance is more related to a Queer Theology, because T-Theology tends to homogenise a God Creator with acts of resemblance, as if creation could be a mere reminiscence of God or an act of memory, a transcendental mimicry of God and a culturally mirrored scene. It is that resemblance which Octave wants to confound by questioning the 'essence' of the gender role – that of the 'mistress of the house' – in the bourgeois universe of Klossowski's novel. As Klossowski remarks that nobody knows who the hostess is (Klossowski 1989: 16) we should also remark that nobody knows either who that 'master' is. At this moment, as the intention of transgression of presupposed 'essences' progresses, it is important for us to understand that this story is no more about a husband offering his wife for sexual intercourse with a stranger than Jesus having a vicarious death, that is, a son given to his killers by his own father. *Roberte ce soir* is about the production of desire and relocation of pleasure in theology by the use of perverse materials accessible to the theologian as a builder or *bricoleur*. For instance, by breaking the law of sexual property or decency, the theology of fidelity is exposed in its more transcendental dimensions. To whom shall we be faithful? To the master (God) or to the stranger at the gates? How can the ultimate kenosis of God occur unless God is consumed by an inner desire for submission? And in the final analysis, who is God sharing with whom, and who are the strangers at God's gate representing liberation? At this point we need to think about subversive affective gatherings. We need further reflections on God the Trinity and in the kind of infidel thinking present in Klossowski.

Following our story, Roberte has been denounced by Octave, the theologian, as an unbeliever. She is in fact, according to her own description, an atheist but not a pervert, as Octave claims, who seems to equate the two things. In Roberte's own words: 'Perverse, you insult God to make Him exist, therefore you believe in Him, that proves you secretly worship Him!' (Klossowski 1989: 70). The argument seems to be one in which post-Christians usually get entangled, because they have the deep belief that Christianity does not admit infidel thinking; that is, that Christianity is defined in a certain way by certain traditions and therefore feminists, liberationists or black subversives in theology are not representative of real Christianity.[2] Klossowski accentuates this infidel thinking in the novel by portraying Roberte as an 'inspectress' trying to get Octave to be rightfully disciplined by a 'Censorship Committee', especially due to Octave's book on Sade. (This reflects Klossowski's autobiography since his book *Sade, My Neighbour* ran into problems with censorship.) What is not clear is who is a believer and who is an infidel in this story, because in a way, they are all believers and infidels at the same time. This is precisely what we are looking for; that is, the relation of believing–infidelity that we should explore in our understanding of the Trinitarians.

First of all, we need to consider that the Trinitarians' relationship is not a reproductive one but a dissident one. At a certain point in her critique, Roberte makes this point with exemplary clarity: the sin of the doctrine of original sin lies in reproduction (Klossowski 1989: 83). Therefore, the first thing for us to do is to avoid considering reproductive affections or the reproduction of identity amongst the Trinitarians. Octave makes this clear when he says:

> The less you see, dear boy, the nearer you approach the truth: you see no possible communication of her nature for the reason that you fancy Roberte is always Roberte.
>
> (Klossowski 1989: 32)

Or once again, when Roberte says:

> ... Your Victor? Or rather the collection of odds and ends which goes with that name?
>
> (Klossowski 1989: 80)

By bonding them through non-reproductive affections we also mean accepting the Trinity as an open form, a gathering of sexual relationships outside prescriptions. Jo Eadie, in an article on 'Activating Bisexuality: Towards a Bi/Sexual Politics' refers to the idea of a bi-community as 'a collectivity of no secure borders' (Eadie 1993: 142). With this point we should like to introduce a bi/difference into some good models of the Trinity presented as 'friendship models' when they have, lurking in their midst, the name of the Father (linked to the family model) or a reproductive, profit orientated idea of community behind them. This is obvious in the theology of liberation model, as presented by Leonardo Boff. I have already argued elsewhere, following Sedgwick, that there is a pattern of homosolidarity in the Trinitarian models of the liberationists (Althaus-Reid 2000). The heterosexual grid (or 'formal expression', following Deleuze and Guattari: see Protevi 2001: 36) works as the undivided surface of the matter which acquires forms or expressions according to that imposed grid. Let us reflect on this point in detail.

This is the point at which to discuss the Lobster God, and the body without organs of Deleuze (Deleuze 1997) may be relevant to our understanding of the kenosis of heterosexuality amongst the Trinitarians. Deleuze and Guattari speak about the category of strata, as a category for understanding how matter is organ-ised and articulated. In fact they use in a broad way different and sometimes interexchangeable terms such as strata, epistrata, parastrata and so forth. What Deleuze and Guattari are trying to do is to be coherent with a highly materialist philosophical project which is much in tune with a materialist hermeneutical the-ological project. That means that instead of making the starting point of their reflections the conversion of 'the world' into signs, they want to do precisely the opposite, that is, to locate material signs within concrete matter (Bogue 1989: 126). Theologically speaking, this project would be equivalent to a radical queer-ing where the interest does not lie in the conversion of our experiences of God in history into the framework of any given theology or T-Theology. That would not be enough. The challenge would be to find that of God in our experiences and organise a theological reflection there, without conversion and on the spot. For Deleuze and Guattari the challenge is to dilute the bi-analysis of concepts such as 'expression' and 'content' as arbitrary and duplicitous divisions. Following Hjelmsev's understanding of the unsustainable division between expression and content/substance Deleuze and Guattari conclude that matter is also an expres-sion, or the form that individual elements take when shaped by that same matter. Expressions are forms in themselves and also substances, created by the imposition of content-forms. (Bogue 1989: 126). For Deleuze and Guattari this matter is also a material substrate to content and expression or a 'body without organs' or body of consistency. A body without organs is a body without rules or codifica-tions. It is a sexual Trinity without heterosexual thought or a lesbian Trinity without lesbian thought (when both heterosexuality and lesbianism are projected via authoritarian, heterosexual ideological constructions).[3] It is basically a desta-bilised sexual body where identity and sexual praxis become relative terms. The consequences of this are so far-reaching that the kenotic process is extreme: noth-ing of God is left over; this is a disembowelling of the Trinity.

Premature ejaculations: God in transit

> ... he who intrudes between you and me, between me and Aunt
> Roberte, between your aunt and yourself ... And this third person is a
> pure spirit
>
> (Klossowski 1989: 22–3)

At this point, the risk of a premature ejaculation of God (in the metaphorical sense of the self-emptying process or Trinitarian kenosis) is something we must beware of and avoid. Sexuality needs to be the point of theological awareness; we should not allow conceptual censorship in our theological praxis. Deleuze and Guattari claim in this discussion taken from *A Thousand Plateaus* (1987) that the concept of nature has been inextricably linked to the concept of God, from Aristotle to Kant. As theologians, we must be aware that the discussion at this point exceeds the eco-logical component of such a statement, as important as it may be. This is because from this point we are not stepping into a theology of articulating nature by reconsidering the Christian paradigm of God-Dominion but disentangling a relation by articulating God and nature in a different way. The discussion on the 'abstract machine' is very complex and extensive, but we are going to focus only on the points which have more relevance to us from our perspective of kenosis, and the risk of God's premature ejaculation in the process. For Deleuze and Guattari nature stratifies, that is, codifies, and destratifies by decodifying while at other times it overcodifies. God is an articulation between the interstices of this double process of unity and dispersion. Deleuze and Guattari call this articulation the Lobster God. But the Lobster God is not the whole of it. Let us examine this point in more detail. The idea of the Lobster God is an expression of a coding, over-coding and de-coding process; a double-pincered God articulating content and expression (two relative expressions as we have previously seen; Protevi 2001: 31). Yet Deleuze and Guattari cannot see God in everything, only in part of the movement. Why? Because for them, the de-stratification has its own immanent rules and orders, independent of any transcendental claim. This is the plane of nature but also human creativity and language. This is also the space of a relative kenosis (for according to this discussion something must remain in order to continue). This plane is called by the French philosophers 'the body without organs', that is, a body (political, religious or institutional such as marriage for instance) where there are no organs to negotiate the order. Sexuality is an organ because sexuality is an order. So 'God is not everything' means that God needs to be thought of as in transit, or in a process of extreme heterosexual kenosis or disembowelling simply by acknowledging that God is only a part in the articulation of desire and sexuality. God is not an ultimate or total source. God the Lobster shows us a path of God (the Trinity) as an articulation of a limited exercise of kenosis. Sexuality cannot go completely there, or it will never make a second return. Yet, it liberates us from finding in God 'the source' of sexual identities such as God the Lesbian or God the Genderfucker. No, instead of these 'premature ejaculations', sexuality becomes part of the articulation of God in history, of people and Trinitarians, and the struggles for identity which fit into the interstices of the processes of construction and production of desires. God the Lobster is partial while responsible but does not resemble its own productions – not in the sense that we cannot identify a Genderfucker God – but in the sense that God's sexuality is not to be rendered stable (Protevi 2001: 39). Let us remember here that the Genderfucker may also be straight, even if daring on occasion to mess with the heterosexual closet.

Returning to Klossowski's libertine theological hermeneutical circle, this Lobster God is what is interfering in the interstices of the relation between Roberte, Octave and Antoine. The 'intrusion' (more than an interfering) is related to the act of 'naming'. Octave's strategy is related to the naming of Roberte to the pure Spirit as an act of consecration and at the same time of denunciation. The naming of Roberte is part of a liturgical act still performed in the church, as when Pope John Paul II consecrated Russia to the Virgin of Fatima on 25 March 1987 (Bernstein and Politi 1996: 533). That act of naming, which

Klossowski classifies as 'a denunciation', calls for the presence of a virtual witness to a virtual reality. This happens because to consecrate Roberte to the Spirit is to call a divine witness to know in her name what she does not fully know yet. For instance, that Roberte will become the law of hospitality herself, in the same way that for the Pope Russia will become, after the Pope's naming, a Roman Catholic country. In fact, Klossowski calls this process of naming a denunciation of the inactuality of Roberte: Russia is not Roman Catholic neither has Roberte shown the 'loose behaviour' expected of her as yet (Klossowski 1989: 30).

'Naming to the Spirit' is a knowledge process of claiming hidden (or inactual) divine knowledge. We are witnessing here an important element that can introduce us to acts of Queer spiritual consecrations. A Queer 'naming to the Spirit' of the Trinity is represented by that consecration of the stranger at the gate, by/to a God who wants to reverse orders while revealing Godself in sexual disorder. In our example of the Pope, an icon of the Virgin of Fatima has been located in Kazan, Russia and by that symbolic gesture the Pope can claim that he has named Russia to the Spirit. In the same way, that God, whose sexuality is independent of heterosexual speculations and not stable, has become the witness of the consecration of Roberte to a Vatican ambassador, Count della Santa-Sede, whom Klossowski has identified in his novel as the stranger at the gate. That stranger at the gate is an image of marginality which resists incorporation, because in the law of hospitality what is theologically posited for us is that the Trinity would give hospitality by becoming the stranger and trespassing beyond the border of current theological discourses. In that sense, we find the sacramental aspect of the queering of the Trinity exposed in its real scandalous praxis: the unstable and varied sexual relationship amongst the Trinitarians is subjected to multiple exchanges outside our well known straight town's policies. This does not mean, for instance, that a lesbian Christian woman encounters the Trinitarian spirituality as a S/M experience and as a result, the gospel becomes incarnated in a S/M–lesbian theological praxis of the divine. It is more than that, for queering the Trinity in this way means that in reality it is the Queer at the margins who is entering into a dialogical healing of the Trinity. The Trinity is then as lost as the Queer at the gate before they realise they need to give hospitality to each other: the radical kenosis of the Queer and of the Trinity means that God is manifested here as a (sexual) relationship, unstable, multiple and Queer, and cannot come out unless that stranger at the gate appears and gives God God's place (which is a marginal position). In reality, she is offering God a dis-placement and facilitating the betrayal of Godself in the heterosexual Trinity structure. It is no longer a Trinitarian economy but rather a self perpetuating exemplary (sexual) form of organisation, production and distribution of Sexual Theology; no longer mono-monotheism claiming to accept diversity but fixing the meeting place; no longer 'active interpenetration of the divine Persons amongst themselves' (Boff 1988: 239) but rather more diverse ways of relating and claiming each other as part of the community of God appearing in our theological reflections.

The law of hospitality gives us several Queer theological entry points on which to reflect. However, there is one important element which we need to discuss here. In narrating *Roberte ce soir*, Klossowski has made of the law of hospitality not only a consecration but also an act of sexual consecration. After all, it is a woman (heterosexual, as far as this can be identified in the narrative) given to the stranger by Octave, the theologian. It could have been Antoine. It could have been Roberte offering Octave to della Santa-Sede. This is the sharing of the theologian's wife: a sacrament of the struggle presenting the visit of the stranger as salvific, pre-conditioned by a consecration which names the inactuality of theology. Yet, the gender issue presents us with the addition of a gift economy, neither completely alien to Christian theology nor yet a novelty. An economy of the gift is obviously present in the sacraments. It is present even in the church's self-deceptive practices of the logic of (divine) exchange, which legitimates the role of calculations alien to gift-logic (Bordieu 1997: 233). There is no doubt that theological calculations have managed to reduce the list of those invited to the gift-festivities of the sacramental acts to a select number. Sexual calculations, to be more specific, are very alienating in the gift-economy of, for instance the Eucharist. Jesus Christ crucified has also been the subject of gift-economic reflections, for the body of the Messiah seems to have been seen according to Kristeva as agape, the 'edible gift' of God manifested in incarnation (Berry 1998: 323). It has thus fulfilled somehow (in that old-fashioned form of the 'vicarious death' reflections) the rule of women's hospitality. However, the Messiah's femininity as a God-commodity used, exchanged and consumed in order to secure the soul-surviving of certain groups is invalidated by the fact that the name of the Father is associated with the commodity. Thus the sacrificial value of the Christ-commodity differs so much from the sacrificial value of women-commodities in church and society, but it does relate to men's sacrificial sense of value. This may be the simple theological reason why the virtue of self-sacrifice is understood so differently in Christianity between women and men, to the point that it exalts men while it destroys women.

Let us start then by considering this point, that historically it is only women who are the exchangeable commodities upon which societies and divine systems are built (Irigaray 1997: 174). Following Irigaray's analysis in her article 'Women on the Market', we may agree that women are the providers of the organisation of social and cultural infrastructures through the usage of their bodies, their consumption and public circulation. Thus, the following dialogue between Roberte and Octave illuminates the point with a twist:

ROBERTE: You, Octave, you confuse the absence of a revealed truth with the situation of the human being who has got to forge a truth for himself because no God has revealed it to him...

OCTAVE: (*suddenly frightened*) Roberte, you have nothing but a body to back up your word!

ROBERTE: (*letting out a curious laugh*) And to keep it I have nothing but a spirit.

(Klossowski 1989: 88–9)

If Klossowski presents Octave as a Queer man in struggle with a straight theology, Roberte's body circulates theologically by providing its traditional adjudicated value made of the two components: usefulness and exchangeability. Roberte 'understands' this by saying that the spirit is the only keeper of her body. Her body is the only locus of herself as a commodity, essential to the life of her group, in this case, the theological community of Octave or that base community consisting of Antoine, the Vatican ambassador and herself. This is what Irigaray would call the cult of the Father, or Sedgwick 'the family' (Irigaray 1997: 179; Sedgwick 1994: 6); the name of the Father who not only authorises the phallic exchange of women-commodities but also manifests itself by such exchanges.

Yet both usefulness and exchangeability are confused, which makes the exchange of the 'Roberte-theological commodity' particularly immoral and indecent. That is, the private body becomes a public body and in this sense Roberte, the intellectual wife of the theologian, is the equivalent of a prostitute, for it is prostitution which confuses the use value of women by producing a break between use and exchange: the value of the prostitute is her use (Irigaray 1997: 185) What we have then in Klossowski's theological account is not only the exchange of women as commodities but the use of the whore (as a category) in order to undertake what Dean has called the angry attempt by Klossowski to force God to manifest Godself (Carrette 2000: 70). Therefore Roberte is a theologically constructed and circulated whore, but not only that, because she may be here the Whore of Babylon, that archetypical enemy of God and the one who opposes the teleological order of God in the narrative of the Book of Revelation. Moreover, as Gerda Lerner has pointed out, the Babylonian prostitutes were the carers of the goddesses (Lerner 1986: 239) and therefore the reason for the theological disturbance in the order of other gods such as the Judeo-Christian. This is a dispute of identity. However, as Deleuze and Guattari have noted, for Klossowski God is always the final enemy of identity and identity in plurality (Deleuze 2001: 292). The whore is here the theological equivalent to the Body without Organs of Deleuze and Guattari in that confusion presented by Irigaray's Marxist analysis of the prostitute, where use (as in the extensive use of a woman's body by men) increases value, that is value is adjudicated and further promoted to a destroyed (woman) commodity. This provides a woman with an identity of value-continuity by precisely the opposite, that is, discontinuity through actions of derangement committed against the valuable. That is the location of disorder and promiscuous organisation of the prostitute identity in the Western culture in our times. Therefore Roberte, as the whore, represents the Trinitarian body without rules; the dis-organised body or more precisely the body outside the law of Godly organisation. The Trinity (or the Trinitarians) is God rebelling against Godself only if we understand the Trinity as the body without organs – an already disembowelled God. In this we find the real intention of a queering of God: the reclaiming of the right to non-originals, or to a departure of the imprint, just as Klossowski has tried in his own theological project to discontinue the relation between the original and its copy(ies) or model and image (Deleuze 1994: 66).

We are redefining not only the role of the theologian which in *Roberte ce soir* is communitarian but also the path of Queer Theology itself. For queering theology requires, as Klossowski has argued, a cutting and reversal of Platonism (Deleuze 1994: 312). In his book *Difference and Repetition*, Deleuze organises his argument on the Platonic Dialectics and Klossowski in the following way:

- first of all, there is a selection of difference;
- second, a mythical circle is put in place;
- thirdly, a foundation is established; and
- finally, the question–problem complex is positioned.

However, the prevalence of the order of the Same in Platonic dialectical thought is so strong that the Same becomes the arbiter of difference. Moreover, as Deleuze highlights, the identity which differs suffers destruction (Deleuze 1994: 66–7). For Klossowski, read through Deleuze, difference cannot be subordinated to the final judgement of the same, or the 'Original model'. The reversal of Platonism is then a doxology of simulacra, or celebration of images and copies. Even the 'eternal return' is for Klossowski not a copy returning to an original model, but an original which originality lies, precisely in the act of returning; or the art of making a copy without original.

Where is the simulacra and the effacing of original copies in *Roberte ce soir*? In the last chapter and as the final words of the novel, after her sexual encounter with the Vatican (ambassador), Roberte gives him a pair of keys which the Count refuses to take. Those keys are the keys of the hostess, the material sign of the location which gives identity to the mistress of the house but not to the guest as visitant. Octave's theological strategy has been to produce a radical exchange of identities: that the host will be the guest, and the guest the host in what we may see as a scene of truly Eucharistic exchange. However, paraphrasing Deleuze we may say that the presence of the different is not to be found in dyads, that is, it does not necessarily lurk between host and guest (or copy and original). Moreover, the master/mistress/host, functioning as the central locus in the act of receiving the stranger at the gate, must resist becoming original identities, but remain as simulacra. By remaining as simulacra, the right to disparity is gained. Is the Trinity, then, a Christian theological attitude about God's resistance to an original? This will force us to question the political standing of the Trinitarians' economy. For that purpose we need to ground our reflections in the underlying processes of production.

Metrosex: Trinitarian under-groundings

To walk is to lack a site.

(de Certeau 2000: 110)

We turn our attention now to two aspects of our present reflection: first, the walking distance from Octave and Roberte's house to the gates where the stranger should appear; and second, the issue of the 'grounding' of the Trinity. In an illuminating piece entitled 'Walking in the City', Michel de Certeau takes us to that 'practice of everyday living' as he puts it, such as walking (de Certeau: 2000). Walking is a powerful metaphor for doing theology. For instance the theology of liberation uses the metaphor of walking when referring to the *caminata*. Although we are talking here about what we could call the geography of rhetorics, it would be useful to think about Klossowski from the point of view of de Certeau. De Certeau, like Deleuze, is interested not in 'the production of difference but in different productions'. (Buchanan 2000: 99). That is to say, neither de Certeau nor Deleuze pursue genealogic studies of production. Our equivalent would be to say that Queer Theology may have little interest in the genealogical or archeological trackings of how and by which processes certain cultural forms are finally associated with power or the lack of it at certain historical moments. That is to say, from the perspective of queering the Trinity our interest has not lain with the genealogy of the Trinity, although much ecclesiastical history deserves to be queered there. The history of the production of differences has an important place in theology.

However, the point is that a Queer Theology, even if in need of doing a Queer genealogy of dogmas, still needs to pay more attention to the location of those 'different productions' which de Certeau queries, through the study of representations and behaviour (Buchanan 2000: 99). As I have said elsewhere, if we want to consider the role of Mariology in Latin America, it is more important to concentrate on *Marianismo* (popular Mariology) in order to understand what people actually do with the Virgin Mary's representations, than to study the complex archaeology of, for instance, the Virgin of Guadalupe (Althaus-Reid: 2000). For de Certeau, this is the area of studying and celebrating people's everyday rebelliousness and breakthroughs against the official story of interpretation. For ourselves, reading the Trinity from Klossowski's *Roberte ce soir* works in a similar way. This is what Deleuze calls 'ungroundings', which are not to be confused with de-contextualisation techniques. On the contrary, for Deleuze ungrounding is the 'freedom of non mediated ground, [and] the discovery of ground behind every other ground' (Deleuze 1997: 67). What he is saying here is that contextualisation must still imply difference, that 'grounding' (for instance, the Trinity) does not mean that the Trinity is an original to copy, or that there are originals at all, or that Trinitarian copies are exact photocopies of God. Ungrounding the Trinity disauthorises a family original, or the original name of the Father, while it reflects on issues of the sexual production of God by focussing on a theology without an original imprint.

The post-colonial question of the encounter at the gate is then informed by these ungrounding differentials. For de Certeau, walking in the city is a practice of space and memory, a return to old sites, but in theology the walking is also a site of excruciating pain and paralysis. This is the walking of the host to meet the Queer at the gate and for the Queer 'to come home'. It is a painful, costly experience of walking without knowing where one is going and for how long. We lack a site: this is why we are walking with hope, but with pain too. As Carter Heyward has put it, this is the conflict experienced by people speaking truth when truth is unwelcome (Carter Heyward 1989: 30–1); in this case, walking the road of the theological *caminata* is dangerous, especially if the *caminantes* (walkers) are despised.

Queer Theology is a road of joy and of suffering at the same time. The joy of speaking truth to power and the pain of the lack of love with which that truth may be received. In a way it is very similar to the experience of people in diaspora and of theologies in exile from the centre, a centre which establishes dogmatic 'originals' where we must all participate in the 'grounded' ecumenism which excludes the strangers and the ungrounded. In an example from Latin America the Trinitarian reflections of Leonardo Boff work around a God who may be a society but in this case a particular construction of a patriarchal society. Therefore, what Boff calls the communion of the Trinity as the basis for, say, social and political transformation works as an ideological 'original' by which Latin Americans need to forgive the church's simulacrum of community. Boff's claims of the 'the three *differents* in communion' (Boff 1988: 151) are nowhere incarnated in Latin America, where to be different (and sexually different) has not been permissible in society. To unground this interesting, if surreal, concept in the practice of the church, people should perhaps begin to ask if the word 'different', as used in this and other theological contexts, really means 'different' at all. Or does it simply refer to the adjudication of gender, sexual, racial and/or class roles historically accepted in any given theological discourse?

Going back to *Roberte ce soir*, while Octave the theologian had planned to overturn this colonial host-guest dialectic, he has done it in order to facilitate what we have called God's own ultimate betrayal in God's house of (closeted) heterosexuality. In order to do so, the Trinity can never be anything other than an emptying of bodies expressed in a kenotic emptying from heterosexual Trinitarians of the form of relationships and theologically stable assumptions which derive from the family-based, re-productive dyad represented in the Trinity. Because although a triad is a world of enriching loving possibilities, trinities are not about numbers, even less about the number three.[4] The Trinity has never to ceased to be a dyad for the same reason that a community does not depart from the field of binary thought simply on account of its numbers. In her theology of relationships, as presented in her book *Just Good Friends*, Elizabeth Stuart has claimed that we are all part of the Trinity (Stuart 1996: 244). By this she is considering how our passionate and 'mutual dances' are also part of the dance of God. There is a call to maturity and interdependence in the Trinitarian dance, but the most extraordinary aspect here is the idea of participating in the movement of a relational Trinity. Linking this to the theological community imagined by Klossowski of Roberte, Octave and Antoine we could add that the encounter at the gate is a constitutive part of this mutual dance amongst friends, because friends ought to embrace also the different in order to forge a real friendship which is not simply a mimicry of themselves. The concept of participation in the Trinity means that the Queer strangers can now take over and talk of God from hidden experiences and distrusted knowledge. For the Trinity to be left at the gate means true kenosis, a kenosis where God does not grant Godself privileges and thus discovers the meaning of incarnation.

However, the most interesting insight in all this may be the displacement of sexual theological knowledge, in the sense that the heterosexually disembowelled Trinitarians can embody lesbianism, while lesbians at the gate can embody the knowledge of bisexuals or transgendered people. This would mean that all these suppressed, displaced embodiments of knowledge could feel at home in the Trinity, just as the Trinity should feel at home in gay bars and S/M scenes, displacing temporary hegemonies and allowing a real plurality of religious experiences and theological practices by giving hospitality to strangers, in the most radical way.

Mladen Dolar, in his article 'La Femme-Machine', in which he discusses issues of sexual identity in Mozart's opera *Così fan tutte*, has concluded that 'when there is no Master, everybody is interchangeable, a substitute for the *unique Subject.'* (Dolar 1994: 49; my italics). In Mozart's opera this is related to clothes, and to what Dolar calls the worship of the master's clothes. The eighteenth-century obsession with clothes as disguises (a libertine favoured route to transgression via different combinations of genderfucking) is reflected in Mozart, according to Dolar, in the exchangeability not only of social status but also affectionate status. This can be seen for instance in the exchange between lover and beloved but also in the exchange of couples (irrespective of their compatibility) in operas such as *Così fan tutte* and *Fígaro*. It is obvious that we are here close to Butler's seminal point about performatives, in which gender roles are adjudicated to clothes, sexual and affective performances (Butler 1990: 33). In the Trinitarian construction, there are clothes of power and effectual power but these are not as exchangeable as one might suppose. That is to say, the Holy Spirit is phantasmatic and produces languages (angelic languages). Or again, that Jesus had a sphere of direct healing with people in his time, a face-to-face encounter and disencounter with power quite different from that found in the narratives of YHWH in the Hebrew Scriptures. The names differ too. The Son gave birth to the Father, and both of them originally come from the Spirit. The names establish a genealogy of power and of affections not to be disturbed, a fact that Trinitarian discussions know well, in their attempt to re-adapt the gender roles of God, for instance, the shifts from Father-gods to Mother-gods. This is a very encouraging, if limited, exercise unless there is a real challenge to sexual assumptions. However, what we are proposing here goes far beyond gender exchanges in God: we are proposing an end to the worship of clothes or, as in Klossowski's novel, locations of power. In order to do this, the strategy should be relatively simple: undress the father of power and glory and leave God sitting in the cold while the Queer community occupies the Trinity. The exchange of dresses of power and the habitat of affection can be surprisingly transformative. To say do not worship God's male attire leads on to exchanging it for fishnets and high heels. It is to ask for a radical destabilisation of the gender and sexual performances of God as community which in turn opens up the vast implications this may have for our understanding of the uniqueness of God and God's presence in our sexual and political history.

In the next chapter we shall explore these ideas of sexual knowledge giving hospitality to God, linking them in what David Cunningham has called 'the practice of Trinitarian theology' (Cunningham 1998). This is a way to think about different ways in which Trinitarian conceptualisations can be re-imagined, displaced and re-organised, including the role of the liturgical as an important part for a theology in which praxis means social justice and fair relationships in the community. As far as our project of queering God is concerned, our next chapter will be dedicated to consideration of the practice of a Queer God as hermeneutics. This will be linked to some extent to the Klossowski model which we have discussed but also to the work of Bataille and the Marquis de Sade. The project is still one of hermeneutical permutations, or radical kenosis at the gate of biblical and libertine stories.

5

PERMUTATIONS

The lover's discourse is, by definition or by default, what overshoots the four other discourses ('the forms of the social tie': Master, University, Hysteric, Analytic) that, together, try to make up for its absence.

(MacCannell 1994: 25)

As lesbians, gay men, bisexuals, transgendered and seeking people, do we really want to 'take back the word'? And if we do, what 'word' is it we want to 'take back'?

(Tolbert 2000: vii)

Re-entering the patriarchs: the law of love

Looking with a friend at a reproduction of a curious painting of Marx and Engels having breakfast (with newspapers strewn around on the small table beside the coffee pot and Marx's pocket watch lying at one side) I pointed out to him how 'Latin American' Marx's complexion looked in this picture. My friend, as always very well acquainted with Marx's biography, commented that Marx's daughters used to call him 'the Moor'. I must have followed this observation with a comment about another topic connected with Marx, namely the so-called suicide of Eleanor Marx. The thought of Eleanor's suicide has always caused me grief, not least because of the irony involved. Eleanor was an intelligent, well-educated young woman, knowledgeable of her father's main criticism to modes of productions and the mechanisms of alienation produced in people's lives through them, but yet, she needed to succumb to a woman's loving fate in patriarchy. That is, Eleanor succumbed to a cycle of love and betrayal, and finally was induced by her false lover to commit suicide by a pact that only she respected. Her lover, meanwhile, was never prosecuted for handing her poison and continued his life with his wife. My friend's only comment on this story was that 'they were people like you and me, with their passions and contradictions': just the same.

I am tempted to think that the patriarchs were also people like Marx and Eleanor, 'people like you and me', people of passions and contradictions, of awareness and innocences, people of closets and secrets. Levels of consciousness and contextual limitations aside, did they not know about love? I am not saying that they did not have partners, in their tribal forms which, if not equivalent to our specific concept of marriage, were accepted forms of social organisation of sexuality and reproduction. I am not saying that they did not have pleasure and affection, but did they also have love 'outside the law'? Considering a point from Derrida, we may say that there is no possibility of justice in love unless law is transgressed (Derrida: 2002). This is, by the way, Derrida's argument in relation to the deconstruction of law, but not of justice and their mutual relationship which is based precisely in the destabilisation of one of them, in this case the law. This comes about because laws are replaceable and the justice discourse depends on this deconstruction so that it is not subject to the fixity of laws. So Derrida says 'without a call for justice, we would not have any interests in deconstructing the law' (Caputo 1997: 16). Disruption then, fulfils the law.

Queering the Bible and queering the patriarchs are projects of similar vocations. To start with, they are projects of love, that is, concerned with love (sexual, personal, collective, communitarian) because it is love which usually survives when the symbolic chains do not (MacCannell 1994: 25). That means that love always exceeds the limits of words (and the Word) and also the limits of law. Queering is also the art of deconstructing laws in search of justice, an art which comes from experiences of love at the margins of the lawful or, to use Christian terms, outside the redeemable. Nevertheless, how can a Christian Queer hermeneutics of the Bible get started if not precisely at this point of the irredeemability of sexual subversions in Heterosexual Theology? Were the patriarchs people just like Marx, Eleanor, you and me, leaving Queer traces of their lives in their stories and times? Did they deconstruct laws for the sake of pleasure and justice in forbidden loves and pleasures? Were the patriarchs trans-sexuals in the sense that they were trans-border travellers, that is, patriarchs in a journey of crossing (or desiring to cross) the borders of the law of sexuality in their times? When we consider any hermeneutics of transgression we also need to consider issues of love because love is the first transgressor of canonic sexuality and the commandments regulating the flow of affections. As Mary Ann Tolbert has said, what we need to consider is what 'word' of the Bible we want to take back (rediscover and appropriate), because it may be that the Bible has narratives that we should problematise in the light of the 'law of hospitality' (Tolbert 2000: vii). What we need to consider is that in many cases what has been presented to us is a false hospitality where the strangers at the gate have not been the guests, but on the contrary, the familiar heterosexual construction of hermeneutics has only welcomed people to the law of the Same. However, if 'to take back the word' means, as Tolbert indicates, to take back justice (while queerly deconstructing the law), then our possibilities of resisting what Tolbert calls 'textual harassment' in the Bible might have a better chance. This does not mean producing another definitive re-reading of the Bible and Tolbert might be right in pointing out that a Queer reading of the Bible can never be by definition another authorised, final version which in time could became another Sameness. Hesitant, tentative, deeply contextual while sexually suspicious of any notion of stability, the Queer Bible may be read as an incomplete story, partially and momentarily filled with our own stories, but searching not for the straight versus Queer to dislocate, or the straight to bend to presume sympathy towards us from the world of the patriarchs. Instead of that, recalling de Certeau, there are the different productions which we need to facilitate. We need them at the crossroads of libertine epistemologies and Queer understandings of love, justice and life.

The non-essential: Queer hermeneutical circles

The Word of God, following from our previous discussions of Klossowski, may be defined – with good will – as the 'Word of the Simulator'. In Klossowski/Deleuze, as we recall, the simulacrum is the event of liberation of references in the signs (or 'the original'). God (the Trinitarians) is/are as simulators, free of ultimate lawful references, and therefore liberate us from reading the Bible as a collection of 'originals'. Far from that essential originality, the Queer Bible should be considered as a collection of copies in which identities are complete, fulfilled as *copies*, as non-essentials independent of the original matrix of closeted heterosexuality. The re-reading becomes then a true dialogue without a continuous confrontation with a superior original to match, an experience which is oppressive even in the terminology of the Hebrew Scriptures itself: reading the Bible with/for an original can make us feel pressurised to accept what we cannot accept if we are not to retain a dignity of life, imprisoned in the closing of horizons. The oppressive reading weakens us and even 'robs' us of our sense of identity. A simple search into the broader semantic field of the word 'oppression' in the Hebrew Scriptures should be the first step for a Queer hermeneutician to reflect upon in order to clarify the starting point of her re-reading.[1] As Tolbert says, 'the word is powerful and powerfully dangerous' (Tolbert 2000: xi). The same experiences of oppression in the Bible can apply perfectly to the traditional experience of reading the Bible from Queer lives.

Therefore this is the first step in our Queer Circle of Interpretation: the realisation that the Bible itself condemns any reading for death (dissolution) and alienation. That may be part of a subversive supplement to the Bible, or just a Queer pre-supposition, but it needs to be taken into account because it is even more important than to declare what is the place of the Bible in our lives as individuals or communities. The point of authority should be a secondary issue, if it is to be considered at all. The awareness of the possibility of reading for oppression should always be the first issue because from there we can be on our guard against the possibility of a reading for bewilderment and alienation, which can be deeply destructive. The awareness of mechanisms of oppression when reading the Bible should be considered as an important part of that first moment of guessing or intuiting in community. By this we mean that when a community reads the Scripture, the process starts with a coming out of fears, hopes and identities. Reading in community is an important liberationist stand-point which can lead towards a hermeneutics of solidarity, but we must also be aware that Queer people do not always have a community around them. The Queer communities may be of collocation or dispersed around us; we may be Queer, solitary practitioners because we may feel that re-readings of the reformation biblical tradition are not enough and we need re-readings for transformation instead (Carter Heyward 1989: 47). Or we may be part of a community that is bonded by homo-solidarity and therefore excludes *us* while including, for example, our beliefs in justice and peace.

This suicidal situation is, by the way, quite common if bewildering. We may belong to a group which supports (more or less) all the right causes – justice, peace, struggle against poverty and against human rights violations – but find however that this is a community bonded around a covenant of patriarchal justice. In practice it may mean then that our beliefs in a gospel of justice may be welcome as long as we (as people, or as the strangers of theology) are excluded. Our ideals of peace and justice as rooted in the gospel may be treated well and offered a chair in a meeting, but meanwhile we, as people, are forced to take our Queer identities outside and die. At the end of this process, if it is successful, we may end becoming holograms of ourselves. The reading for oppression (even in the name of just causes) has thus been successful in eliminating us in the process even if we are still there. The original has displaced us.

To do a Queer reading of the Scriptures may loosely follow a deconstruction pattern. After all, we have said that we want to deconstruct the patriarchal law of love. The deconstruction process to which Derrida has introduced us follows some basic steps as follows:

1   There is a need to diagnose elements which stand in some form of opposition through the text to elements related to heterosexual thought (for instance, dyadic hierarchical structures).
2   Once these thoughts have been localised the relationships need to be inverted, dispersed and disrupted. One hermeneutical clue is to pay attention to Queer experiences such as denigration. Denigrated terms are fundamental to the processes of hierarchisation and privileging of other terms/concepts. For instance, slaves make the master; women make men; women make God the Father; Queers make straights; sinners make 'the saved'.
3   From that point, we go back to the text and re-inscribe those terms in which we can see more clearly how what de Certeau called the different is produced.

However, sexual deconstructive re-readings of the Bible are problematic because they need to be continually queered further. Basically, we need to do that in order to try to avoid assimilationist trends in biblical interpretation, working around some basic understandings from Queer Theory, such as the following:

A biblical re-reading without a teleology

By this we mean the understanding that what we can call the Queer Circle of Interpretation is a trajectory and is moreover a coalition of elements in movement. These coalitions of interpretative clues and perspectives may appear and disappear (and re-appear again). It is more important to find a re-reading coalition consisting of different kinds of knowledge such as critical bisexual readings in coalition with, for example critical lesbian readings, or a critical transvestite praxis of interpretation in coalition with a gay hermeneutics of suspicion. These re-reading coalitions do not presuppose a teleology and therefore do not aim at eternal life. Moreover, the coalition reading may prove to be conflictive. The experience of lesbians oppressed by gays, or bisexuals oppressed by almost everybody, may produce tensions and differences which are not reconcilable, which may need to stand side by side as simply different, even unfriendly. And yet in such cases what Robert Goss has called 'to act up' may be the first step towards the praxis of coalition hermeneutics (Goss: 1993). The attempt to situate our hermeneutical circle of interpretation around Queer solidarities, might allow us to discover what resistances are possible in the reading of the Scripture as a continuous, novel process, but also foster the resistance that we need to find amongst ourselves as Queer people of God in order to let go of patterns of subjugation of the Other.

Incoherence

Reading through the grid of heterosexuality provides coherence and stability. A Queer reading may want the opposite, in the sense that once the heterosexual grid is perceived, the 'mis-matches between genre, sexuality and desire' can be easily localised (Jagose 1996: 3). In practice this would mean that, for instance, we should literally apply the principle of 'heterosexual incoherence' to any reading of sexual identity in the Scriptures. However, since in Queer Theory we can not presuppose natural, given sexualities, we should be aware that the questioning of 'who is who' in the Bible cannot easily be determined. Malehood does not need to be our current understanding of heterosexual masculinity. By the same token women do not necessarily need to be mothers, nor men fathers. A sexual genealogical biblical project may even find racial codes under the sexually conferred identities of biblical personae, uncovering the processes of sexual identification produced, not around YHWH, but around the tribes of YHWH.

Location of sexuality

Heterosexuality is ubiquitous and 'unremarkable' (Jagose 1996: 16). It is only identified by comparison with 'what is not' and as such heterosexuality is a derivative or a second act of homosexuality, as Jagose observes, following Jonathan Katz in *Gay/Lesbian Almanac* (Katz 1983: 147; Jagose 1996: 16). The fact is that heterosexuality marks locations and places in the Bible which function like the seventeenth-century concept of the 'molly houses', places where a Queer culture is in process of developing and where people become Queer in community. In the New Testament we can identify the places of the deviants, places of specific activities such as eating and drinking or gender and/or sexual misconduct, where a class of people were made in a community process in opposition to the religious law (or in the case of Jesus, in a deconstructive relation to that law). The Queer places may be vague and temporary in the narratives but they can be recognised by the element of 'safe space' (even if provisional) that they provide, as if they were deviant sanctuaries not necessarily of dissident behaviour, but of dissident identity.[2]

The challenge of finding the molly houses or places for locating the Other cultures of sexuality in the Bible remains a Queer one. These were perhaps the locations (as places and as knowledge webs) where the patriarchs learnt by difference. These may have been also the hetero-unremarkable places which worked according to Lyotard's theory of locals, as 'island(s) of determinism' (Lyotard 1997: 59) secretly nurtured though by a sense of contradictions and struggles.

Straightening Sodom

... I have two daughters ... do to them as you please.

(Genesis 19: 8)

The criminals treated me more gently than humans have ever done. But I was homesick.

(Acker 1988: 159)

If the meaning of the biblical text is to be found, as Ricoeur has said, in the in-betweenness of the reader's community, the community of production and the redaction of the text, as in the dialectics of appropriation (Ricoeur 1991: 86–7), then going Queer in our hermeneutical circle of interpretation needs to start by re-creating different kinds of in-betweenness, that is, to change the expected interrelationship. In the text Queer analysis destabilises and releases incoherence by a strategy of coalition readings. We ourselves as part of our Queer communities bring about that coalition. Yet we must add something else, the work of permutations. Continuing our previous comments on strategies of 'location' we might add that according to Foucault, these are 'sites of fleeting articulation' (Foucault quoted by Punday 1998: 1), that is, locations are sites of theological articulations but also complex constructed sites. They are not transparent locations. The question is then how to interconnect those non-transparent, dark locations. For instance, in the biblical narrative, we might ask how we should interrelate sites of menstruation with Sodom (disordering reproductive and wasteful spaces of sexuality), in order to allow us to present a hermeneutical suspicion and ask if Sodomites were straight, or if angels had a doxology of menstruation. What needs to permutate are sites of Queer location which can irrupt and discontinue other sites of representation. In order to do that we need to encourage the most unusual dialogues in the biblical hermeneutics of relationships.

Suppose then that we organise the space of in-betweenness to bring together our re-reading of the Scriptures with libertine texts, or texts of disruption and difference such as are to be found in the novels of Kathy Acker. We could permutate intertextualities: Acker's *Empire of the Senseless* and the biblical story of Sodom. We could read them with Sade's *Philosophy in the Bedroom* as a hermeneutical clue, or with Klossowski's *Roberte ce soir*: the choice is ours. Basically what we are proposing here is that we should use Acker's own strategy of location to permutate Queer sites by understanding the 'circumscription of those sites and by establishing connections between individual sites' (Punday 1998: 2). Queering the biblical texts is basically about destabilising locations of identity formation. The female body in Acker and the sense of male hegemonic control over the female life may be closer to our understanding than the story of Sodom and therefore might illuminate it, since the story of Sodom is about bodies, cultured, sexed bodies struggling in hegemonic settings. It is in this sense that Sade could be valuable for our reading, since Sade provides us with an understanding of sodomy as a clue to interpretation.

Let us start by reading texts in a parallel fashion, as in an encounter between strangers and then interrelate the sense of Otherness in them. *Empire of the Senseless* is a novel written by Kathy Acker in 1988. The story concerns a family romance which is situated in Paris, presented as a decayed city of the future invaded by Algerians. The story is narrated by the two protagonists, Abhor (a black woman, part woman, part robot) and a pirate called Thivai. The novel is based on other novels. It is a re-voyage of other literary memories such as a science fiction novel (*Neuromancer* by Gibson) and an American classic *(The Adventures of Huckleberry Finn* by Mark Twain). This is the richness of Acker's novels, she rewrote other fictions and stories as she wrote her own, mixing and interconnecting complex locations in a Queer intertextual play. It is in the same Queer way that we want to re-read the Bible, rewriting other stories alongside our own and re-creating the mythical in our lives, as if meeting strangers at the gates.

In *Empire of the Senseless*, the romance between Thivai the pirate and Abhor is mediated by cybernetics, but also by technology and multinationals which construct political and sexual bodies. In the novel, Abhor ends up succumbing to male hegemony and becomes a slave (like Jim the young slave in *Huckleberry Finn*), locked up in an attic in order to become a writer who would write down how she was eventually rescued by Thivai and a friend (Acker 1988: 201; Punday 1998: 3). In his article on 'Theories of Materiality and Location', Daniel Punday identifies (along with Robert Siegle) the function of a group of characters, 'the sailors', as a model for ex-centricity, a position in confrontation with society. They are a 'philanthropic group' and a group of poor people who refuse to join the consumerist society (Punday 1998: 4–5). The novel is powerful in the use of language and its deconstructive model. Sex is excessive; sex saturates everything without a trace of romanticism. In this sense, *Empire of the Senseless* is truly Sadean. There is no (obvious) love in it; moreover, love only permeates the novel through unstable desire which destroys that 'useless, virulent and destructive disease named heterosexual sexual love' (Acker 1988: 64). Apart from that, *Empire of the Senseless* is a novel of exile, of the pain of sexual exile, the exile of love and the need to struggle against patriarchal enforced exiles such as our bodies of thinking, and acting.

These are the sites from Acker's *Empire of the Senseless* that we are going to permutate with Genesis 19:1–14 (the story of the Sodomites). That story is well known, but we are going to read the unknown story as though it were gossip circulating around the gay bars. We are going to read the unknown in Sodom in the company of the traversing themes of death, waste (as in sexualities beyond the ethos of reproduction) and also irony. Consider the biblical story. Two men visit the city of Sodom. Their status in relation to divinity is unclear: men of God, or 'angels', perhaps Vatican ambassadors such as the Count della Santa-Sede of *Roberte ce Soir*. Their presence brings infallibility to the sexual textual exegesis of terror. In a way they represent the Pope from Rome, or to be more precise, the Hetero-Pope visiting Sodom and evidently looking for Queer company. Like many visitors before them, they had apparently chosen to spend the night sleeping in the town square. That place was a site of hospitality in itself, since it was common for travellers to sleep there if there was no other place to stay. However, Lot, who happened to be at the gate when these men arrived, observed the law of hospitality by insisting that they come to his home. He broke one rule of hospitality (town hospitality) to impose his own. Perhaps Lot was accustomed to going to the gate to check on travellers arriving in Sodom for whatever purpose. Perhaps he liked to invite such men to his house. This, of course, we do not know. Later that day some people from the town went to Lot's house and demanded *to know* the men. Whether this use of the verb 'to know' is figurative speech for homosexual intercourse or not has been debated for some years. The most progressive of biblical exegetes prefer nowadays to conclude from the attitude of these men that it was the 'violation of hospitality law' which constituted the sin of Sodom. Thus a Sodomite would be the person who refused to have a guest room at home and that it is this practice (rather than a sexual culture) which defines the biblical meaning of 'a Sodomite'.

Little is known of the origin of the name Sodom, which is linked to an old root meaning 'abundance', especially of water: Sodom, etymologically speaking, is curiously linked to fluids. Yet we know that Sodom was a Canaanite city. Homosexuality at least (for little is known about other sexualities) was part of the Canaanite cultural and religious life. This makes Sodom a cultural site where homosexuality was more than a form of sexual behaviour, but rather a style of living, of relating and also thinking. And of course it was also a form of spirituality. It is precisely from this point of departure – Sodom as a Queer cultural site – that we wish to read intertextually Acker's *Empire of the Senseless* and the story of the Sodomites together with Sade. Acker will provide us with a place from where we can read this particular chapter of the Bible; for instance, a way to read from a dungeon. We should like to consider Sodomites (that is, the inhabitants of Sodom) in a context of non-straightforward sexual identities forged in struggle, sometimes involving processes of definition against other or self-definitions (Weeks 1995: 32). Apart from that, we must consider that the traditional way of exegeting Genesis 19: 1–14 has been precisely a work of narrative saturation, based on a particular form of sexual behaviour, as if the rape of Dinah or Tamar could have made of heterosexuality an execrable (hetero)sexual identity, calling for God's destruction of whole populations. This point has been already made by Robert Goss when he classifies Genesis 19 as a 'text of terror' and of phallic aggression 'as in the rape of the concubine in Judges 19' (Goss 1993: 90–91). In the usual framework of understanding heterosexuality as a given, it is interesting to notice that little has been said of the Sodomites as people with a particular and respectable sexual culture and tradition. By doing that, biblical hermeneuticians have been systematically straightening Sodom, that is, eliminating agency from sexuality. We say this because in thinking sexualities, we need to think the people who constitute them and the praxis involved in, for instance, ambivalent desires. Such desires may function sometimes as forms of deconstructing laws, perhaps even religious laws in the case of the Sodomite community. In this way of sexual re-thinking (as in a critical bi/theology), other forms of sexualities can learn much. It is as if a Hetero-Pope decided one day to visit a cultural site, for instance a gay café, to reflect on issues of communion (communication, community and the sacred) and found his sexuality relating to a loving community such as the Sodomites. He would then understand difference and communion and as a result of that, his soul would be salvaged from the entombment of the Other (the Queer) in himself. The reading of Sodom is, no doubt, complex and Queer. It is about entombments in a man called Lot and the nature of sexuality. But at this point we need to bring Sade into our hermeneutical circle.

(Sub)missions in the bedroom: the Bible

How can we talk about Sade and biblical interpretation? What kind of sexual intertextuality can we expect from a text such as *Philosophy in the Bedroom*? How to account for the submissions and (sub)missions by the reification of women which appear in all of Sadean literature? These are questions which a Queer hermeneutician needs to address by using non-straight processes of action and reflection. The first question, why is a woman theologian like myself using Sade, needs to be asked simply because Sade still functions as a site under surveillance.[3] Sade is the room where state interrogation joins theology. Marcel Hénaff refers to that when he says that the name Sade 'is still intolerable, still unredeemed...', a name which belongs not only to the realm of literature but to the 'realm of scandal' (Hénaff 1999: 1). However, Hénaff wishes us to consider that after all the images of horror, when all is said and done, Sadean literature is fictional – and, we might add, non-canonical. Sadean novels are as fictional as the Bible in the sense that although every metaphor and narrated plot has some resemblance with known (or dreamed) realities, the deeds and dialogues from a book such as *Philosophy in the Bedroom* may be read in the way that Tamar's dialogue with her brother in her own bedroom is read in Sunday school. After all, both *Philosophy in the Bedroom* and the story of Tamar aim to deconstruct God, although in different ways, either by using Queer strategies in the case of Sade, or by heterosexual strategies in the biblical story. The Queer strategy in Sade can be seen as an angry protest against power (church and state alliances). It is a challenge to the ecclesiastical metanarrative of dis-pleasure in his time, but also a gesture of defiance against structures of political control. The heterosexual strategy by contrast works in a different way. As women are reified in the patriarchal (divine) narratives, the logic of the heterosexual may consider that objects do not appeal to the heavens concerning crimes committed on earth. As we are well aware, in the reification process of the biblical writers God becomes constructed as inefficacious. In the story of Tamar, his reference (deliberately using the male pronoun in this case) is absent. In continuing with the question of why or how to use Sade for a re-reading of the Bible, we can conclude that if it is true that women are reified, so are men. In Sade, the subversive characters are not men or women from a heterosexual paradigm, but sexual transgressors (bisexuals, cross-dressers, gays). When we decide to use Sadean categories as hermeneutical tools in reading the Bible we find there is much to be gained from the categories of sodomy and submission.

Sodomising hermeneutics

What is sodomy as a hermeneutical clue? For a start, in theology sodomy belongs to the space of the non-productive, or subversive pleasure. There are however some theological contradictions in this definition which deserve to be discussed, such as the relation between love and sodomy and love and heterosexuality. If (biological) reproduction is what distinguishes sodomy from the idealised sexual practices of the heterosexual (vaginal penetration) then God in the Hebrew Scriptures is a Sodomite. This can be said because God only metaphorically 'reproduces' Godself. Therefore, God's love belongs to the Sodomite kind, for God's love is not biologically procreative. The specific case of Jesus requires further discussion: whether and how we can still use the terminology of a 'son' of God in relation to a woman, or whether this 'relationship/sonship' is of another kind. However, there is more to being a Sodomite than having a particular kind of sexual relationship. We may ask if God finds Godself at home in a culture of grace, that is of pleasure given and received in a free community, without the expectation of any sort of final product or profit. If so, then also in cultural terms God is a Sodomite.

The other characteristic of sodomy as a hermeneutical clue is that it works as a 'key sign' breaking the diverse institutional forms of control over the reproductive body (Carrette 2000: 71). In this way Carrette sees in Sade how sodomy becomes a testimony and a moral one at that, concerning the announcement of the death of God. Here Carrette is following Foucault: we do not possess our own bodies except 'in the name of institutions' (Foucault quoted in Carrette 2000: 71). The entry point for subversion which opens up from this is that a Sodomite God seems to be the one who refuses to carry God's own body in the name of the institutions of church, or T-Theology. At least this is a God who can choose other institutions or forms of organisation and orders at the margins. This happens because a Sodomite God, following a Sadean epistemology, is a courageous God who dares to commit suicide (an ultimate kenosis) and stand free of theological (reproductive) expectations while announcing the death of the biological (reproductor) God.

The second hermeneutical clue from Sade is submission, but taking into account the fact that sexual submission in Sade is generally the submission of heterosexuality, presented in a kind of theatrical stand against heterosexual political and religious praxis. At this point we should consider if the Sadean confrontation with God, represented in his novels by acts of transgression and excess, occurs in women (as might appear from a surface reading). Is Sade's spiritual corporeality based on misogyny, as Carrette seems to imply? (Carrette 2000: 74). Although it is true that there is misogyny in Sade, it is also true that Sade never develops his fictional characters and narrative plots from scenes of heterosexuality. On the contrary, as Hénaff has pointed out, the Sadean characters are constructed without exception from the margins of heterosexuality (Hénaff 1999: 38). All relationships portrayed in Sadean literature are irredeemably Queer (homosexual, lesbian, bisexuals or S/M), fluctuating and also promiscuous. Sade's literary strategy consists in occupying all the possible zones of transgressive sexuality at the same time and from that point we could argue that in the Sadean novels men are not men, neither are women women. What happens is that in Sade we have no subjects: only transgressive desire is the real subject while transgression represents the ruin of the law of binarianism (Hénaff 1999: 40). In this there is a libidinal post-colonial hermeneutic, queering us about what is a woman and what is a man. Reading Sade, women are deconstructed by sodomisation because their biological identity is destabilised, and women are thought about outside of reproduction. If there is something important in Sade it is that the deconstruction of men and women occurs in continuous exchanges of gender and sexual roles, as if one of his main objectives was to produce the submission of heterosexuality in order to allow the emergence of 'ugliness', or to enable the reprobate body (the different body) to become visible (Hénaff 1999: 36).

Using sodomy and submission as interpretative clues we might say that if the kenotic process that we discussed in the last chapter is ever meant to take place, then God avoids submission. God the Father should then submit to the de-heterosexualisation of God's own body, because libertine desires change and unveil the possibility of different theistic structures (the institutions of God). God the Sodomite belongs to a different logocentric order of the soul, very different from Leibnitz's concept of the monad based on simplicity, true being and unity (Hénaff 1999: 34). The Sodomite God, like a libertine Sadean body, is a far more complex God whose pleasure may be to engage in multiple combinations and exchanges reflecting that face of the Queer God which can be seen amidst the Queer people of God at the margins of the church and T-Theology.

At this point, we can start our work of biblical permutation following a rhizomatic network of exegesis. This should work by connecting elements according to our own heart's desires, without consideration of pre-privileged structures or hierarchical paths which have been put in place to guarantee exegetical results in a frame of hegemonic unity and harmony (Deleuze and Guattari:1976). A rhizomatic way of reading a structure is by definition opposed to an arborescence: it displaces the 'root-tree' model of thinking and searches instead for horizontal connections, almost unlimited in the sense that there is no privileging conceptual movements or class systems of connections amongst the different elements of our exegesis. Using the rhizomatic model in the work of Kathy Acker, the Hebrew story concerning the fate of the Sodomite culture and the Sadean epistemology of *Philosophy in the Bedroom,* will have space in which to have a Queer exegetical dialogue to address us and start other multiple queering processes of interpretation.

Let us start with the Queer subject who is reading this text, or remembering it, since Acker's *Empire of the Senseless* is so deeply located in transgressive understandings of life and God. Abhor, the protagonist of this novel, was a kind of warrior who ended up as a slave. As a nomadic reader, a Queer person is more or less the same. We are sexual and class warriors who need to beware of the danger of ending up in confined, narrow spaces of reflection (our little jails) when reading the Scriptures or God. The Queer reader becomes a warrior when she persistently disorganises the fixed protocols of incommunication between different components of the reading which are deliberately kept apart. The warrior reader builds guerrilla paths between scenes and concepts. Abhor was part robot and part woman. She was kept in by men who wanted to make her into a writer of science fiction novels. However, Abhor did not know how to write: she needed to be taught first to inscribe a language. Queer theologians are also kept in attics or in dungeons, because we can say that after we have been taught how to do the rudiments of a theology, we discover ourselves in a grammatical dungeon. There, the spelling of a systematic theology and the accent and punctuation systems become over-privileged and, by default, transgressive thinking becomes illogical, illegal or 'irrelevant'. This is the question of the *écriture féminine* in theology. We may reflect on the *écriture féminine* as it has been posited by Hélène Cixous in many of her works such as, for instance, in *The Newly Born Woman* (Cixous 1994) or *The Laugh of the Medusa* (1981). Does such a thing as Queer writing exist? Or is a Queer theological writing, to be more precise, an attainable goal? For Cixous, the *écriture féminine* cannot be a place of stability, but of bisexuality. It is a 'writing without contours' (Cixous 1994: 44); writing is in itself 'the very possibility of change, the space that can serve as a

springboard for subversive thought' (Cixous 1981: 249). In a curious Queer
way, to legitimise and thus impede that possibility of change will be also an
unethical standpoint for nomadic theologians. Let us consider here an ethical
point concerning theology in jail, which comes from Thivai the pirate character
in *Empire of the Senseless*:

> Corporate executives commit atrocities. Must we act like them, sexually,
> in order to fight them successfully? No...Acting like shits will only make
> us become shit. Greedy and maniacal.

> (Acker 1988: 94)

That arborescent process of the Same which we have named T-Theology may be
compared to an act of corporate atrocity when seen as a hegemonic alliance
between dual patterns of power and the traditions which perpetuate them. An
elite theology, which makes of rebellious theologians part humans and part
robots, with 'artificial memories' implanted (as in Gibson's *Neuromancer*),
makes us believe in the false grammars and distorted memories of a theological
praxis which is based in an ideal and not in a critical reality. Elizabeth Stuart
makes the point that theologians consider themselves to be the followers of a
theological 'experiential' path when, for instance, they adopt the method of the
influential nineteenth-century German theologian, Friedrich Schleiermacher.
Stuart, following Winkist, points out that this can hardly be the case since none
of us has ever had the spiritual and intellectual experience of Schleiermacher
(Stuart 2002: 5). We only have Schleiermacher's theological grammatology,
pasted over with (our) false memories. False experiences (which does not imply
that no one has ever had them, but only that they are not as 'ours' as we may
think) join the church's traditions and traditions of theological language.
Paraphrasing Thivai's question, shall a Queer Theology reply with an 'eye for an
eye' mentality? Are we allowed to fight sexually with the grammar of T-Theology
using the same hermeneutical tools which include binary oppositional thought,
sexual stability premises and the legitimisation of a sexual epistemology to the
detriment of others? The answer is obviously no, but at a cost. The cost is the
permanent attempt by Queer theologians to work on a Random Theology, using
a concept such as *voicinage*, to redefine our location of doing theology. *Voicinage*
is a concept related to the idea of neighbourhood (Deleuze and Guattari 1994:
19) and refers to the overlapping of conceptual zones. The fact that there are
neighbourhoods of unclear demarcations or *zones de voisinage* speaks to us not
only of the complexity of conceptual forms, but also of solidarity and friendship.

For instance, are we reading the story of the destruction of the Sodomite culture
from the dungeon in Sodom (struggling within the confinement of the theologically given and encountering the walls of sexual class wars in theology) or are we
located in another biblical city, for example Zoar? Elsewhere I have made the point
that Queer Theology is not and cannot be neutral in terms of the theologian taking
sides (Althaus-Reid 2000: Ch. 2): that to be a theologian is a similar act to putting

our heads through funfair cut-outs and adopting a variety of cross-dressing identities all the time. Deciding where the theologian is to be kept to write an exegesis, whether in Sodom or in Zoar, presents us with this and other ambivalences. It is like the experience of many bisexual people in relation to their identity, which makes them question themselves sometimes whether they are going too straight or too gay in their relationships and therefore whether they are 'not being bisexual enough' (Eadie 1993: 144). However, as Eadie suggests in his article 'Activating Bisexuality: Towards a Bi/Sexual Politics', this is part of our difficulties in dealing with zones of un-policed sexualities. Can we enter the story of Sodom without a policed apparatus of sexual theological control perspectives? If so, we may realise that the Sodomite culture was not an island in itself: it was a neighbourhood (*voisinage*) where that culture was shared or somehow coexisted with other similar sexual cultures with which it had at the very least some common element.

Therefore the Queer theologian is sitting in her dungeon somewhere in the neighbourhood of a network of Canaanite physical, cultural and religious spaces. The dungeon is not Canaanite: it is contemporary; it is Binary Theology. It is trying to make us straighten out our theological praxis by an alliance amongst the false memories of heterosexual traditions and systems of thought. Are we Christian enough? Are we becoming too Queer? Can theology or God exist without a prescriptive sexual centre around which we should gather as a community to celebrate our struggles for justice and peace in our lives?

If for Sade sodomy is the ultimate transgression announcing the end of that reproductor, the God-biology of Christian Sexual Theology, then the story of the Sodomites may be read from a different angle, a rebellious movement directed against a hegemonic theodicy. In the biblical passage Lot is portrayed as a man and a heterosexual concept that can also be related to a whole patriarchal *voisinage* in itself, organised around what can loosely be described as his heterosexual culture (represented by his family entourage of daughters and wife, plus the symbolic divinity of male visitors). Lot's *voisinage* is a theological entourage of beliefs, conceptual frames and ideas superimposed and mixed in the story. Thus we have here one of the many creations of the theological concept of the Other in the Bible. Following Deluze, we may think that this is not only a history concerned with the understanding of God and cultures which we are confronting in Genesis 19, but a series of new connections created in the story which render sodomy as a neighbour's concept of the God of appropriation. In all probability Sodom was not what we would consider a 'homosexual city'. Sodom was a city where people probably had a more ample understanding of sexuality and divinity than Lot's people. As Bataille has said with regard to a Foucaldian perspective on Sade, there is a need to understand here the relation between transgression, politics and the (libertine) discourse (Bataille 1995a: 4). The difference could be underlined by Bataille's analysis of the categories of excretion and appropriation in relation to Sadean literature (Bataille 1995a: 20). The act of appropriation is constituted by a homogenous process organised through norms, prohibitions and the liturgical aspects of action realised in the sphere of the sacred. The objective of appropriation is to produce what Bataille calls a static equilibrium which is enacted through laws, and several 'profane facts'. This category also applies to tools of production and we may include here the instruments of theological production. Heterosexuality is in part a tool of theological production but also a result of the process. Heterosexuality has been produced by an alignment of elements such as dualist thinking, hierarchisation and colonial processes of displacement localised in different spaces, such as those of sacred and civil society. Bataille has called God 'the simple paternal' sign of universal homogeneity and this is what the sacred culture of Lot is trying to appropriate at the level of neighbourhood: the sexual elements which cannot be assimilated into Lot's system. It is obvious though that those sexual dissidents were unassimilable in terms of Lot's sacred production (or that of the writer of Lot, to be more precise). The Sodomites represent in the text (not in history) the process of excretion which Bataille defines as revolutionary or heterogenous (Bataille 1995a: 28). They are subverting, as Sade does, the law of the Father. Not that we can say that the Sodomites were members of that Sadean literary invention, the 'Society of the Friends of Crime', but the narrator of Lot has seen in them the menace of a different political and sacred economy.

Theo-Apocalypse now: blind God

The pervert pursues *the performance of a single gesture*; it is done in a moment. The pervert's existence becomes the constant waiting for the moment in which this gesture can be performed.

(Klossowski 1995: 42)

Finally the Algerians won Paris. Except that more than a third of the city was now ash.

(Acker 1988: 80)

… God will remember them and do justice.

(Goss 1993: 111)

Is there a lack of hospitality in Genesis 19 and, if so, what is it? The answer to the first question is probably yes, there is a lack of hospitality. Where to locate that lack is, however, problematic. At the level of a superficial heterosexually centred reading, the Sodomite culture is inhospitable. From a Sadean perspective, it is Lot's culture which lacks hospitality. Lot's God is then the one who cannot accept the menace of heterogeneity and transgressive productions in its midst and who therefore closes the doors of the house of hospitality. There is no point in denying the fact that this text is saturated with violence. Men from Sodom against these particular visitors; a father against his own daughters, and God against almost everybody and everything, threatening to destroy people and environment alike. The issue of violence in this text is regrettable but that includes God's violence too. Underlying this violence, there is another level of discussion to engage with: the issue of hospitality and violence as a 'single gesture', that is, as Klossowski says, a waiting for a divine performance of exclusion and destruction.

Here we have a kind of theology in the bedroom, that is, a displaced Sodomite Theology outside the frontiers of Lot's house and public discourse facing the retreat provided by intimacy. The borders of this monotonous narrative compound are made up of a single-sex god and monotonous messengers, together with subjected women who work in the theological production as part of a system of divine exchange. How many women are for the mono-loving gods? What value needs to be adjudicated to make an equivalent (virginity, for instance)? Still following Bataille on Sade, we can consider how, as seen from our present context, the Sodomites provide us with a base of materiality where the individual can find her own identity, not in the civil society but in the interstices of theological, economical and moral encodings (Bataille 1995a: 7). It is in these interstices that Lot's God of utility, conservation and procreation is contested by a different life drive. As we have previously observed, the narrative element of threats of violence against the messenger's of Lot's God are not relevant. Heterosexual violence, rampant throughout the whole Bible in stories of rape but also in metaphors of God's violence against women (such as in the prophetic account of Hosea, but also disseminated amongst all the prophetic texts) had not invalidated heterosexuality. The traditional reading of Genesis 19 is an excuse to establish a basis for what is effectively a struggle between different orders of heterogeneous and homogeneous nature. But the text is confusing. The breakdown of hospitality may not have come necessarily from the Sodomites, since the men of God were not stopped by immigration controls and a free place for the night – in this case the square – was provided for those who did not have their own accommodation. The lack of hospitality came from Lot's divine messengers, involved in a mission of policing sexuality in the neighbourhood. The evil gestures come also from Lot's God, the gesture of the destruction of the sexual culture of the Other. Nothing is good amongst the Others and as in the disquisition of early Colonial Theology, not a single 'good' (that means 'same') person could be found by the monotonous, mono-loving God of destruction. In Sodom, they were all different. The destruction of Sodom functions then as a colonially minded epopee of annihilation in which every thing needs to be destroyed in order to start a new (although 'same') genesis. This is cloning-warfare. Hybridisation processes need to be counter-attacked at an early stage. Who then has expropriated life and who owns the sign of the Sadean gesture of destruction which heralds the incessant new beginning of Sadean scenes? The God of Lot. As the Algerians have taken over a half-destroyed Paris in Acker's *Empire of the Senseless*, making of victory a dubious sign, so Lot's culture did the same on a biblical scale. Lot's culture took over diversity, took over a nation of different good and bad people who could be, if not entirely peaceful, at least less violent than Lot's God. The victory in this Theo-Apocalyptic narrative is frustrating, because we can realise now that only the ethical perspective of diversity (and specifically, sexual diversity) could have provided what the biblical heterosexually interpreted project did not have, that is, dialogue in community to self-criticise and to balance the Bible's own excesses of the sameness nature. The scenes after the destruction of Sodom speak for themselves: a woman who refuses to forget that life was different, disobeys and turns her face back to see what has been done. In this she acted like the mothers of the Plaza de Mayo who dared to commit the maximum offence that a person can do against a fascist system, which is to remember and to challenge the false memories of a symbolic tale of the reproduction of sameness. Lot ends by having sexual intercourse with his own daughters, an incest scene which continues the incest theme in the theology of God's male messengers. Divine men who procreate men, or to be more precise, the Bataillean single sign of universal homogeneity called God who now reproduces (by cloning) himself in male heterosexual culture.

The Queer theologian may have become a statue of salt, as did Lot's wife, by remembering the destruction of heterogeneity in this foundational biblical exegesis (for that is what biblical stories are: written exegesis of other oral and/or written stories). She did not perish in the destruction of Sodom neither did she reproduce the father. She represents diverse, promiscuous love: the erotic love which does not discriminate, in contrast with the agapian, which marks off categories of the loved and the unloved.[4] The Queer theologian is now exiled like Abhor, but not knowing from which identity she is exiled (Acker 1988: 63). She is not a statue of salt, but she moves in different ways, in diverse memory rhythms that are not recognised or able to be decodified by the culture of sameness and Lot's God. The cry from Abhor, 'raise us from the dead' (Acker 1988: 39) becomes then the cry for the resurrection of the Sodomite people and their human rights (and our rights and needs) to be different amongst the destructive sameness which would in due course become the divine economy of Christianity.

We may end these reflections by saying that the God of Lot was blind and the victory obtained was a sad one. Queer theologians in the dungeons of systematic T-Theology cannot forgive and forget, as if we were involved in an appeal for amnesty in the case of Pinochet or judging the 'final solution' (*punto final*) in the trial of those responsible for the disappearances in Argentina during the 1970s. The Sodomites must be resurrected one day and, as Goss says, 'God will remember them and do justice' (Goss 1993: 111). By them, sexual justice will become a key hermeneutical clue for any reading on the sacred and people's lives.

6

THE ECONOMY OF GOD'S
EXCHANGE RATE MECHANISM

Not one word which you read in my work has a reason beyond that of faith. With this I mean that the Scriptures are for me not only printed paper; every time I am given to examine a body, I see in it the work of the Almighty and on every inch of that body I read the Divine Words, and my spirit is moved.

(Andahazi 1999: 170–1)

That is the significance and the enormity of this insensate little book: the story brings in God himself with all his attributes; yet this God is a whore exactly like all other whores. But what mysticism cannot put into words (it fails at the moment of the utterance), eroticism says ...

(Bataille 1987: 269)

Transcendence in brothels

If God is a God of history and resurrections therefore also happen in history, we need to consider the role of permutations in Scriptural readings. The category of prostitution in the Bible, with its heavy theological investments, needs to become part of a dialectic of exchanges and transmutations with the divine. Permutations are related to genderfucking (gender exchanges) or transsexualism (sexual exchanges) but also to economic processes. Reading God and prostitution in the Scriptures permutes first of all the partners in dialogue from the prostitute and the religious community of sexual authority in the Bible to the prostitute and God. Second, the dialogue is between God and Godself, because Queer theologies consider relationships as the ground from which we think God.

Reading Bataille we find that God may be a whore and this opens a whole new world of symbolic exchanges and experiences to consider in the unveiling of God as a stranger. For instance, in Bataille God the Whore acts outside an economy of capitalist exchanges. God is a whore in a potlatch system which has replaced (or perhaps put into its right place, that is, re-placed) divine grace. For Bataille eroticism and religion have a common ground of experience (Carrette 2000: 82) and in that sense Bataille's embodiment of God in a completely theological Other (such as a prostitute) makes of *Madame Edwarda* an important hermeneutical key to consider in depth. We must be aware that the erotic and economic theological challenge present in *Madame Edwarda* is a challenge directed precisely to economy, that is, to the exchange rate mechanism of the God of Lot. That God who wanted to exterminate the different in its midst can be identified by specific biological traits and relationships of re-production (as in cloning) and therefore by belonging to the order of hegemonic ownership. Instead of that Bataille confronts us with a powerful transgressive image of God, the God in the brothel, or the Whore God of the streets and alleys. In this we see the nude God who emptied herself in a brothel's kenosis of sexuality, poverty and violence. That God is Madame Edwarda. Continuing with our queering of the Scriptures we shall continue reflecting theologically on Madame Edwarda as the God-Whore of Bataille, while advancing with our proposal of doing a permutative kind of reading. This time we intend to use several biblical stories. The narrative of prostitution which we shall privilege will be the story of Rahab, the prostitute who hid the Israelite spies in her house (as found in Joshua 2). In reality, we do not have stories of prostitutes as such in the Bible, neither in the Hebrew Scriptures nor in the New Testament. What we have are women identified as prostitutes, that is, whose identity is linked to prostitution even if this has been done for the most part in dubious ways. For instance, in the Hebrew Scriptures Gomer, the wife of the prophet Hosea is identified as a harlot, but in the story she can only be seen as a sexually independent woman (or adulteress, according to the text) somehow also identified metaphorically with Canaanite worship. However, even in the few cases such as the story of Rahab in which women are identified as prostitutes, the text seldom gives us an account of their humanity. The prostitutes do not talk and we do not have theological insights or reflections coming from them. We do not have episodes taken from their daily lives (familiar or otherwise) and we do not know anything of their reflections about God and their societies. In the New Testament the 'prostitution' of many women is mainly of an exegetical (not biographical) character; such examples include Mary Magdalene and the Samaritan woman who becomes involved with Jesus at the well. Their prostitution is part of the exegetical imagination of the biblical interpreters for instrumental theological purposes. In reality the focal point is seldom the so-called prostitute but rather an agenda of ideological issues which requires the use of the body of a prostitute to make a political or religious statement. Rahab is one of the few texts where we can get a glimpse of a woman and her sexual survival in a difficult time.

Also in Rahab we find a story related to that category of the law of hospitality which we have encountered in Klossowski's *Roberte ce soir*, permutating with the narratives concerning the destruction of the Sodomite culture. Rahab and also Hagar (the woman who received a theophany in the desert) will be stories on which to reflect. We shall also be considering for our readings of permutations some Latin American writers. From two Argentinian writers, Alejandra Pizarnik and Federico Andahazi, we shall take elements concerning the positioning of the body of Rahab in the biblical story and issues of sexuality and nationalism.

Specifically from Pizarnik we shall be using the representation of the female body in her poetic narrative, which is made up of a complex collage of images of madness, death and disintegration (Foster 1997: 103). In Pizarnik we find a poet who was, beyond her narrative, a threatening political presence during the years of the military dictatorship in Argentina, for she was a Jew living in the midst of a strong anti-semitic culture, a young lesbian woman at a time during which her sexual identity could not be easily articulated even as part of a literary fiction. Moreover, her medically diagnosed schizophrenia which forced her to live in clinical institutions during the last years of her life has given us an insight into the dialectic of reason and madness during the times when state terrorism rationalised and re-categorised madness, especially women's madness.[1] Pizarnik's early death when she was 36 years old, by an accidental or deliberate overdose, came at the peak of the repressive government under which her work circulated in an almost clandestine way. This in itself was also somehow a statement of the transgression which marked her work, for suicide is still to this day an offence against the law in Argentina (Foster 1997: 96). That unique and precious identity that Pizarnik could not circulate publicly, except in a limited way during the years of the brutal project of univocity and hegemonic appropriation which characterises military dictatorships, is not so different or distant from that lack of articulation of the figure of the prostitute in the Bible, both in the Hebrew Scriptures and the New Testament. For instance, the prostitute did not have an explicit life in a constituted narrative about prostitution; she was configured only as a piece of religious and political propaganda. If the perversion (in the negative way) of God could have produced the gesture of destruction which annihilates the Other's culture, that divine state terrorism could also have re-organised an economy of bodies which would force into clandestinity the bodies of the prostitutes in the Scriptures.

The other Argentinian writer whose writings we shall use, Federico Andahazi, was a more recent protagonist in a minor scandal in puritanical (although democratic) Argentina. In 1996 Andahazi received the first prize from the prestigious Amalia Lacroze de Fortabat Foundation for his novel, *The Anatomist*, only to be threatened with having the prize taken away when someone discovered its highly erotic and controversial nature. *The Anatomist* is a Queer medical novel mixed with the ethos of the Conquest of the Americas. The story narrates the incidents leading to the discovery of the *Amor Veneris* (the female clitoris) in the sixteenth century by a man whose life was dedicated to seducing a famous prostitute of the time.

In his search for finding a formula to make a woman love him, the anatomist finds the locus of female pleasure and attracts towards himself persecution by the church and threats from the Holy Inquisition. The discovery is seen as demonic. The words pronounced by the anatomist to his tribunal imply that what has been discovered by him is more than pleasure. So he says: 'to present a thesis on the body implies, inevitably, another thesis concerning the soul' (Andahazi 1999: 171). The book is deceptive, and it seems to be worked upon layers of social and religious subversive messages, mixed up with patriarchalism. The theologically patriarchal atmosphere of the book, located in Italy in the sixteenth century, not only confronts the main character with censorship and the Inquisition but somehow does the same to the reader. Dissent and subversion come in oblique ways through the violent and anti-clerical reading.

There are two women in this novel: Inés de Torremolinos, in whose body the anatomist discovers the *Amor Veneris*, is a virtuous widow consecrated together with her three daughters to a monastic existence. They function in the text as a kind of Queer Trinity who end up being burnt as witches. The discovery of her own source of pleasure by Inés makes her abandon the convent with her daughters and start a prostitute movement (loosely suggesting a kind of prostitutes' monastic order), whose success was their liberation from the love of men via clitoridectomy. It is a novel about death where love is an impossibility and God only moves through destruction. The permutations between a captive Trinity (the widow and her sisters in the monastery) and their independence (affective and economic) requires, in a patriarchal religious culture, a mutilation of their sexuality, under the threat that female sexuality could be discovered and controlled by men.

The genre of sexual transgressive literature in Latin America usually assumes a powerful critique to the social, religious and political systems of that continent. There is another important contemporary writer whose work is relevant for our per-mutative re-reading of the prostitute in the Bible, namely, the Brazilian writer Hilda Hilst. Hilst is a pornographic poet, playwright and novelist who has produced some of the most important contemporary discourses in the area of destabilising sexuality, politics and theology in Latin America. One of her books which is particularly rele-vant to our present work is *Rútilo Nada* (1993; literally, 'Glittering Nothingness' or 'No Brilliance Whatsoever'[2]). In this novel Hilst confronts the reader with a game of multiple homosexual transgressions related to economic power in modern Brazil. In this novel a homosexual man, forced by his father to marry a woman, witnesses the martyrdom of his gay lover. The homosexual lover becomes in a theological reading, a paschal lamb, while prostitution can be explored in relation to the construction of marriage, the homosexual body and capital. The public and private service of/to a homosexual body and the annihilation of the transcendental in the process is a key theological element in reading *Rútilo Nada*.

Pubis-Liberation Theology

... 'class struggle doesn't exist' since 'there is no element deluding it' – we cannot apprehend it 'as such', what we are dealing with are always the partial effects whose absent cause is the class struggle.

(Žižek 1994: 110)

... *E hoje, repetindo Bataille:*
'Sinto-me livre para fracassar'
(And today, repeating Bataille:
'I feel free to fail')

(Hilst 2001)

Slavoj Žižek, in his analysis on the forms of sexuation in Lacan, as found in his article entitled 'Otto Weininger or Woman Doesn't Exist' (Žižek 1994), explains how the masculine and the feminine are structured, making use of the Marxist concept of the class struggle. According to Žižek every position that we adopt in the class struggle, that is, every point of participation and insertion we have in it, is already the class struggle. This means that any militant theological practice (for instance, Robert Goss's 'act up' Queer manifesto; Mary Hunt's 'Water Alliance' or Tom Hanks's 'The Other Sheep' ministry in Buenos Aires) implies an 'ourselves' taking sides in a particular moment of the struggle. This we can say somehow, but no more, for the simple reason that we cannot delineate what is the class struggle 'as such' in itself, beyond the praxis of which we are part and the praxis which preceded us. Only our participation or commitment to the moments of the struggle count (Žižek 1994: 109–10). Interestingly Bataille may be confronting us with a similar theological argument through Madame Edwarda. Following Žižek's argument, we can say that every universal notion of theology is related (or rooted) in a particular sexual moment of the struggle. This happens because theology elaborates its universal claims through specific sexual modalities which work as a surplus of something universal, that is, bigger and inclusive, an omnisexuality. In *Madame Edwarda*, the God Whore who manifests herself in a Parisian brothel, we have this particularity of Sexual Theology reflecting something unique and universally encompassing at the same time, since 'each particular has its *own* universal ... contains a specific perspective on the entire field' (Žižek 1994: 110).

God the Whore is then a unique revelation of God and yet part of a broader field of God's revelation, perhaps as the Sodomite God (God outside utility and reproduction), a moment in the struggle to reclaim the outing of sexuality in Christian theology. God the Whore is perhaps only a moment in the representation of God in Queer Theology yet it is all we may have when we want to see the presence not of a God of the margins in the Scriptures, but of a truly marginal God.[3] That is, a God who is not searching for that form of bartering commerce which is redemption in a colonial order of Grace,[4] but rather a God sticking to God's own marginal identity. Sexual identity may not be the only base of God's own identity but it becomes so when it intersects with so much political power that it could be said that God in Christianity remains clandestine more than marginal. From that perspective, to re-read God as a clandestine figure (for instance, a whore) in the Bible is a project doomed to failure, but we should feel ourselves free to fail. Not being afraid to fail is, however, much more than courage which rejects profit. It is also what Cixous, in *The Laugh of the Medusa*, calls not being afraid of *lacking*, that is, doing theology while trying to distance ourselves from a Christian phallocratic symbolic order (Cixous 1981: 248).

As in Sadean literature, the main objective of a clandestine God may be to transgress, not to settle down, to remain more un-lawful in order to keep the flow of justice moving and not to be a God re-inscribed in the official order of T-Theology. The objective is to transgress whilst remaining Queer and not just kinky, that is, to have in the words of Elizabeth Wilson, a suspicion about what also qualifies as transgression (Wilson 1993: 116). For transgression to be truly transgressive it must carry tactical elements sufficient to be transformative of our lives, or to be 'acted up' (Goss 1993: 147). Transgression is about agency. That is perhaps something which, in the re-reading of the whore in the Bible, is going to be important for us, because the streets are full of women and men subjected to several forms of prostitution including suffering violence and poverty and there is a need to queer God both outside and inside that particular structure or combination of patriarchal oppression. Our re-reading needs to be one that retains the moment of unveiling God's clandestinity of sexuality, poverty and violence while respecting God's determination to remain in the streets and alleys of theology. Reading as Queer theologians, not as just kinky theologians, would mean that in the biblical Rahab we should be able to see a particular moment of the presence of the divine and a particular strategy, which may be different from the one we require now, yet which may still open our road to reflect in a queerly different way.

We have already considered some of the main elements of the story of Madame Edwarda in a previous chapter. An anguished man (Pierre Angelique, the pseudonym under which Bataille wrote the story and at the same time, the main character of the novel) finds himself in a scene of theophany in a brothel, where the revelation of God, that is Godself, is a prostitute called Madame Edwarda. This is a body-theophany, and the revelation of God through a female pubis. It could have been a sexual theophany, and as such inspiring and challenging, but the materiality of Edwarda's pubis as an agent of revelation gives a taste of what is the meaning of the divine incarnation at the edge of heterosexually constructed margins of messianship: the (male/straight) God who is poor (but not so poor that he cannot afford to keep himself decent). As such, this piece of Pubis-Liberation Theology helps us to think about a reversal of God's theophanies in the Bible. For instance, it may be considered that the scene of Hagar in the desert is the only female theophany in the whole Hebrew Bible, that is, the only narrative of God manifesting Godself to a woman in an individual setting (Genesis 16: 7–12) and in a framework of a face-to-face dialogue. There are other collective theophanies in the Bible such as the story of Sodom which we have re-read, in which some 'men of God' were there in public view, visible to straight and Queer alike, including the women of Lot's family (whose sexuality we ignore as the text does not specify it). As women's faces and voices tend to disappear or become invisible in patriarchal communities, so any interaction between women and God is simply not acknowledged in the communitarian narratives of biblical theophanies. The God of Lot is a profit-making re-productive divine being. Hagar receives this theophany because she is pregnant. She is a woman whose womb has been doubly blessed (in the terminology of pregnancy as a blessing in these ancient texts), by a son and by God's presence in the desert. However, we want to pursue God outside the framework of re-production. We need another kind of God and another kind of love. It has been pointed out that in the Hebrew Scriptures the verbal root of one of the terms used for God's love is *rhm* (womb).[5] Thus, Phyllis Tribble has correctly made exegeses of images of God's love in the Hebrew Scriptures as 'love from the womb' (Trible 1987: 45). This added elements which were required in biblical exegesis, such as a reflection on God and compassion taken from a feminine imaginary. However, as Queer theologians we may wish to move away from this point and take critical distance from a God related to wombs (which is, patriarchally speaking, a disputable honour and perhaps, in this case, a sign of sexual appropriation by a He-God) because we sense that here we are still in the theological land of reproduction and utility. We have argued against this position in the previous chapter, following a reflection inspired by a Sadean perspective on a very different economy of sodomy.

Through Madame Edwarda Bataille gives us, instead of theological wombs, divine pubis. Instead of love from the womb, we have now a God whose love is love from the pubis. This works out as a powerful hermeneutical clue, not only because Edwarda is a Woman-God, but because in her we have the female divine body (and a marginal God: a battered, impoverished, drunk and sick body) which represents the blessing of (and to) the pubis, not just the womb. This is the Woman-God of non-reproductive and non-profit relationships and as such, in Her there is a multitude of powerful signs of transgressions of a sexual and economic nature.

The whole story of Madame Edwarda as written by Pierre Angelique may be read as a Christian ritual, requiring a reading of theological substitutions. Foucault pointed out the need for rituals in the religious discourse (Foucault 1970: 225). He chooses Edwarda as his sexual partner for the night. He first approaches and later follows Edwarda to the brothel. The brothel's hall is full of people, prostitutes and clients. For Stoekl, this scene is evocative of the 'Mass of the Catechumens' because it is open to the non-converted or to those expecting initiation – in this case, erotic initiation (Stoekl 1995: 81). This is also the space in which the theophany occurs, for while kissing Edwarda in the brothel's hall, Pierre Angelique is surprised by the presence of God. Madame Edwarda reveals herself as being God to Pierre Angelique not only by words but by a corporeal, liturgical sexual gesture of showing him her genitals with the following words of intimation:

– Would you like to see my rags (*guenilles*)? ...
– You see, she said, I am GOD ...

(Bataille 1973: 21)

The blessed pubis of God has appeared to Pierre Angelique and he has understood it. The liturgical movement then needs to proceed. A female voice intimates to the clients that they should go to the rooms upstairs with their chosen partners and he now follows Edwarda to the bedroom to make love. Later, he will follow her to the street, when her desires lead her and force Pierre Angelique to go also. It is in the street, seeing Edwarda standing still under a door, that Pierre Angelique receives the second revelation (this time as an inner sense) of Madame Edwarda as God. At this moment in the novel, the reader is told that Pierre Angelique's drunkenness has been dissipated in the fresh air of the night. He is now sober enough to realise that the theophany has really happened, that it was no illusion of his senses. Suddenly, as a consequence, he is afraid that Edwarda may leave him and disappear into the night, that God will desert him. But Edwarda suffers a fit, insults him and, just as he realises that she is not only God but also a mad God, she calls him a 'dirty priest'. After that, the reader is told that Madame Edwarda (God) remains silent. Finally the novel ends with a sexual scene in a cab. Madame Edwarda is now making love to the taxi driver, while Pierre Angelique is a priest who contemplates the scene. In Stoekl's analysis this is the scene of recognition in the novel: not only does Pierre Angelique see that Edwarda recognises herself as God but at the same time, as the impossibility of God. As God, she has transgressed the ultimate margins, revealing herself as God in the 'disgustingly' different (Stoekl 1995: 89). It ends with Madame Edwarda and Pierre Angelique, her only follower or believer, in a moment of communion given by a voyeuristic recognition of God.

Rahab in a brothel in Paris

… she tied the crimson cord in the window.

(Joshua 2:21)

Sales de tu guarida y no entiendes
(You leave your hideout and you don't understand)

(Pizarnik 1968: 54–5)

The story of Rahab in the Hebrew Scriptures is one of colonialism and betrayal. It is the story of a woman who conceals two Israelite spies in her house and embraces the Israelite faith and colonial quest, thus saving her life when the walls of Jericho fall (Joshua 2:1,3; 6:17, 23, 25). The biblical text presents her as a prostitute and although this is disputed (Josephus for instance considered her to be an innkeeper), we are going to follow the general biblical story for the purpose of producing a permutation between this text and Bataille's *Madame Edwarda*.

If we were to locate Rahab ('the wide one') in a permutation with Bataille's story, we should probably place her laughing in the street with some friends, with God (Madame Edwarda) in the midst and of course in the brothel. However, Rahab is not Edwarda; on the contrary, she is the one who rejects the law of hospitality, although the text would like us to believe the contrary. Let us start with the argument of hospitality and proceed from there to one of sacrificial rituals.

Madame Edwarda inaugurates the reflection on the public potlatch of God, which means that God's presence is non-negotiable even if some sort of transactions

101

(interactions) are an integral part of a theologising of God. But the God-whore of Bataille is a re-distributive divinity who has emptied Herself without expecting payment, not even that of attributing a purpose to the kenotic movement. This happens because the potlatch economy seldom leaves leftover residues. Everything is consumed, like having sex with God in public. When Pierre Angelique kisses Edwarda's pubis in the brothel's hall, the private devotionary practice is obliterated from the life of the believer. The divine potlatch is equivalent to the scenes from Klossowski's *Roberte ce soir*, in which the law of hospitality struggles between the balance of a restrictive and a general economy of expenditure (of Roberte's body or of Madame Edwarda's body of God). However, the circuit of exchange in the law of hospitality in Roberte belongs to another category of grace and non-profitability, that is, to the theological realm of useless expenditure where everything is 'consumed' or disposed, even the mere memory of the expenditure. This is the scene of God as Madame Edwarda giving herself and not leaving even a memorable trace to be remembered and, therefore, leaving 'something' of Godself behind. In Rahab, the law of hospitality occurs in territorial possession.

It was Hélène Cixous who associated phallocentric language with cultural orders organised around possession and property (Morris 1993: 119). Following this argument, the book of Joshua and this particular episode, which stands as a prologue to the possession of the promised land, contradicts the logic of the potlatch. The exchange contract which specifies the gift of life for Rahab and her family (through public recognition: her house is marked for life and the following prosperity of the invasion enterprise) remains in the patriarchal dialectics of exchange for power and control. If, as Cixous suggests in her 'Medusian' way of reading texts through hierarchical orders, we try to follow Rahab and the spies in the places of binary logic in the text, we may be able to see where they are hidden. The strategy followed by the narrative of Rahab is one which emphasises the heterosexual logic of conquest and masculine profit.

At the outset Rahab is located in a site of what is constituted as a domestic/public space. Her house doubles as her own brothel; her house is her place of business. It is a site of prostitution and it is at the same time a site of domestic (family) life. It is in this domestic/public space that she receives the two men who are in the city for a political reason (to spy) but nevertheless want to visit a prostitute for the night. A series of sexual and economic exchanges happens in the text after that, which challenges the original bi/texuality of Rahab, not only in her home/brothel location but also in her capacity for doing politics apart from sex with strangers. We need not suppose that she had sex with the spies for free, but even so, the whole text is one of interlinking the giving of gifts with the ultimate gift, namely the gift of land (associated with God), but in the framework of what Cixous can call the plus-value of virility: authority, control, possession, pleasure (Cixous 1994: 44). Rahab gives the men the gift of hiding them and they pay her back by promising to hide her in turn. The exchange of hiding however is deceptive in its apparent simplicity because for the men hiding presents an opening, or public appropriation of lands and culture (a colonisation process), while for Rahab it represents a further development in logocentrism. That is the explanation of the declaration of logo-faith that the biblical writer puts into the mouth of a woman who belongs to a religious group other than the Israelites. In order to survive the prostitute becomes a heterosexual text and forgets her original bi/textuality. We are confronted in this text with a new, anti-Sodomitic style gesture of destruction by appropriation by the God of Israel, a new beginning, creationist story. It is at this point that God can be rightly called a God of the Fathers since from Lot to Joshua the divinity has re-produced itself intact in the same commercial exchanges, that is, without challenges to the divine identity built around colonial hegemonic desires.

Rahab gives hospitality in her body and in her house but in a constructed logocentric economy of exchange which obliterates her in order to save her. Femininity in the text will be displaced from her to the country to be occupied. Going back to the question posed by Cixous, 'Where is she?' (Cixous and Clément 1994: 37), the location of Rahab leaves her body too soon in the story. This occurs because (as elsewhere in the Bible) something surprising happens to prostitutes. Prostitutes in the Bible are, by name, only subjected bodies. They are bodies of transgression and enemies of the law of the Father, but bodies. To think prostitute is to think a body. Yet the body of Rahab did not give place to an inventory. How do we then know that she had a body?

In order to find Rahab's body and understand the logic of hospitality involved in the text (including its denial) we need to read from another place. Suppose we are now located in a place which gives us access to observe not the spies plotting the destruction of Canaan, but the almost incipient bi/textuality announced as the location of Rahab. From this standpoint we want to reclaim her body from the interpretations of heterosexual plots and give it a Queer identity. Suppose that we have a Queer reference by which to undertake the surveillance of the game of strategies of colonial success in the text. That bi/textual location may be given to us by Alejandra Pizarnik's poetry which can help us to see how Rahab might have fallen into ignorance and forgetfulness in what could have been for her a place of revelations. Pizarnik reminds us of the experience when she says in a poem:

Caer como un animal herido en el lugar que iba a ser de revelaciones
(To fall as a wounded animal in the place which was going to be of revelations)

(Pizarnik 1968: 43)

Pizarnik's usage of defamiliarisation techniques includes gender vagueness in her poetry (which, in Spanish, is an almost impossible task) by a displacement of the tradition of the female voice in Argentinian poetry (Foster 1997: 97). Also in her work the body is continuously present, mentioned even to the extent of corporealising the non-human universe. Everyday things, familiar objects, even the sky itself are mentioned in an interminable inventory of body parts. Eyes, mouths,

103

breasts, hands, legs, tongues, pubic hair, hearts, brains: they are constantly mentioned and repeated in different combinations in Pizarnik's work, because as she says in one of her poems 'your body should always be / a beloved space of revelations' (Pizarnik 1965: 10). 'No one knows me. I speak my body' (Pizarnik quoted in Foster 1997: 94).

A reversed bodily revelation happens in the biblical text though, since it is Canaan which is feminised (silenced, open to multiple violations and located as a natural embodiment of sin) while Rahab is masculinised. Rahab has exchanged a body for a mouth and is now a logocentric confession of faith, no longer a woman of promising ambiguities. If at the beginning of the narrative her location was the domestic/public house in which she lived and worked, now her displacement is both from the public and the private, though she will remain in the private scene for a while. This is a process of virginalisation of Rahab, for any previous cultural, religious and sexual exchanges are now undone and the economy of excess promised by the bi/textuality of the narrative restricted. Curiously, by allying herself to the patriarchal economy of 'nothing for free' (or for grace) she has been redeemed in the (hetero)sexual exegesis of the text and survived in more than one sense. Let us examine this point in more detail.

The story of Joshua is the story of colonisation of the Other's lands. It implies destruction. We are still in Sodom but the difference here may be that Rahab is presented as heterosexual. Cixous' brief commentary on Genesis, from her essay 'Extreme Fidelity' (Cixous 1994), is pertinent here. According to Cixous, the story of Eve read as a social punishment to women in control of pleasure begins a 'you-shall-not-enter series' (Cixous 1994: 134). For Eve has entered the law and defied an absolute prohibition. We could say that Rahab's femininity is threatened by this same eviction brought about when she took the side of the God of the conquistadors. With the feminisation of the natives it is her own country which will live under the 'you shall not enter' prohibition, and in dereliction: her fate will be diaspora, migration. The economy of exchange in this text is also the economy of the sacrificial where a victim is needed. As in the story of Sodom, the victim is a cultural one: Canaan. We could read the story of Rahab and her two clients through Bataille, for this is a story of sex and death, of eroticism and the sacrificial. With Bataille, we can see here that the story starts with sex between a woman and two men and ends in 'the last taboo' or object of eroticism, that is death. The sacrificial victim is not Rahab, if only because her death would not be as revealing as the death of her culture, a culture she has now betrayed (Bataille 1987: 82). Now from beginning with the prostitute we have arrived at the sacramental act of the destruction of Jericho, which provides the continuity of the God of Israel by a re-union of the sexual Same in theology.

Human sacrifices: do walls ever resurrect?

As Rahab declares herself heterosexual – that is, dis-assembles herself from that we have called the Sodomite culture, from her religion and values, from her life as a prostitute, to become a mono-loving person, declaring mono-fidelity to the mono-God of the foreigners – she saves herself from being sacrificed and gives that place to her nation. Through her closed windows the cry of destruction must have reached her but she could not leave her house until nothing remained outside. At this point, our permutative reading needs to turn to the story of the sacrifice and martyrdom of a homosexual lover, as presented by Hilda Hilst.

Hilda Hilst, in her novel *Rútilo Nada*, has portrayed the sacrifice of a homo-sexual man by a heterosexual father. In this novel, a young man (Lucius) falls in love with the boyfriend (Lucas) of his own sister. The love becomes mutual and they establish a relationship. However, the father of the jilted woman (the father of the boyfriend of her ex-boyfriend), who is a powerful banker, hires a group of men to kill Lucas, his son's boyfriend. The men go to Lucas's apartment, sodomise him by force, beat him and leave him badly injured. After that, the father arrives and suggests that he should commit suicide, which he does. In that way the prosperous banker is able to regain his decent standing in society, in both the public and private spheres of his life according to his own desires. The final scene of the novel is the wake of Lucas. The father kisses the body of Lucas on the lips, while Lucius can only do it through the glass of the coffin. The novel ends with seven poems from Lucius on the theme of walls; walls as 'barriers, as prisons, as the backdrops of repression … as entombment' (Foster 1997: 51).

Let us now look at Rahab in the light of Lucas's story. Her fellow countrymen have been killed and she herself is also obliged to commit some form of cultural suicide. A wall of repression and entombment begins to be created around Jericho, for the walls have teeth and can bite and dismember identities. The Word of God has become a mask: the mask of Lucius distanced from the one who died for him and the mask of Rahab, giving her back to the beloved coun-try. Did not Pizarnik say just this in one of her writings?

> Not to call things by their names. Things have toothlike edges … But who speaks in the room full of eyes. Who bites down with a mouth of paper. Words that come, shadows with masks …
>
> (Pizarnik in Foster 1997: 155)

From now on, the readers of the biblical text will not be able to kiss the Sodomites on their lips, except through the glass lid of the coffins, distancing themselves because they consider it dangerous to be publicly recognised as lovers, that is, as people who love in a different order, made of plurality of desires and heterogeneity in theological praxis. For Rahab to have remained faithful to herself, would have needed to find first of all pleasure in herself and that includes her culture and lifestyle. Between Madame Edwarda and Rahab there is an ocean of divinity, of one exchange ruled by freedom and grace and another by profit and re-productions. While Edwarda has remained as God who gives herself completely, until the end of her sacrifice of kenotic obliteration, Rahab has become straight. Far from allowing herself to enter the self-emptying process of which we all need to be part at sometime in life in order to grow wiser, she fills herself with the sexual myth of hegemonic nature which is part of the foundation of the Bible and colonialism. The whole discourse of imperialism is based on Joshua (Prior 1997: 36) and imperialism is mono-love in arms. What now is called evangelisation (and then Conquista) is based on the sexual theologisation on the art of making 'straight' peoples and cultures.

If the Queer theologian looks at herself, she may still find an opening, an exit door (*sortie*) to her situation in reading this story of eroticism and betrayal (and/or the betrayal of the erotic) in Joshua 2. Her writing does not need to reproduce the plotting of the spies but, instead of that, following Morris's comments on Cixous' proposal of subversive reading, might 'release the potential bisexuality' of the text (Morris 1993: 125). In other words, it might re-locate the texts of a woman (Rahab) amongst other women and men outside heterosexuality, that is, in Sodom. If the Queer theologian meets Rahab the prostitute at the site of her pubis and reads from the perspective of Sodom, she may find subversion and joy in her own clitoris and that may be the beginning of a pubescent biblical theology, a new disorder of imagining Rahab as part of a community of women prostitutes, where she might find many.

The final exit of a difficult text which may be inspired by the imaginary community of prostitutes is Federico Andahazi's novel, *The Anatomist*. In this novel, the main character, an anatomist called Mateo Colombo, a man inflamed by his love for a famous prostitute, Mona Sofía, has made a discovery. That discovery which he equates with the discovery of a new continent (for he is a new Christopher Columbus discovering *América*) is the *Amor Veneris* or the pleasure of the clitoris. He discovered it by chance in the body of a woman called Inés de Torremolinos. Inés would also discover herself and fall deeply in love with the anatomist. But Colombo warns her, 'It is not me whom you love' for Inés had found the source of love in herself, in her own body (Andahazi 1999: 234). Once she had understood this, she adopted a radical solution to her sentimental troubles; she carried out her own clitoridectomy in order not to love men anymore. That is, by the way, not the solution that the female reader might have anticipated, for the liberation from the impossibility of love with men might be found in precisely the opposite direction. This alternative is seen in Irigaray's discourse on female sexuality where a new holy Trinity of clitoris and two lips can be enjoyed and theologised; the beginning of a post-colonial Sexual Theology anticipated in the speech of the lips which are one and sufficient in their dialogue. 'A woman "touches herself" constantly without anyone being able to forbid her to do it, for her sex is composed of two lips which embrace continuously' (Irigaray 1980: 100). However, Inés and her daughters (called by Andahazi 'the Trinity'; Andahazi 1999: 249) are pragmatists. In fact, they found happiness and success by teaching other women to commit a sexual suicide. The Trinity, who was oppressed and ill in the monastery, discovered her clitoris, her love, but those were not times for loving. The Trinity destroys herself and it is destroyed (burnt at the stake) but there are no regrets. And so with Rahab; it is easy for us to read texts of sex and death outside the context of war. Women must guard this secret: men should not be allowed to discover their female sexuality. In *The Anatomist*, Inés sets up brothels and fills them with women whom she educates in the art which she has discovered of liberation from pleasure and love in a world of men and god-men.

Might it not have been better for Rahab to cut out her heterosexual site of fear and her respect for men's power, to live as a woman of many multiplicities, rather than be finally reduced to one culture and faith whose adoption means the betrayal of herself and her nation? Is that not a theological and cultural clitoridectomy in itself? Did she not cut Sodom from her body, as an *Amor Veneris* and in doing so did she not cut herself from herself? What had happened in the sexual encounter with the two foreigners (at the beginning of her story) which filled her with so much fear? The site of sacrifice should have been not Jericho, not this Sodom, but a woman's tendency to survive by heterosexuality – imperialism, colonisation and the rule of the mono-loving God. There is a lesson here for the Queer theologian. She should remain faithful to the theo/logics of the potlatch by declaring her site at the margins as a non-negotiable site of Grace and freedom. Rahab is an example of a woman saving herself and her closed community (her family) without being herself a salvific presence. Instead she excommunicates her nation. For one thing leads to another and one betrayal leads to the entombment of nations and the destruction of the walls which circumscribe the loving communities of the Other and their neighbourhoods.

Queering the Scriptures will always be a project related to re-reading the patriarchs, for patriarchy is not a transcendental presence but has agents responsible for its order. To deconstruct the patriarchs means to deconstruct their law, for justice requires the vigilant revision (new visions) of the ideological construction of the divine and the social. Justice and the search for just orders in theology and in society is after all the only link element that a Queer community may have and it provides the common ground for a Queer hermeneutics of liberation (Goss 1993: 87). In this way deconstructing the patriarchs becomes part of what we can call a non-essential project of the hermeneutical circle of suspicion. Its main characteristics may be found around the following elements, which come in general, from the experience of queerness:

- The necessity to remove a teleology from the hermeneutical circle, that is, being more interested in the process than in a pre-determined conclusion, and moreover, privileging the discovery of 'the different produced' (following de Certeau) as we read the Bible.
- That 'different produced' needs to be found through a process which allows mismatches and incoherences to resurface from a text which has been falsely harmonised by centuries of homophobic exegesis and hermeneutical methodologies.
- We can then try to locate sexualities, what we have called the exegetical 'molly houses' of the Scriptures, that is, sites of Queer communities evolving, being nurtured, and/or in conflict and in processes of destruction.

In reading Sodom and the stories from Hagar and Rahab we tried to bracket off the pre-visible, exegetical and fairly limited conclusions to these readings. For instance, reading Sodom was done in positive, non-homophobic ways from historical criticism to rhetorical methods of interpretation, pointing to the sin of lack of hospitality amongst the Sodomites and their aggressive sexual behaviour towards the visitors. Rahab was observed to be a courageous, intelligent woman whose intervention in the site of Jericho was of crucial importance. Yet we prefer to work in both texts from a different coherence. The Sodomites had a different sexual and religious economy from that of the people of Jericho: they had a right to live and to share a perspective that for the Israelites was 'different'. To locate sexualities in conflict without romanticising any of them can mean, as in the story of Sodom, the introduction of aggression. In the story of Rahab there are bi/textual elements in the narrative that are both straight and destructively colonial. Neither the Sodomites nor Rahab had clear cut patterns of behaviour. The Bible allows us to find ambivalences and changes due to circumstances. We are reminded of the claim of the Liberation Theologians: the poor are not better than anyone else, but we privilege them in our reading because of their suffering and oppression. Neither are Queers any better, but their claims cry out to heaven.

Permutations (reading in betweenness) use texts chosen from the experience of the reader. It is not a new way to read the Bible and it has been done before, but the basis for the choice of texts is seldom declared openly and they are frequently selected using criteria which could be the subject of disagreement. Queer texts, even if fictional, are able to convey images and experiences which we sometimes find ourselves unable to express. This is particularly true as we struggle for our sexual theological identity while using phallocratic language to speak of God and ourselves. At the end of our hermeneutical praxis we are trying to unveil or re-discover the face of the Queer God who manifests Godself in our life of sexual, emotional and political relationships. This is a God who depends on our experiences of pleasure and despair in intimacy to manifest Godself, but who has been displaced, theologically speaking, by a God of grand heterosexual illusions, phantasmatic assumptions of the order of love and sexuality.

We have said that God is a Sodomite, since the non-reproductive and non-profit orientated sexual structure of the Sodomite culture is a much more appropriate location in which to name God than the site of the heterosexual continuum. It is to that theology that the metaphor of God the Sodomite is offensive: in reality it should not be more offensive than to represent Christ as a Bolivian miner, or a black Christ from Jamaica. However, presenting Godself as a Sodomite involves such a radical change in the politics of God's sexual orientation as to present an almost impossible challenge to the understanding of God within hierarchical structures. Notwithstanding the use of benign metaphors such as God the Father, what we are claiming for the Queer God is the right of God to submit and to betray God's own straight representation in history, without which a kenosis of sexuality cannot happen – neither can Christ happen. We are claiming critical bisexuality as a pre-requisite for being Christian. We are claiming further a critical transgender, lesbian, gay, heterosexual-outside-the-closet, that is, full Queer presence, as a requirement for doing theology. As Thomas Bohache has said in his article 'To Cut or not to Cut. Is Compulsory Heterosexuality a Prerequisite for Christianity?' (Bohache 2000: 235), 'We do not have to circumcise the foreskins of our sexual orientation in order to be acceptable to Almighty God'. On the contrary, we must be on our guard against ending up like Rahab, reproducing a logocentric faith, or like Inés de Torremolinos in *The Anatomist*, performing a clitoridectomy because she had no options. She sacrificed communion, that is, she excommunicated herself from pleasure to keep her female *jouissance* as a secret outside the male world and the sufferings implied in her life as woman.

Queer and political: condemnations

He decided to approach someone and to ask: *¿Conoce Ud. al Señor Jesús?* (Do you know the Lord Jesus?[6]). He had learnt to say [this phrase] in Spanish ... However, as an American, he did not know that '*señor*' is simply a word used to address someone, and that '*Jesús*' is a very common name amongst people here. He then decided to address a man he saw walking in the streets of Guatemala city. However, when the man replied to him with courtesy: 'I am sorry but I don't know him. I am also a foreigner here', he felt very discouraged ...

(Cano *et al.* 1981: 22)

Our final reflection needs to be on the area of condemnation, as a hermeneutical site or option. Queer hermeneuticians may have differences in their approach or methodology for reading the Bible, but they do have a commonality: the struggle against theological resemblance. As the above anecdote, taken from the life of a missionary from the United States living in Guatemala, might highlight, we should start by asking who or what are theology and traditional hermeneutics determined to resemble?

Let us examine this point in more detail. Historically, T-Theology has assumed a fundamental hermeneutical principle in reading the creation account in Genesis 1:26–7. Whatever the differences may be, it seems that we are always encouraged to read the Scriptures and reflect theologically from the standpoint of resemblance. However, we might reflect with the Italian philosopher Georgio Agamben that there is no such thing as the resemblance of a *unicum* (Agamben 1998: 49). As we might say from our Queer reflections, there is no unicity in God to be reflected either scripturally, dogmatically or ecclesiologically. What we are trying to do by queering theology and Christian hermeneutics, is to stop what – still following Agamben – we could call the pornographic distribution of bodies in Christianity in a *unicum*'s image and resemblance (Agamben 1998: xii). We have taken, for instance, the resemblance of Jesus to God as the resemblance to a quality of singleness in God, or a solid uniqueness without fractures, sexual modes or pluralities. For that reason masculinity is not the main Queer question we have for the reading of Jesus, but the fact that it has been assumed that Jesus, if resembling God, needs to resemble a single heterodivinity without fluid borders and desires which grow in restlessness. Biblical hermeneutics has traditionally assumed resemblance as a hermeneutical key to understanding. Re-readings may exceed some borders (as liberationist and feminist readings have demonstrated) but they still require to remain in the likeness of God's representation, composed of elements of homogeneity and indifference.

The theological tragedy behind this resemblance substratum of T-Theology is one of political proportions. Agamben makes the interesting point that beyond the politics of resemblance there is a capitalist link in which bodies and images are manifested, for instance in the spectacle (Agamben 1998: 50). The risk of these portrayals of people in the capitalist world of fashion (homogenisation of appearance) is that real bodies, hungry, ill-treated, sad and isolated bodies in our midst, are forgotten. If Queer theologians are condemned for disapproving of the economics of resemblance in traditional biblical hermeneutics, this is also part of our political stand against idealism and the theological commercial values of profiting by not identifying multiplicity. The different bodies of the people of God reflect precisely the multiple bodies of God in the Trinitarian kenosis of omnisexuality and the presence amongst us of polyamorus divine concerns.

Resemblance hermeneutics implies always a commodification of the body: theological, economical and political. However, if the current capitalist system requires a global identity (Agamben 1998: 86–7) a Queer hermeneutical option does not require anything instead. It is a work for free, for the camp potlatch, for the grace which does not expect any return and a community in which – still following the thought of Agamben – we can say that everybody could 'co-belong', without being forced to choose or assume a sexual identity. It is at this point that Queer and kinky part company. By that we mean that the Queer theologian's attempt to work with theological transgression is costly: it is neither a fashionable game nor an occasional transgressive sexual distraction. There are real bodies present in our discourses and these are bodies of economic suffering and sexual oppression. Theologies and hermeneutics located in the body are demonologies, contested sites of possession, ambivalence and struggle. They are also sites of exorcism. Queer theologians struggle in areas of the unnameable in theology, yet Queer and straight alike, these are areas of our common hell as humanity.

However, Queer theology needs to continue its hermeneutical route of interpretation not only by opening the Bible from the closures of previous readings, but also by re-reading humanity and intimate relationships in search of the face of the Queer God in a context of poverty and oppression. Such is the issue of our next chapter.

Part II

QUEER PROMISCUITIES

7

POPULAR ANTI-THEOLOGIES
OF LOVE

The 'transformation of the world' of Marx includes the 'change of life'
of Rimbaud; it is not limited only to the socio-economic area, to the
modification of the property regime, but to all levels of human existence, to change in human relationships, interpersonal bonds and the
upsurging of a new ethics.

(Sebreli 1990: 162)

Under colonial domination monogamy takes on a particular social
importance. The strong patriarchal family and "good" women's enclo-
sure within it provide the time-honoured consolation of strict home
rule for male society humbled by the conqueror's yoke. It is even more
essential for the rulers themselves who need to maintain a docile, well-
ordered subject population as well as the social cohesion of their own.

(Dowell 1990: 48)

Bodies in love in theology: where have all the Queers gone?

We are referring here to the body, but not just to anybody, because we want to
refer to the body in love, which has been notoriously absent in theology.
Christian theology has been and still is a theology of controlling the love for
other's bodies, but we are now aware (particularly under the current globalisation processes) of the extent to which the sexual integrity of the poorest of the
poor is being undermined politically and theologically today. Germaine Greer
has made this point in relation to the control of fertility in the exploited nations,
and Susan Dowell, commenting on this in the context of her study on
monogamy and Christianity adds that the sacramental Christian dimension of
our sexual lives lies not in particular imperial Christian teachings, but in the
sacramentality of honouring the ordinariness of sexual lives (Dowell 1990: 196).
This highlighting of the 'ordinariness' of love and sexuality as done in a materialist theological framework belongs to the order of Others. This is an order of
many people's everyday lives which gets lost when we do our arithmetic of the

body in Christian theology, for instance, when recounting how many times the word 'body/ies' appears in theological discourse, such as the body of Christ, the body of the church and its tension with the discourse from the academic theological body (as bodies in opposition). Dogmatics is the Christian *Corpus* (literally Christian Body; in Spanish it is *Cuerpo Dogmático*) which organises the relationships between the divine body of knowledge that theologians have and the body of the community. Those bodies are organised, regulated, redeemed or condemned in a permanent theological discourse of bodies in loving relationships. However, as the Brazilian theologian Jaci Maraschin once suggested, these theological bodies have usually been bodies without flesh, without bones or brains, bodies without nervous systems or blood (Maraschin 1986: 27–8) – and, we may add, bodies without menstruation or sweat or without malnutrition and bodies without sexual relationships. Moreover, as Richard Collier has argued, heterosexuality has not been analysed within political and social theory as a 'historically, culturally specific given concept' (Collier 1999: 43). Thus Latin American Political Theology has been ignorant of the non-heterosexual body and non-heterosexual loving patterns of relationships which exist outside that theology of relationships from the centre which has become normative. If that theology has privileged in its discourse a grounding of its reflections on the perspective of the poor, the perspective has been a limited one, namely that of heterosexual bodies in (ideal heterosexual) relationships.

In order to give some concreteness to the reflection on bodies in theology and to engage them in a dialogue within the framework of the discourse of a Liberation Materialist Theology we need to particularise these bodies. It is particularly important here to identify personal bodies by their names and stories and special characteristics of dissidence and adaptation in our contemporary history. Latin American Liberation Theology has already identified in its theological discourse the concreteness of the *Da* of *Dasein*, or the being-there of our reflections when it declared that the poor were the *Estar* of the *Estar y Ser Ahí* (presence and 'being there') of theology: the poor were the existential locus of the theological discourse and its habitat. In Queer Theology the grounding of the theological reflection lies in human relationships for, as we have argued in previous chapters, it is in scenes of intimacy and the epistemology provided by those excluded from the political heterosexual project in theology that unveilings of God may occur. In this chapter we shall be queering people's loving relationships which, in Latin America, stand at the margins of Christian definitions, in particular the institutionalisation of the decent (as normalcy). The poor in Latin America provide us with reflections of a very Queer nature, emerging at the intersection of economic oppression, racial discrimination and forbidden manifestations of sexualities. Once again we are using the term 'poor' in the broader sense of Liberation Theology, as a site of marginalisation which goes beyond simply economic circumstances. We define Queer as a site of struggle where people's oppressed sexualities have become a locus for the struggle for justice in their communities, that is, of denunciation and/or annunciation of alternative ways of being communities and societies.

114

The theological reflection which queers loving relationships at the margins of the understanding of the social contract of Christian marriage and also the search for Queer signs in its midst, provides us with more than one subversive theological strategy. First, it helps us to locate Queer Theology in the context of political and economic marginalisation. Elsewhere I have already criticised the tendency of Liberation Theologies, and particularly Latin American Liberation Theology, to de-sexualise the communities of the poor, while trying to normalise intimate relationships in a colonial attitude towards the margins (Althaus-Reid 2000). While the churches have been interested in documenting and even encouraging some gender challenges to the structures of relationships, sexual dissidence has been silenced or displaced into a discourse of normalisation. Even the fact of speaking about 'marriage' as such could be incongruent in the vast cultural context of Latin America and as irrelevant as speaking of marriage (in the dyadic structures of husbands and wives) in the context of the Hebrew Scriptures, because the forms of loving and productive relationships we are discussing need not be related to what is a relatively modern Western understanding of the particular legal and theological structure called marriage (Mies 1997: 75–85). As Mies has argued, 'family' is a bourgeois, private territorialisation of relationships, which includes co-residence and withdraws women from public life (Mies 1997: 183). Obviously we do not need to seek similar equivalences even in the patriarchal politics of territorialisation of women in Latin America.

Our aim is to consider the surviving presence of a Queer Theology of relationships amongst the traditional cultures of Latin America. Some of them may have been heavily repressed during the past five centuries since the *Conquista*, even domesticised, but they all continue to retain a core of the sexually different in their organisation. Also, we intend to consider love in the poor urban culture of big cities such as Buenos Aires, while asking ourselves if the present conditions of social and economic exclusion brought by the globalisation processes of capitalism have had some influence in a re-imagining of sexualities. The point is that since exclusion has become a form of civil death for vast sectors of the population of big cities, sexuality also has become somehow de-regulated. However, what is difficult to say is what is new and what is just re-surfacing from centuries of Colonial Theology in alliance with a heterosexual state. As Gramsci has discussed already in relation to the sources of the study of subaltern groups (Gramsci 1970: 491) we are always confronted with the challenge of finding methods of reflection which may expose the fragmentation of the excluded as a group, while resisting the reabsorptive tendencies of theology and church elites. Our interest is in the social practice of loving relationships and elements of consciousness developed through them. The libertine epistemology which informed our previous chapters and the reading by permutations need to continue, now grounded in the convergence of the multiple oppressions of class and gender of the Latin American people. This is an epistemology of *libertinaje*, or the 'popular libertine thought' where Queer transgressions are part of a centuries-long strategy of spiritual and material survival. It is also a location, an answer to our question: where have all the Queers gone? The answer is simple: they have gone nowhere. They are firmly rooted in our folk social traditions and in the ways in which the old religions are still trying to negotiate a different social order. The popular libertine thought is bargaining with Christianity and popular theologians, and this can be seen in the new religious manifestations which come from the creativity of the people at the margins in rural areas as well as in the big cities of Latin America.

The problem we face is that colonial assumptions about affective indigenous relationships and sexual understandings are very pervasive. Marriage, as if there was only one conception of 'marriage' (without pluralities of models) amongst indigenous people, has been viewed in the churches from the Western model of marriage which developed in societies with very different structures and cosmovisions. In fact what we usually have is a Christianisation of traditional models of marriage which in many cases have succeeded in re-presenting them while interfering with the creative possibilities presented by different ways of establishing relationships. Thus for example in the Andes *Servinacuy* is a union approved by elders in the community, in which two people live together for a time before making a major commitment. But where the making of such a commitment has been re-presented in the church, it has been seen as a part of the process of (Christian) marriage. This implies that marriage is expected after the *Servinacuy*, which becomes a trial period for the couple to become accustomed to each other before a legal (and Roman Catholic) ceremony of marriage. However, this is not the reality of *Servinacuy*: there are people living together after many years of *Servinacuy* without any desire to enter into a different form of marriage. Women enjoy more protection against family violence and may have more independence in their traditional form of dyadic union than in Christian marriage with its complex legal implications for women in terms of property (as body-property as well as territory).

In some indigenous communities, marriage (as a legal and religious institution) is seen more as a rite of passage between a type of life with few responsibilities and another that is more mature. Therefore, eventual separations between the couple and re-marriages are not considered to require more legal ceremonies. If a person has already been married once, that is, has passed through the rite of passage from singlehood to maturity, any subsequent new unions or separations require no new rituals. The problem is that in Latin America, theology has incorporated these traditions into Western Christianity but has not valued the creative and disruptive forces within the tradition. What is more meaningful in social movements for deep transformations (as the ones encouraged by Liberation Theologians) is their ability to produce a different social logic. Such social logic is frequently and sadly also theo/logical, and as such manifests a confrontation between people's understanding of spaces of sexualities and loving relationships and the colonial thinking of Christian theology which still pervades the continent.

Peter Drucker, in his article 'In the Tropics There Is No Sin. Sexuality and Gay-Lesbian Movements in the Third World' (1996: 75–102) considers the policing of sexuality in the colonial world, and how indigenous sexualities have been replaced by 'new, unique sexualities' (Drucker 1996: 76), that is, by a monopoly of the master's idealised sexual model of society. Not only forms of transgender sexualities and same-sex relationships existed in Latin America and the Caribbean, but also different understandings of heterosexuality manifested in different structures of marriage. After the centuries-long struggle of Christianity, mainly in the form of Roman Catholicism allied with states, for the political control of sex and souls amongst the natives, the sexually different still exists and manifests itself even in the midst of Christian indoctrination. Sometimes, as in the case of the Canela indigenous people who inhabit the central Brazilian Plateau, different customs concerning sexuality outside marriage have been hidden from foreigners for fear of criticism and disapproval (Crocker 1974: 192). Our main concern is precisely the uncovering of some of the traditions of marriage in Latin America in order to further develop our epistemology of the sexuality at the margins and to continue in this way searching for a Sexual Theology of the Other. The following are issue-based reflections on key sexual cultures which defy Christian heterosexuality (or take it out of the closet) such as:

- bisexuality and the structural organisation of life in a town in Perú;
- issues concerning the different understanding of body-property and the theological untranslatability of 'fidelity' in the tradition of the *Soq'a* in the Peruvian mountains and amongst the Canela people.

God and sex in the mountains: bi/town theology

Let us start by queering the organisation of space and of sacred space in a structural way. If the dual gods of the Incas did not survive very well the Christian pervasiveness of European politically imposed cosmovisions, it is important to locate that spiritual duality also outside the old liturgies, that is in some space of praxis or transformation of structures such as social structures. After all, it is in the social space that our gods live and act and it is in the challenges to stagnant ideological orders that we find them taking sides and announcing by their presence, tensions and struggles. The space which we propose to consider for our theological reflection is Moya, a town located in the mountains of Perú. The Roman Catholic theological structures had colonised and superimposed upon the town space a variety of liturgical gestures which, amongst other things, ensured some resemblance to an order of homogeneity. There are cycles of festivities and Roman Catholic saints' names given to the communities (*Ayllus*) which constitute the town, but the interesting thing is that the indigenous organisation of space and time has resisted colonisation. Moreover, it defies the order of Christianity by maintaining alive its own and different sexual religiosity, such as sacred bisexuality. Our challenge is then to reflect on Moya as an indigenous town in which bisexuality has an important divine and organisational place. The Christian faith which has pervaded the townspeople and their everyday life, as is evidenced for instance in their Christian calendar and devotions, cannot hide completely that difference in Sexual Theology which is rooted in the social organisation and the spatial division of the town. For these reflections we will follow the study on Moya made by the Peruvian anthropologist Alejandro Ortiz, as presented in his article entitled 'Moya: Espacio, Tiempo y Sexo en un Pueblo Andino' (Ortiz 1982: 189–208).

The town is called Moya and the translation of the name has already been the occasion of disputes. *Moya* is a word that could be rendered as 'garden' if it derives from another word spelt *Muya*. But there is another similar term, *Mulla*, which seems to be related to directions or even to the ways of courtesy amongst relatives, like an uncle addressing a younger nephew. A noun derived from this last term is *Mullaypa*, which means a triple cord or a rope thrice plaited. According to Ortiz, it is this last word which matches symbolically the social and religious structure of Moya as a town, precisely by this element of triplicity implicit in the word (Ortiz 1982: 189). Moya is a sexual Trinity. However, people from the region have always translated Moya with the phrase *macho copulando con hembra* (literally, 'male copulating with female' or 'male copulating and inciting others to do the same') which may emphasise the sexual characteristic of the town organisation (Ortiz 1982: 193).

Moya's religious system, the one around which the town is organised, is constituted by three divine mountains. Mountains (the *Wamanis*) are in the Inca cosmology sexual divinities, which can be male, female or bisexual. Mountains are believed to establish loving relationships amongst themselves, can eventually get married and even procreate, forming extended families. Mountains may open themselves to receive a woman they like as a temporary partner. She may, for instance, return home after one year with a child (a child of the mountain). In Moya's divinity systems the mountains are three simply because one important element of the Andean community has been and still is the trialogue (*kimsan kamachicuy*). This trialogue is an understanding of the three basic principles of spiritual relevance for the everyday practice of people in their communities (Quicaña 1994: 103). Such triple principle is composed by the *Ama Suwa* (honesty and faithfulness), *Ama Llula* (truthfulness) and the *Ama Quella* (joint strength). This is the trialogue of the *Tawantisuyu* or Inca Kingdom, which regulates political and economical exchanges as well as social and religious relationships amongst its people. Also, in this cosmovision, the universe is divided into three regions: these are the dwelling place of the people as animals (*Kay Pacha*); the dwelling place of the just who are rewarded after death (*Hanaq Pacha*) and the place for the wicked who disobey the trialogue (*Uku Pacha*) (Quicaña 1994: 105). Therefore the three mountain-gods of Moya simply follows the religious beliefs in the trialogic organisation of sacred, communitarian and personal spaces of life. Moya's religious trinity is composed of male, female and bisexual.

The bisexual divinity of Moya is the hill called *Apu Yaya*. In relation to the entrance to the town, its back is said to be masculine while its front is feminine. The Christian tradition has renamed the *Apu Yaya* as San Cristóbal (a masculine patron saint of the Roman Catholic calendar). However if the *Apu Yaya* is represented in a human image, it usually takes the form of two physically beautiful elderly people, male and female, represented as a couple walking together. The other two mountains (of less importance than the bisexual *Apu Yaya*) are masculine. Theologically, it seems that the main reflection which comes out of this divine configuration concerns the redefinition of bisexuality as a 'conciliatory' or intermediary sexual category (Ortiz 1982: 189). The 'mediatory' role of the bisexual mountain has been stressed and has frequently been seen as a symbol of the importance of the couple in Andean life. That is, the couple as a dyadic family and as the community by extension are more significant than the individual for the Andean community. Doña Matilde Colque, who is a *Yatiri* (a wise woman), speaks about the strength of 'man-woman' in the resistance to oppression in terms of an intimate reciprocity which subsumes at some level the two gendered sexes into one (Rivera Cusicanqui 1990: 171–2). Putting this in context with the bisexuality of some gods, it may be that this indigenous concept of bisexuality is not a Western one. In the Andean context the category of intermediary has been dismissed in favour of allowing bisexuals to claim their own unique identity outside the mediation role of heterosexuality. Yet, our theological task is to reflect on the concept as it is presented in this community and its implications for people's lives.

The indigenous religious system of the people of Southern Perú (where we find Moya) is based on a mountain cosmovision. In this system we find the *apus* (spirits of the mountains); the *awkis* (spirits that inhabit the rounded hills called *moqo*); the *allpa* and *Pachamama* (spirit or Goddess of the earth); the *tiras* (evil spirits from cliffs) and the *ñust'as* (spirits that inhabit emerging stones called *wiñaq rumi*). This religious system is structured around the figures of the *Roal* and the *Pachamama*, two primal spiritual forces related to the forces of nature and the earth (Nuñez del Prado 1974: 238–9). The spiritual world in Moya is perceived by people as very close to their ordinary lives, actively intervening in every facet of their community life, from having children to harvesting. Rewards and punishments are also understood in relation to the approval and disapproval of people's behaviour. It is interesting that in this context the Roman Catholic institution of confession has become acculturated in their traditional religiosity not as a ritual to forgive sins, but as a medium to secure good (diplomatic) relations with the Western god (Christ or the Virgin) (Nuñez del Prado 1974: 244). This is also part of a colonial process of religious and political alienation. Unfortunately, it has not been Christ's own qualities as liberator which have brought Andean people to this conclusion but the alienation of law and justice by the Christian elite who conquered them and rule their lives even today.

Many mountains are considered to be the residence of the *Roal*, thus having great spiritual power and influence upon whole populations. The spirit mountains are sexed; they may be male, female or bisexuals: the latter being especially prestigious. One of them, the mountain of San Cristóbal or the *Apu Yaya*, is the bisexual mountain spirit which presides over Moya. The conceptualisation of the

Apu Yaya as a bisexual divinity, as an intermediary divinity, can also be seen in the understanding of reciprocity and complementarity among the Andean people, as illustrated for instance in the yearly religious rituals performed by the community. However, some of the rituals also speak about bisexuality as a sexual identity which conflicts with others, in the sense of a displacement of gender roles and attributions. There is also a sense of deference in the understanding of bisexuality (as never fully defined) but also an explicit sexual hierarchy in worship: the three mountain gods who are the guardians of the community can be worshipped individually, in their respective *mesas* or worship-sites, or can be ritually approached through the *Apu Yaya*. This means that the *Apu Yaya* is in a dominant position in this Andean Trinity, and if we consider these three gods as if they had a family structure, we could say that the *Apu Yaya* disrupts the privacy of the relationship between believers and the other masculine gods by providing hospitality by inclusion in itself. It is not only the *Apu Yaya* to which bisexuality is attributed: the river Willca, which is one of the rivers of the town, is also believed to have a bisexual spirituality. The Willca has been seen as 'a river of dubious (ambiguous) sexuality' (Ortiz 1982: 190) and it is identified as a border between death and life; this is the river that the dead need to cross as it functions also as a kind of limit between the world of Moya and other worlds. Bisexuality, as a thought concerned with fences and borders, is present in the representation of the crossing between life and death.

One of the challenges presented to theologians when reflecting on bisexual mountains and rivers, or on the whole sexed universe of the Andean people, is that in Christianity sexuality is strongly defined around the praxis of genitalia. If rivers do not copulate and give birth, or if they do not have orgasms, how can they be bisexuals (or male or female)? However, here we are confronted with sexuality defined by gods and a sacred sexualisation of nature, which participates in the order of society, thus opening areas of transgression and the space of possibilities. The *Apu Yaya* represents the face and the gate of Moya and its spirituality pervades the social structure of the town. How does this happen? By a triple distribution and organisation of the town into three *ayllus* or communities which correspond to three sexualities: a male, a female and a bisexual.[1] The bisexual *ayllu* is called *Chaupi* and is perceived as sacred and prestigious (Ortiz 1982: 195). *Chaupi* literally means 'in between' things or time and it also refers to the social composition of this *ayllu* with its mixture of indigenous people and *wiracochas* (white people). But more than that it refers to an identity created by giving space to the contradictory or different co-residing together. People traditionally understand the *ayllu* as an affinity community, considering their members to be the descendents of a common spirit, for instance a *Cóndor* or a mountain. In this case, *Chaupi* people are descendents of a bisexual mountain and have inherited a symbolic mediation role in their lives, such as the identity blend in their midst, already mentioned.

Bi/Christian festivities

However, as we previously observed, to reflect on the possibilities involved in being a descendent of a bisexual spirit we need to look at the religious festivities where issues of sexuality become more evident. It is traditional that in the yearly cycle of town festivities, the three *ayllus* each honour the (Christian) patron saint of the others. *Chaupi* used to have a male and a female patron saint, in an attempt to Christianise bisexuality (San Pedro and La Virgen de Candelaria), but it has now only one female patron saint, La Virgen del Carmen. The Virgin Mary has sometimes been identified by communities in this region with the *Pachamama* (Nuñez del Prado 1974: 246).

There is a distribution of leadership during the different days of the ceremonial cycle of Moya which starts in January and ends in September, but also a marked ritualisation of the sexed universe of the town. In the feminine *ayllu* women have a leadership role and in the masculine *ayllu*, men fulfil the role of major-domo. There are days when rituals are dedicated to the feminine, for instance, 2 February is the day of the Virgen de la Candelaria, and also days on which the masculine is celebrated. Other days in Carnival are dedicated to ritual fighting between men and women, ending in rituals of reconciliation. All of these festivities end with the drinking of *chicha* (maize liquor) and the people celebrate their sexual freedom, to the point that there is a name for children born after the festivities. They are called *wawa fiesta* (children of the festivities).

The more specific bisexual rituals become manifest during the Easter festivities. Between March and April there are festivities related to the handing over of power to the new authorities in the three *ayllus*. Bisexuality is represented in this power exchange by the symbolism of rituals which allow an interpretation of relocation and redistribution of gender roles in the communities. For instance in the ceremonies we are describing the location of women becomes a political one. Women from the *ayllu* who are the wives of the new authorities symbolically occupy a masculine space such as the town plaza, together with children. However, although occupying a masculine, political space which is not theirs by social structures, they still fulfil a feminine function from there, such as distributing bread to the people. From the margins of the plaza, they have come to the centre to distribute bread, but in the ritual of doing that, they incur a symbolic transgression. The bread is kept by each woman wrapped in a traditionally masculine garment, the poncho, and is then distributed to the people from this 'masculine' symbolic location. As Ortiz observes, men become marginal to the political and religious space of the plaza by the temporal disorder symbolised by the presence of women and by the ritual cross-dressing for the distribution of bread (Ortiz 1982: 198). The hierarchical sexual order of Moya gives bisexuality the higher position, followed by the masculine and third the feminine. A mythical explanation of this can be found perhaps in the founder hero of Moya, the *Opa Laywe*. The *Opa Laywe* is described as 'three siblings' (male, female and bisexual), as a giant who was a mute leader of the people, a cultural creator who

121

ended in failure (killed by its enemies). The name *Opa Laywe* has linguistic roots meaning 'a lack', 'virtue' and 'ambivalence'. It is a name which invokes the presence of something as primordial as a female vagina, and a principle which divides, reorders, changes and interchanges while it teaches at the same time.

In many studies by feminist Liberation Theologians, including my own early work, the scene of the Last Supper at which Jesus distributed bread has raised questions in the Latin American context, especially the alienation of the product (bread) from the producers (women) by the intermediaries or distributors of goods in society (in this case, men). The consecration of the sacramental bread is still performed in the Roman Catholic Church in Latin America by male, priestly hands. A sacramental act such as the Eucharist is, as in the case of the Moya ritual exchange of the town authorities, a location of power even if, as in a gift economy, it functions by demonstrating the instability of (divine) power in the name of a Jesus Christ who is, as with the *Opa Laywe* also an ambivalent god of failure and exchanges. What the Eucharist lacks is what in the festivities of the plaza is suggested, that is the symbolics of the exchange and the transgression of an order (as shown in the cross-dressing ceremony of women distributing bread while wrapped in male attire). The dialogical suggestion which we can take from this is that of a Eucharist in which the excluded of the sacred space of the priest, such as women, may take the role of distributing the bread and wine to the people (including the priest), while using elements which suggest the inclusion of other sexualities and their current power disbalances in society. For that we shall require a theological understanding of the plurality who is God and the sexualities included in God, claiming for representativity and a voice in a divine redistributional, sacramental act of power. Sacraments are more than enclosed encounters with God: they act as ways of understanding love, or even ways of having voices of protest symbolically heard. Heterosexuality seems to have interfered with the Eucharist by introducing its own ordering of society in oppositional ways, thus domesticising the figure of God the host as a mere intermediary of heterosexual religious productions.

The question before us now is: How does a sacred understanding of bisexuality work in the life of the people of Moya? Does it have any influence on structures of marriage and loving relationships? How bisexual is the bisexual *Apu Yaya*? Or is it bisexuality as seen from a hetero-window? The answer cannot be definitive. The structure of marriage in Moya is endogamic and matrilineal and the situation of women in it unfortunately does not reveal anything distinct from the general structure of women's subjection in the indigenous society. However, in the Moya community, we are confronted with a religious system which has a sufficient number of elements to assure different relationships amongst people, including loving relationships. The ethical values which inform the life of the community (which come from their bisexual understanding) are those of reciprocity and exchange as a form of re-distribution. Gender re-distribution is also a possibility announced in rituals. What then has neutralised the epistemological potential of the triple sexed town? It seems that reciprocity as a value without a clear and distinctive sexual identification of the different (bisexuality, in this case) can not work as 'reciprocal' at all levels of the organisation of society.

We might ask whether the Christian Trinity is also a case of a theology based on a concept of mutuality and reciprocity which has been historically inefficacious. The deep attachment of Christianity to a non-reciprocal system such as heterosexual patriarchy shows clearly how a theology done from within a system of domination (as in the sense of an everyday doing of theology), ends as a theology of domination (Dussel 1988: 224). Only by substantially modifying or 'outstripping' (as Dussel says) the prevailing practices of domination in society can the prophetic aspects of theology (Andean and Christian) act as agents of transformation. A lack of specification in the sexual identity of our divinities may produce effects of subordination when reciprocity is formatted by heterosexual reciprocity. What we can call the Queer difference disappears when it asserts its own sexual rights in accordance with the heterosexual system. What happens is that theologically speaking, we have not recognised as yet the different boundaries of what has been declared legitimate or illegitimate in sexuality. Consequently the challenges to a totalitarian Christian theological worldview are very few. The indigenous communities, as 'political bodies', are still constituted in theology by forms of inclusion which obliterate and discourage any theological thinking from Christianity where for instance, a bisexual god can nurture a new Christian eschatology. Such eschatology needs to be manifested by an overturning of limits and not by remaining in a static divine project made by the crosscurrents of sexual ideology. If it is true that to think 'universal' in theology is to think in a monotonous philosophy of identity, a postcolonial theology needs to take seriously the sexual gestures of difference which inform the Sacred, while allowing the same sexual different to participate in the construction of new ecclesiologies and a different concept of marriage, for instance. So much of Christian liturgy emphasises transmission without change. The festivity rituals of the bisexual *ayllu* have a potential teaching role of transformation of hierarchical thought in our churches. We could wish that one day the Christian liturgy might be built around the symbolic exchange of priestly clothes amongst people as an act of redistribution of power and responsibility and that the Eucharist might involve children distributing the bread amongst people. The church's sexual spaces might become de-sacralised by producing a re-positioning of the different in the discourse of 'normalcy' of theology. If gender and sexuality (and therefore patterns of relationships in society) are taught and reproduced, Christianity in Latin America would only be able to abandon the colonial Sameness project by creating new gestures, such as bisexual gestures in its praxis, as learnt from the people it claims to represent.

Holy Spirits: on seduction

El Soq'a Machu

Spirit, old daddy,
Your face is like a mouse
The tip of your nose has been eaten by moths ...

From a poem to the Holy Spirit (Lara 1960: 138)

Any theology impregnated of the doctrine of the Holy Spirit should offer us the grace of being able to overcome our own incapacity when faced with absurdity ...

(Camps Cruell 1994: 46)

The theme of change and transformation in theology, especially in Latin American Liberation Theology, is a theme related to the praxis of the Holy Spirit. In the Andean world the use of the word 'spirit' or 'spirits' is ambiguous. 'Spirit' may mean the soul, or the emotional state of a person. It may mean the soul of the deceased, of a mountain or the Christian Holy Spirit albeit in some particular sense. The Holy Spirit, depending which indigenous community we are referring to, may or may not be different from the Virgin Mary or from a saint. It may even include several concepts together in one (Wisley 1973: 159). However, the differences between saints and spirits are minimal and what in Christian theology is identified as the Holy Spirit can be identified by Andean communities as a 'principal spirit', sometimes called *Dios Espíritu* or *Tata Espíritu* (God spirit or Father spirit). This is a form of identification of the Holy Spirit independent of the spirit of the deceased, but associated with issues of fecundity (amongst animals or women).

Considering that the Christian definitions of the Holy Spirit are not translated literally amongst Andean communities, and looking at some of the interrelations amongst them, we could synthesise them in the following way: a spirit is a miracle doer; it helps when in trouble and gives blessings manifested in good harvest, healthy animals and children in the community. As there are many saints, so there are different forms of holy spirits (*espíritus santos*; in Spanish there is no conceptual difference between the terms 'holy' and 'saint'). Moreover, every saint has his or her own talents and they are also considered to be mischievous (not 'saints' in the sense of having only goodness in their characters). Such mischievousness is manifested, for instance, when the spirits take revenge on people who do not fulfil their religious promises (Wisley 1973: 162). Our present reflection is related to a spirit called *Soq'a Machu* which belongs to the general category of spirits who intervene in the life of people and in relation to issues of fecundity (unwanted pregnancies amongst single women). The *Soq'a Machu* is a particular sexually mischievous spirit which belongs to the category not of the deceased coming back, but rather of the spirits of some primordial beings which existed before humanity. They are to be found in the region of the south and central hills

124

of Perú, and traditionally are called *Soq'a Machu*, *Ñawpa Machu*, *Machula* or *Machu y Awki* (when referring to masculine spirits) or *Soq'a Paya*, *Ñawpa Paya* or *Awlay* if the spirits are supposed to be females (Flores Ochoa 1973: 47). In Andean religiosity, these are the spirits of beings who lived before the actual creation of the world, whose graves are identified with ancient pre-Columbian graves still to be found in the hills or at places characterised by humidity and darkness called *phiros*. These spirits are affected by the light of the sun: the myth of their creation is linked to an enmity with God and a dislike of the sun which debilitates them. They are therefore to be found in the evenings and at night. These are spirits 'who have refused to give an account of themselves to God' (Núñez del Prado 1974: 240). Although the encounter with *Soq'as* is considered to be negative, bringing all sorts of illnesses and problems to the person who has had contact with them, they may also have a liberative sexual role. Such is the case with women in sexual encounters with the *Soq'a Machu*. It would be interesting for us to reflect, from a perspective of a Sexual Theology, on how the Holy Spirit might intervene in people's sexual stories, bringing liberation from oppression in an actual social praxis of solidarity.

The case study we are going to use comes from Jorge Flores Ochoa's article 'La Viuda y el Hijo del Soq'a Machu' [The Widow and the Son of the Soq'a Machu] (Flores Ochoa 1973: 45–57). Flores Ochoa refers to a *población* (small town) of little more than 200 inhabitants located near Cusco, Perú (Ochoa 1973: 46). The forms of social control in the town, particularly directed towards young people and their sexual exchange, seems to have been very intense at the time of the case study. Many youngsters were leaving their homes looking for freedom in other towns. The forms of social control towards widows were still very strong in this town; widows were forbidden to remarry and if they did, people expected catastrophic consequences for the town whose widows had children. Droughts, earthquakes or disastrous harvests are attributed to the sexual activity of widows. The community perceived a close relationship between the lives of widows and the destiny and prosperity of the town, including issues of remarriage and inheritance.

Adela was a 35-year-old widow with three small children and a series of economic difficulties which she tried to resolve by engaging herself in several commercial enterprises which forced her to travel outside her town. One day she became pregnant and when people started to ask her what had happened, since she had not remarried, she told them that the *Soq'a Machu* was the father of her child. She had been travelling in the area of the puna, felt tired and decided to sleep in a cool place where the *Soq'a* found her and had a sexual relationship with her. The *Soq'a* played a 'joke' (*chansarusqa*) on her and therefore in the eyes of her community she was immediately cleared of any guilt and did not need to face any of the social consequences of a widow's pregnancy. However, many in the town harboured the suspicion that Adela's pregnancy was the result of a sexual relationship with a man rather than with a spirit. The belief in the *Soq'a* made the widow's pregnancy acceptable to the community, but not the child that she bore.

Along with belief in the *Soq'a*, abortions and infanticide were accepted as part of the reality that the children of the *Soq'a* do not survive: inheritance problems are resolved by accepting the death of the child as the fate of children of the spirits. In this case the child's life put at risk the security and prosperity of the whole town giving rise to forecasts of calamities of all kinds and prophesies of disasters to their harvests. The separation between reproduction and production does not exist in this small town and this story further demonstrates the intimate relationship between the public and the private. These nuclear families are public families whose behaviour threatens the whole community.

What the belief in the *Soq'a* provides here is a way of moving beyond the model of the scapegoat. It presents the possibility of the redemption from sexual deviancy of a woman in a community (or a man, if he claims to have been seduced by a female spirit and thus led to spend time away). This scenario recalls the narrative in the gospels by which the Virgin Mary explains her pregnancy. The Spirit takes the initiative and also the responsibility for a woman's pregnancy. In the case of the *Soq'a* the account normalises the relationship between the woman and her family and between her and the people in the town. The seducer spirit fulfils a salvific role, securing not only the life of a woman who has trespassed the limits of sexual contracts in the community, but addresses also issues of fecundity for the town in terms of good harvests and animal welfare. The *Soq'a* is a spirit whose presence supports those who trespass the limits of a sexual economic society. In Christian theology if the Spirit has any liberative role or is associated with freedom, it is the lack of spiritual intervention in the concreteness of the situations of people's lives and moreover its oppressive moral overtones which in the end defeats liberation. In the life of this town, with problems related to interrelations and economy, the Spirit *Soq'a* is theology in action. The spirits can do it in the Andean world, because – like the mountains themselves – they are sexed.

The sexuality of gods may have been a limitation in Christian theology in the past, only because it was organised from a He-God and a heterosexual patriarchal Trinity. Any small difference, such as introducing a non-heterosexual perspective or a spectrum of major sexual representation into the community which God is supposed to be in Christian theology, may prove to be efficacious for change. The story taken from a small Peruvian town concerning the *Soq'a* does not seem to provide great changes in social attitudes towards the control of women's sexuality. It only provides a 'way out', a means of normalising a sexual transgression in society. The Gospels present us with the same difficulty. For Jesus the way to deal with an alienated woman was to cure her of her menstruation, not to challenge the Jewish laws on menstruation. However, in the Andean world, the liturgical transformative element may prove to be more efficacious in the sense that sexuality is acknowledged as a reality which participates of the divine in itself. The normalisation of the transgressive may be a moment in a process of further understanding a higher consciousness. Flores Ochoa draws an interesting conclusion from his study when he claims that in reality, neither the townspeople nor Adela believed in the *Soq'a*, or to be more precise, they did believe in the spirit and in the whole story but only as part of a process. They believed it when it was needed. Later on, through talking with the people of the town, it transpired that as time went by they were becoming more able to face the truth of Adela's supposed sexual liaison with a married man from another town. In this story, the Spirit has become as an intermediary in a process of thinking and acting. Otherwise, it might have cost Adela her life.

What can a Queer Theology learn from this example of a popular Sexual Theology in an Andean town in the twentieth century? First of all, a different approach to the Holy Spirit, which needs to be sex-specific although allowing for all sexual identities to be represented. As in our previous reflection upon the bisexual *Apu Yaya*, a Trinitarian sexual identity is necessary for a theology which is trying to uncover the face of God in scenes of intimacy and loving relationships. Without that identity, theology becomes inefficacious and self-neutralised by totalitarian heterosexuality. Reciprocity becomes hetero-reciprocity; solidarity becomes homo-solidarity (Althaus-Reid 2000: 89–90). But from the *Soq'a Machu*, which comes from the theology of a people for whom the Holy Spirit is a more flexible concept than for us, we can learn that efficacy in theology means intervening historically in people's conflicts of sexual transgression. The point is that a liberative Holy Spirit needs to be a Queer Holy Spirit, incarnated in our communities of resistance in something of the same way that the *Soq'a* is in his/her own community, not to normalise but to support acts of defiance to structures of sexual and economic injustice. In this way a Queer Holy Spirit may provide us with a praxis of transformation by allowing us to move from words of comfort to political resistance. The *Soq'a* is, at the end of the day, a religious story more of colonisation than of forgiveness. Claiming to have been under colonisation processes allows us sometimes in Latin America to continue without challenging our own participation in structures of oppression. In Latin American Theology, the Holy Spirit is the colonisation of the Other in community, that is, absorbed, silenced, disempowered for the sake of the supposed normalcy of a community. It is well illustrated in the story of the UN Women's Decade Conference in Nairobi in 1985, where Kenyan women stood up during a discussion on lesbian issues claiming that in their country they did not have lesbianism. They found an immediate response when a group of Kenyan lesbian women entered the room shouting 'Yes, we do!' (Drucker 1996: 96–7).

To decolonise the Holy Spirit, we need to hear the 'Yes, we do!' voices amongst us which claim for themselves the right to transgress structures of oppression as part of the intervention of the Holy Spirit in our lives. We need a more ambivalent Holy Spirit, moving with flexibility in our lives and challenges, taking away our internalisation of oppression (such as guilt, for instance) while giving us back our voices of dissent. To queer the Holy Spirit might then be an important task of a Sexual Theology trying to renew a faith in incarnation, that is, in the historical presence of God in our struggle and in our own cultures which are also sexed cultures.

Polyfidelity: building community solidarity

It was the voice of a young woman finishing a postgraduate degree in theology in the University of Edinburgh which created an awful silence during a conference where issues of marriage were being discussed. She was an indigenous Latin American woman who claimed that in her culture the concept of marital fidelity, as known by Western Christians, did not exist. The reaction of the other participants was not, as one might perhaps have expected, one of moral outrage, but rather of disbelief. It was as if anything could be doubted in Christianity today except the rule of body-property in marriage and the sacred theology of jealousy which supports it. Yet there are cultures in Latin America in which 'marriage fidelity' is a concept that defies translation. One of the most interesting examples comes from the lives of the Ramkokamekra-Canela people from the northern edge of the central Brazilian plateau. In common with other Canelas (such as those from the Ecuadorian jungle), extramarital sexual relations are encouraged, practised and form the basis for an identity based not only in consanguinity but also on sexual affinity (Whitten 1976: 110; Crocker 1974: 184). The Ramkokamekra-Canelas were a group of nearly 400 people speaking Jê and already during the mid-1970s they were struggling to keep their identity against Christian beliefs and patterns of relationships imposed by non-indigenous people. They were socially organised in matrilineal and matrilocal groups, were monogamous and divorce was extremely rare among them (Crocker 1974: 185). Both women and men spent most of their adult lives married to the same partner, yet they also enjoyed open extramarital relationships which may be brief encounters or fairly long affairs. It is interesting that married women not only had this right (or duty) to have extramarital relationships but they also initiated them by approaching, through a chosen mediator, the person with whom they would like to have sex.

Their attitude towards sexuality was taught from childhood in what has been described by anthropologists as a 'context of fun' (Crocker 1974: 186). Such a learning context was composed of open conversations amongst adults about sexuality in the presence of young members of the family, suggestive types of dances and other festival activities in the community. Sexuality was awarded a high value and taught as such from an early age. The two main prohibitions amongst the Ramkokamekra-Canelas were incest and fighting: both crimes were severely punished.

As issues of sexuality and property are closely linked in people's lives, it is not surprising that the Ramkokamekran did not have a concept of private property as such. This comes about because in this social system of intersexual relationships everybody is related by affinity to everybody else. Therefore, a man would call every woman of his own generation 'my wife' (*iiprō*) and also the children in the community would be called 'my children'. The obligations towards these wives and children were substantial in terms of services, gifts and considerations. This is one of the reasons why women in the community were relatively more independent than other indigenous women. Through the matrilocal facilities for living space and the extended network of husbands by affinity, they could enjoy economic and affective support throughout their lives. Thanks to this system even single mothers in the community were allowed to live with economic security and the support required through the system of community service (Crocker 1974: 189–91). This system therefore provided the Ramkokamekra-Canelas with a culture of high community solidarity. At the same time, a different attitude towards property implies a different emotional response to jealousy amongst partners engaged in this form of polyfidelity relationships. This contrasts with a familiar biblical contractual model: the relationship with the 'Jealous God' of Israel is linked to particular forms of understanding property and the body as property. The 'proper body' is taught and organised widely in the contemporary understanding of Christian marriage as a secret body, that is a body that is concealed. As such, the married Christian body is not only hidden away but kept from discovering any forms of sexual organisation which might contribute to different economic organisations. Amongst the Ramkokamekra-Canela, 'jealousy' as the emotion which links us to the concept of the secret body was dealt with through a different form of social organisation of people in terms of property and emotion. Partners shared their love life with their own families, therefore secrecy and concealment did not exist. Yet, they also used language forms and structures of socialisation in ways that avoided confrontation and the possibility of jealousy amongst partners.

Property issues are part of the love-talking theology that Latin America, by force and by its own will, has accepted during more than five centuries. Theologically, we are confronted here with a case of the Other's love/knowledge which produces solidarity and high morale amongst people from a community, yet it differs so basically from the adopted Christian customs in relation to marriage and sexual relationships that we must wonder if it is love that we are talking of here, or if it is something else. It is not only love that has been demonised amongst the indigenous nations of Latin America, but also knowledge and forms of social organisation and understanding which have much to do not only with society but with ecclesiology. In the testimony of an Auca man,

> They taught us passivity and love ... meanwhile ... they stole our lands and exploited us daily. They eliminated us little by little, taking away our land, where our ancestors lived. All the communal mechanism has been destroyed.
>
> (Cano *et al.* 1981: 291)

The demonisation of the Other in Christian theology has produced dominant understandings of love in support of agrarian expropriation, or to be more accurate, a love that belongs to the same country as agrarian expropriation in that privatisation movement towards sharing fewer bodies and fewer food resources. Queering Christian jealousy as a theology which came to Latin America with the

Conquista means to reflect on the praxis of different forms of being, in this case, a heterosexually based community. It may challenge us in reinterpreting Christian faith and practice with more theological imagination than has been used until now. The Peruvian writer MarioVargas Llosa wrote in *La Utopía Arcaica* (Vargas Llosa 1996) about the role of ideological fictions. For Vargas Llosa life is a literary genre in itself and the function of literature is not to repeat it with realism, but with critical realism. That means that literature needs to speak truth and lies at the same time. Expressing a fictional account, literature expresses and re-discovers truth which could not be expressed in real life in another way. So it is with theology: theology's main function is to be fictitious. It aims to lie in the sense that its mission is to express the inexpressible, the utopia of the Kingdom, the intuitions manifested in vague suspicions and intuitions of different orders in sacred and human society. That is the real meaning of the prophetic role of the church, understood in a critical way. Queer Theology, by basing its reflections in libertine epistemologies, rescues different forms of imagining love which exist amongst us and which may lead us to different and better understandings of God and life outside the patterns of, for instance, high property values, which are inscribed in Christian theology. Different forms of loving mean different forms of valuing property and exchanging solidarity amongst men and women too, and might contribute to another step in the process of the total kenosis of God and also of the structures of organisation of the church.

Tenderness as a currency: the *ayni*

Transgressing the borders of the dyadic, highly individualist Christian family also means transgressing the theology and the economy of the market by people who have little if any power to do so. In the past years the differences between *campesinos* and *hacendados* (peasants and landowners) in Latin America and in particular in Perú have been diluted by other factors. Peasants have been increasingly divided along an axis of production resources and technologies and less so along traditional ethnic and other lines of divisions. However, even if relationships amongst *campesinos* have changed in the sense that there are serious divisions related to the control of land and orchard properties, traditional relations of reciprocity have demonstrated considerable strength and have even challenged the market system. The institution of economic reciprocity used at the level of peasants' interchange is called the *ayni* (Fioravanti 1973: 122). This is another form of ritualised friendship from the same traditional spiritual and social root and operates at the level of relations of production. The *ayni* relies on very complex formulas and rituals, which include special words of greeting amongst peasants, exchange of food and presents and shared dress codes. When someone needs a service related to work, a relative (or a neighbour) can be asked to perform that service, with the proviso that the person who is soliciting the service will, when required, reciprocate by offering her or his own services. For example, if a *campesino* needs help during the harvest he might visit a relative or any member of the community to ask him or her for help with the work. To do so, other family members would accompany the person asking for the service, and they would bring an offering that in Spanish is called *el cariño* (love; tenderness). The 'love' usually consists of *aguardiente* (a traditional alcoholic drink), cigarettes or any other present (Fioravanti 1973: 122). The person whose service is required takes this 'love' and an intimate friendship based on reciprocity starts a new cycle between two people and two families. In this way, by mutual service, the relation between employers and employees is changed and even celebrated in the traditional fiestas with which people celebrate the end of such service. Impoverished peasants are able to employ workers in this way to help them at harvest time. Even when people with access to economic resources pay workers, they still tend to respect the *cariño*, by taking offerings of friendship to the future paid workers and making sure that there is a fiesta to celebrate the end of some piece of work in the community. This needs to be done because in Peruvian communities, the element of reciprocity needs to be somehow present in the organisation of labour. The use of machinery or tools of work can also be exchanged for labour and in this form the *ayni* keeps extending its many forms of creative reciprocity across the working life of the community.

In some cases a family is able to move between regions considering different pieces of land, thanks to the help provided by 'spiritual relatives' who, in turn, can expect any of their needs to be met at a later date. The *compadrazgo*, the tradition of good parenting in the community, is at the base of the *ayni* and similar institutions such as the *makipura*, which is an *ayni* with a small salary added and reciprocated by the person who is employed when her/his moment to employ someone comes (Fioravanti 1973: 124). As the *compadres* belong to different social classes and have different places in the economic systems, the help they give to each other produces a face-to-face approach to issues of poverty and disempowerment.

El compadrazgo and the *ayni* is then part of the reciprocity system of many Latin American communities, but its challenges penetrate deeply into the social and economic structure of the market economy by introducing its relationships of community and solidarity. Theologically we are challenged by the presence of God in the midst of another different way of conceiving family relationships. In fact, the best of Liberation Theology comes from these traditions of reciprocity in service and solidarity in labour, which are accompanied by joyous days of festivity. It is from these traditions that the praxis of Christian solidarity has been and needs to continue to be elaborated and not vice-versa – since there are no examples of Christianity in Latin America with original forms of loving exchange such as these. In addition there are other old, traditional institutions such as *el cargo*, in which whole communities would spend all their savings in a yearly communitarian festivity. These present us with a metaphysics of giving without receiving profit: to the contrary, it is a ritual expenditure of the accumulated, given away with happiness (Godelier 1971: 102). This ensured, amongst other things, a form of limit to possible economic inequalities in the community, while teaching a different value system in society.

In theology, as in the world it too often reflects, nothing comes for free. Grace has a price and unfortunately it is not always a price worth paying, but rather a price of normalisation or domestication to the ruling ideological system in charge. Redemption has all too often been reduced to a welcome to an order that should be rejected or questioned. To be Christian implies a minimum questioning of politics and the sexuality which organises our lives and limits our exchanges. However, a hermeneutical circle of suspicion shows us that everything is related: the jealous God who supports monogamous, life-exclusive relationships does not support socialism, nor even the pre-capitalist economies of the Incas. At the root of the Latin American systems of economic and affective exchanges lies a bisexual praxis. For, following Cixous, we can say that bisexual thought carries with it a utopia of completeness in community which may provide us with a unity based on a different order of exchanges (Cixous in Schrift 1997: 156). By claiming critical bisexuality as a praxis, we are contrasting it with a Christian phallocratic way of thinking and acting characterised by exchanges of limited possibilities and lack of flexibility, including relationships (amongst people and/or with God) organised around specific notions of individual profit, that is, hierarchical profit. By contrast the *cargo* is an offence to Christian ethics because it represents waste. The energy and time expended by the Canela people in organising a complex sexual life in community is also a waste. In the creative reciprocity of the *ayni* it is not clear who is who in terms of positions of privilege in production lines, although it is clear that everybody has to keep her place in serving others. Perhaps we are starting to answer our early questions concerning Moya and how a town organised under the protection and order of a bisexual mountain works in the structure of society. The liturgies of sexual identity exchange may be just a small reminder of the great institutions of reciprocity which Christianity needs to consider seriously, although for that theology needs to give up its claim to stability and its place in the space of the proper in society.

8

DEMONOLOGY

Embodying rebellious spirits

Love is the passion of facticity ...

(Agamben 1999: 187)

Queer redemptions

Queer Theology may be a call to reflect one day on a theology of mistresses and
hidden lovers who are also the aliens of theology and Christian ethics. Such a
theology posits for us questions such as: What shall we preserve from the past of
our love lives? How shall we add to love and preserve love? It might inform us on
which memories from meaningful love affairs should be kept alive and thus
redeemed in the history of the contributions of our hearts to the memories of
humanity. Redemption is after all a praxis of our past and a sexual praxis which
accommodates the effects of the love life of people's bodies. This sexual praxis
then begins its own counter project of redemption. Elizabeth Stuart has already
written of the Feminist theological 'attempt to redeem ... the central beliefs of
the Christian tradition from their patriarchal formulation', which is part of her
own Sexual Theology (Stuart 1996: x). The question posited here is one of
redemption with a different cartography of love. Or, to put it a different way,
there is still a need for redemption in our lives, but there is no longer a clear-cut
location for sexual redemption.

A Queer redemption is made to a different recipe. In Queer redemptions
there are other geographical sites where people would like to search, not only for
different routes to God's grace, but also for some of the abandoned routes whose
ancient names we still remember from the communities which preceded us.
There are sadly conquered routes of love, as they were and people knew them
before colonial baptisms marked new religious eras; other naccess to truthcome
from the past and the lives of our communities, some forgotten while others are
hidden amongst the excluded. In Colonial Theology the names of love have
received baptism and confirmation according to Christian calendars of despoila-
tion. The process in itself, as a spiritual phenomenon, has been described by
Stuart in what she claims to be the way by which saints' souls have been stolen
from the people (Stuart 1996: 36). Yet we might still care to remember the other

names of love because without those memories, as Stuart reminds us, there is no possibility of redemption. This might mean though that Queer redemptions, based on the memory of loving friendships as revelatory (Stuart 1996: 84), are not necessarily translatable into imperial theological language. This might happen because their love affinities belong to other geographical logics which might render them outside the limited scope of a theological sexual orthodoxy whose praxis is conversion, conversion seen as the negation of the redemptive act of recovering the memory of love in our lives. Therefore in our alienation we have prayed 'convince us of our sin', that is, vanquish the memory of the names of love and allow us to forget that we have loved. There is a traditional theological art of forgetting the old names of love in theology, as if Christ could only speak to us through the language of the conquerors and the monotonous, ideological speech of heterosexual Christianity. It is as if Christ did not have any memory of his own community, or as if Christ was a *tabula rasa*, thus facilitating the insertion of heterosexual ideologies into his Messiahship.

After everything has been said by T-Theology, to dare to conceive a redemption map which is not preceded by a territorialisation of the sacred (sexual) marks of colonial empires means for us the beginning of a rupture with that Colonial Theology, which is at the same time to mark the origins of something new. That novelty which is heroic (although not sacrificial) comes from Queer theologies. We may see them as announcing the beginning of the end of systematic theologies, while welcoming the birth of a demonology. Let us reflect on this point. The personification of holiness in Queer Theology, that is, its concreticity depends on how we embody rebellions, specifically, legal (sexual) rebellions. Agamben reminds us how for the Greek philosophers the demonic element and happiness were two related concepts (Agamben 1999: 138). In Benjamin's study of Goethe's *Elective Affinities*, the demonic is the inconceivable, the Bi-Theology made up of the human and the sacred, taken together without borders, a 'solidarity of spirit and sex', whose law is represented by ambiguity (Agamben 1999: 149). That is precisely the point for a Queer Theology as demonology, a theology the starting point of which is the knowledge of rebellious spirits, a theology that exposes and accuses the legal sacred order of being constructed and not natural. From this perspective, Queer redemptions also expose the historical role of conversion as a reproduction of a decent or proper order. This also exposes the limitations of Liberation theologies which, while wishing to leave the conditions of redemption as cultural and economic convertibility, fall into the trap of understanding redemption as 'retention'. However, applying critical realism to conversion might show us that non-redemptive paths are meant to be neither reproductive nor domestic. Redemptive practices are those which let the memories of bodies that have been loved outside the limits of heterosexual ideologies to become sacred.

For a Queer Theology searching for the face of the Queer God through the theological rediscovery of knowledge in loving relationships outside conversion, the task is one of understanding sexual constructions as constitutive of existence.

Demonology is the calling of inspiration from the bodiliness and sexuality that Agamben, recalling Heidegger on the constitution of the facticity of *Dasein*, refers to as an original dimension of being (Agamben 1999: 195). How can we reflect on the possibility of a Queer Theology if we do not contemplate redemption, if we do not consider the beatification processes in the holiness of our everyday living, if we do not even reflect on celestial spaces such as limbo and hell, with their iconics of sacred carnival? Following Lancaster and di Leonardo, we might say that any reflection from the perspective of a political and Queer Theology must consider how 'metamorphoses in sexual and gender relations ... linked to political, economic and cultural challenges', are to be located according to the shifts of their practices (Lancaster and di Leonardo 1997: 1). In Western theology, the neglect of reflection on the doctrines of celestial spaces such as limbo, purgatory, heaven and hell has had the consequence of postponing a colonial critique into the systematic theologisation of the afterlife. For this afterlife theology is a result of imperial interventions in the redemption of the Other, and it functions as a colonial landmark representing theological shifts concerning loving possibilities, the scramble for the vast amatory continents reclaimed by heterosexual Christianity. It is in this context that we claim the right of demonologies, that is, the right to listen to rebellious spirits which have rejected the light for the darkness. The transparency of light which carries with it the clarity of imperial logics and the white axis of its racial supremacy, gives a global identity to demons. It is based on the understanding of God's logic as the rock of ages and yet identities which were meant to be unchanged, unmoved and fixed have never, in fact, ceased to wander around. Theological fixity testifies to this wandering movement by a discourse of opposites; this is a process of the language-building of a theological reality. Such have been the political and theoretical assumptions underlying the philosophical discourses of the West (Lancaster and di Leonardo 1997: 5). However, when sexual identities move away from colonial frontiers to reclaim the lands of their ancestors and to enter new territories, the process of redemption is not simply a mirror of the identity problems of the master, nor do the celestial spaces of the afterlife theology remain uncontested.

Let us start by considering how doctrines of redemption have become doctrines of retention. They may differ in the extent of the retention, that is, in the extension of the imperial meme which reproduces itself by reproducing a past. It is not just any past however, but an imperial one, based on imperial knowledge of expansion and strategies of acceptance, such as re-territorialisation and processes of identity unification which include the erasure of the past (redeeming the past by changing it). In all this display of imperial knowledge, the work of Christian redemption functions at its best by disrupting identity and presenting itself as a universal. In this, following Laclau, we can say that redemption as a universal becomes the 'symbol of a missing fullness' (Laclau quoted in Žižek 1994: 105). Redemption then knows of the theological processes of the dislocation of identities, of the lack of hospitality or a proper place for those who by their mere existence resist transcendental hetero-definitions of spirituality (Žižek 1994: 104).

It is true that redemption works as a meme in the sense that it is an idea which is original and creative; the connection created between the theological and other ways of knowing is evident in history. The Doctrine of National Security, as imposed on Latin America, has been organised in Roman Catholic countries around the theme of redemption by blood.[1] Also, women's oppression relates to a theology of an elective sacrificial salvation. The continuation of this process, which relies on a difficult relationship between universals (as containers of truth) and particulars (as identities supposedly in those containers) is not easily resolved. The fascist state may seek to redeem a nation by purging it of dissonant identities; in this case retention is a false 'conservative' position, for what is supposed to be traditional and thus to be preserved, but is in fact a new creation with a recently manufactured genealogy. Other retentive strategies are to be found, for instance, when women's identities are guaranteed as part of an act of inclusion. That is to say, in redemption as retention new identities are not permitted, only those that already exist. And redemption is always, at some level, a case of sexual redemption, as a belonging to a heterosexual, predefined order.

It is relevant to point out that redemption, as a theo-political concept, has been basically constructed around the idea of a supplementary knowledge which includes in itself both the idea of a surplus or an excess and a substitution. The love of God for humanity has been presented as an incomplete text which in time needed to be substituted or complimented by a messianic event. In this way redemption shares with the sacramental, for example baptism, the same considerable amount of distrust towards finalising processes. Bloch and Guggenheim, in an article about *compadrazgo*, baptism and the symbolism of a second birth, have argued that motherhood can be considered devalued in Christian liturgy (Bloch and Guggenheim 1981). The point they make is that we seem to have ignored without questioning the need of a further, finalising ritual of humanity towards the newborn baby, without which birth seems incomplete. The human is not fully human. This point has been developed by other anthropologists cited by Bloch and Guggenheim, such as Fortescue and O'Connell. Baptism, according to these anthropologists, is a liturgical act based on a theology which devalues the human, in the sense that it assumes the incompleteness of the newborn human. However, it is also a devaluation of women, as if women are incapable of giving birth to children accepted by society as fully human. Baptism implies that newborn children are incomplete in some respect. It also asserts that the creative power to complete this humanity lies not with the mother, or with the *compadrazgo*'s ritualised friendship, but with the church (Bloch and Guggenheim 1981: 380). Baptism appears here as a sacramental supplement to birth.

In this context, redemption is also a sacramental supplement of normal processes of socialisation. Christ appears here as either the supplement of divine grace, in the sense of completion, or as some additional divine quality of forgiveness and abundance for human life. The main difference between the Roman Catholic and a broadly Protestant perspective lies precisely in the degree of tension between the law of replacement and the law of the additive in the conceptualisation of redemption. For instance, reading the encyclical *Miserentissimus Redemptor* (Clarkson *et al.* 1973: 198) it becomes clear that the Mass is a liturgical supplement of the redemptive work of God in a second or third degree: the first addition to God's redemption is Christ, the second is the work of the church and the third the Mass as an act of substitution efficacy. Here we have the possibility of the liberation of the imperial meme of redemption, since it need not be only a mechanistic supplementation reproducing an old meme, but it can be also very creative. In this sense, it shares the creativity of sexuality, specifically of masturbation. As Derrida notes in his discussion of Rousseau, masturbation was seen as a 'dangerous supplement': it is a form of sexual activity, constituting an element additional to sexuality in relationship, while at the same time appearing as a perverse substitution for it (Derrida 1977: 157). The dangerous supplement to redemption is not only Christ (as a messianic extra to God and also as a substitution) but also the church. The pleasure of the church in regulating and redeeming sexualities (redemption as universalisation) justifies itself ideologically as a completion of sexual identity, as if sexual identities have only one lesson to be learned, that of the prevalent idealised heterosexual model of the day, an identity normally applied also to non-heterosexual models which have been constructed. But the supplement has multiple applications. If, for instance with Derrida, we see that the hymen can symbolise at the same time both virginity and the consummation of a sexual act (Derrida 1981), we can also say that redemption symbolises the exclusion and the embrace of the Queer as the ever-present and powerful supplement of salvation. For redemption is able to represent both docility towards the hegemonic sexual order of Christianity (a 'coming back' or return from perdition – that is, outside heterosexuality) and the richness of other sexualities which are reaffirmed in this unsettling game of sexual identities. Redemption symbolises both T-Theology (as docility) and demonology (as rebellion).

What then is the point of thinking about demonology if not to reflect on Queer redemptions? One image of redemption as a pact carries with it the church's almost constitutional definition of the family: dependence on the benign attitude of the ruler or *pater familias* for welfare and prosperity, which is in turn defined as a surplus of God's own benign nature. The pattern of community dependence or solidarity is also one which sabotages the free expression of sexualities, for if economic welfare depends mainly on the family unit, sexuality and gender roles tend to be accommodated to a pattern of economic distribution. When family relationships are no longer the only source of the accumulation of goods and the guarantee of wealth or power, sexual diversity can be not only accepted but pursued.

Redemption therefore could be queered not through the model of the patriarchal family, but for instance through the experience of masturbation. Masturbation can present redemption as a form of rebellion. Masturbation presents theology with the challenge of the consummation of grace, but also and simultaneously with its deferral. Masturbation gives us an angle of ambiguity in our sexual reflections on theology, from which sexual ambiguity manifests itself by affirming the community basis of the act of theologising, while enjoying at the same time maintaining a fierce self-sustaining independence. What is happening here is that what lies outside the sexual boundaries of redemption provides identity by default. Masturbation is also part of theological demonologies when it shows solidarity with the rebellious supplement in the struggle with the obvious: a loving solidarity with ambiguity and a sacrament of ambiguity and the inconceivable in itself. However, masturbation presents solidarity as a form of post-colonial strategy because it de-territorialises sexuality from procreation, complicating the easy identificatory sexual colonial patterns of what is what (what counts as sex, as communal or as 'solitary' for instance), problematising the processes of colonial constructions as 'discrete biological and social units' (Stoler 1997: 14) and mixing up rights to pleasure. The solitary act of prayer has a reproductive intention in itself, for God is the invisible partner of the dialogue of prayer. However, we forget that God is also present in solitary sex and that masturbation is not such an isolated act, for as with prayer it includes the same flowing desire and a memory (much richer than simply a retention) of desire to be actualised. Masturbation has a past but also a future. The epistemological frontiers which divide colonisers from colonised can become unclear.[2] The same can happen with the boundaries between the redeemer and the redeemed, or the distinction between what is to be erased or to be remembered. This happens if remembering is no more than a retentive theological practice. The supplement of redemption, what we might call Queer redemption, claims a space in our theological reflections by extending multiple layers of suspicion into strategies of forgetting the old names of love but also into the thinking processes behind heterosexual ideologies.

Therefore, a re-territorialisation of redemption claims that other sexualites should be recognised as redemptive, that is, as participating in the praxis of redemption. This is the sexual gift of the supplement of redemption and it is the gift of Godself in its own kenosis of sexuality. The tragic consequence of the heterosexual redemption role of Christianity has been precisely the outcasting of Godself as a sexual Other, or the colonisation of God, the representation of God as a discrete and identifiable biological and social unity (as in the Trinitarian model). Queer redemptions have the gift of confronting us with alternative ways of loving and organising ourselves socially. They may be the response of contesting the spirit of corporations and the redemptive acts of global capitalism. But global capitalism has its own demonology, that is, its rebellious spirits which may be inspiring the People's Movement worldwide in its resistance against exploitation and participates in the reconstruction of redemption as a spiritual and political category. But for that, we need to reflect on that which heterosexual colonial concepts of redemption have excluded and on just what are the possibilities of the law of exile in redemption.

What is it that has never taken place in the history of redemption? Following Agamben, we could say that what is saved is what never took place (Agamben

1999: 158). The best of the history of redemption (as a demonology and not as retention) has been seen in the disruption not of events to be redeemed (thus, stopping their reproduction and bringing their story to an end) but of whole traditions or modes of transmission (Agamben 1999: 153). Therefore we need to consider that the work of redemption is the disruption of citational processes such as sexuality and gender. 'What never was' in the history of redemption is linked precisely to the salvation of disruption and the destruction of citationality. Jesus Christ as redeemer is not only an ambiguous supplement of divinity but an incarnation of a divine model of disruption of origins. Jesus' birth disrupted the origins of God; his birth devalued the eternal and his project of redemption disjointed the law of salvation by repetition. There is therefore a messianism born of disruption, that is, of a redemptive primal act, which follows the law of exile.

When Agamben says that messianic time and historical time should not be confused, he is making a case for the exilic quality of the Messiah and the messianic law. For the Messiah lives the law of exile by confronting public law, and producing an exceptional law, that is, a law made in a state of exception (Agamben 1999: 168), a law which is characterised by living things as they were (in relation to the religious law) except for a displacement. That displacement is the basis of a diasporic understanding of redemption. Redemption has a displacement quality, in relation to citationality, but in Queer Theology such displacement needs to involve both the salvation of alterity and the alteration of salvation. Redemption can therefore be considered a coming out, an expansive experience and not just a retention of traditions (and sexual traditions) which cannot claim the hegemonic credibility of the Christian theological constructions of the past. In that sense, a Queer understanding of redemption needs also to redeem what never was: the denial of grace and holiness and the presence of God in the lives and relationships of people at the margins of the colonial heterosexual order, but all this according to a new and different creative pattern. Redemption as disruption should never be part of an adoptionist plan, but rather part of an existential exception. It should not be located in traditional theological reflection which makes the ban on different, libertine epistemologies precisely the structure of Christian redemption itself (Agamben 1999: 162).

Queer sainthood: paths to beatification for sexual dissidents

I forbade any simulacrum in the temples because the divinity that breathes life into nature cannot be represented.

(Baudrillard 1996: 76)

Nothing is more fragile than the surface.

(Deleuze 2001: 82)

In the same way that redemption is a theological sexual activity, so is sainthood. Therefore, the paths towards beatification for sexual dissidents have always been treacherous and subject to several editorial changes from high places, such as the Vatican. Paths towards sainthood have displayed all of the characteristics of processes of simulation which, according to Baudrillard, are made up of what can be referred to as four monopolies (Baudrillard 1996: 77):

- The monopoly of reflection: a basic reality is understood to be reflected in an authoritative way.
- The monopoly of masquerading: a basic reality is masked and perverted in its representation.
- The monopoly of reality: the process masks the absence of the basic reality.
- The monopoly of representation: the real, having been excluded, is represented by a sign which does not carry any resemblance or relation to reality. As Baudrillard says, 'it is pure simulacrum'.

The saints whose names appear in the church calendar have become simulacra of sainthood in this order of representation in which, from the sacramental presentation of the 'good appearance' (Baudrillard 1996: 77) or the coherent theological biography of saints, we descend, for instance, into a process of economic sexual exclusion. The whole process is one of concealment, or dissimulation and succeeds, paraphrasing Baudrillard, in producing an epiphany of church power with the 'virtual disappearance of God and of worldly manipulations of consciences ... and the end of transcendence' (Baudrillard 1996: 76). Curiously, demonology as a calling for the holiness excluded in T-Theology has become the only way of transcendence, for transcendence is either Queer or it is a masquerade of the holiness of bodies in Christian theology. Elizabeth Stuart has reflected on the same process of dissimulation and re-ordering of women's holy lives by considering how souls have been stolen in the process of beatification. This has happened by what she calls the 'anti-sexual ideology that has diseased Christianity for most of its history' and the 'anti-body mentality' which has been exercised in the biographical theology of women's saintly lives (Stuart 1996: 17). The saints' lives portray stories of the redeemed but they do not include historicised gestures in the process of sexual simulation in Christian theology. Ché Guevara has been sanctified on T-shirts as a handsome Argentinian with a cigar in his mouth, but as the poem from Arellano 'In Rivas, Nicaragua' says, he was also the slim, foul-smelling *guerrillero* who returned home to relax, and eat rice with chicken while dressed only in his underpants (Arellano 1974: 382). The heroic *guerrillero* provoked the laughter of children in the act of eating rice in the privacy of his own kitchen. That was the Ché Guevara who looked out on the world with big eyes set in a malnourished face, whose body had not enjoyed a bath for months, a body which wanted to be liberated from military boots and combat clothing. That was the fragile, Queer Guevara.

The queerness of sainthood has all but disappeared because people have not been able to witness holy men and women eating with their hands while dressed only in their underwear, or in the underwear of the opposite sex, and certainly praying while removing their underwear. The signs of sainthood – decency and the legal sexual order of T-Theology – have become equivalent to the real lives of saints, eliminating gestures of defiance and the contradiction of colonial geographies of sainthood. The purpose of these manoeuvres into sainthood is clear: by de-queering saints, the church has supported social and politico-economic contracts. This is illustrated in the famous and contentious case of the beatification process of the Italian saint Maria Goretti, who was an eleven-year-old girl who fought off an attempted rape but lost her life in the process. This is a piece of legislation concerning virginity, the stereotyping of female sexuality and the supposed futility of preserving life after rape (Stuart 1996: 12). Even suffering, as Stuart recalls, which has been constructed as an important element in the lives of saints, is not the rebellious suffering of the poor but rather the suffering of submitting to domestication processes deemed as holy projects. This silence of the lambs seems to be the opposite of the call to Christians in the world to rise up against poverty and to 'opt for the rebellion of the poor and for the poor rebels, the uncomfortable poor who claim their rights ...' (*Kairos Central America* 1988: 101).

Here we are confronting again a theology of incompleteness which devalues people's saintly actions for change and reflections, while requiring a baptism of 'renaming' (or retelling) people's lives. The example of the re-baptism or renaming of the life experiences of Joan of Arc which Stuart and Carter Heyward present in their reflections on a Feminist Theology of sainthood is a powerful case in point (Stuart 1996: 73–95). For both of them, revelation is found in the lives of saints through a theology of friendship, as empowering loving relationship. So Carter Heyward, in her *Staying Power: Reflections on Gender, Justice and Compassion* (1995), considers how in the theological biography of Joan of Arc, the 'voices of God' which the saint claimed to have heard and obeyed, were voices calling her to obey her true self, in dialogue with the divine. Joan obeyed but also discussed with her voices what she wanted to do, while acknowledging the embodiment and sensuality of her relationship with God (Stuart 1996: 92). It is only as a result of this embodied and mutually respectful relation with God that compassion – what Stuart calls the refusal to give up connectedness and the challenges posed in relations with friends and enemies – could finally arise.

If we agree with Stuart when she claims that 'friendship is revelatory' (Stuart 1996: 84), we must also consider that holiness is a verb, manifested in events. First of all, let us reflect further on revelation in friendship. We are proposing an understanding of friendship which does not include filiations, the content of which may be judged by T-Theology to be undesirable revelations. Queer disaffiliations make for the subversive cradle of that friendship which stands as an accuser of the sacred legalisation of the alienating nature of friendship in hetero-Christianity. The embodied and sexual friendship model which forms the basis for holiness, as it appears in the re-reading of Joan of Arc offered by Stuart and Heyward, may be concealed by T-Theology – but only for a time. For holiness, as a verb, is manifested in events, especially in body events. This means that sainthood is a theology of being holy. The effects of true holiness, sooner or later, always come to the surface: nothing is drowned for ever. This is a theological issue which could benefit from taking seriously the reflection by Deleuze on surface effects (Deleuze 2001: 4).

According to Deleuze there is a distinction, made originally by the Stoics, between bodies and states of affairs. By 'states of affairs', we are referring to bodily actions or the passions produced by bodies mixing with each other. Sanctity, from this perspective, can be considered as an effect of bodies, that is, the result of actions and passions and a way of being human which includes a re-distribution of beings and conceptual frames (Deleuze 2001: 5). Therefore, we are already saying that sanctity becomes a tradition of bodies, for instance, in disruption of the memories of law (as redemption) and in a prophetically inspired rebelliousness (demonology). That tradition of sanctity in disruption is what comes to the surface of texts of hagiography, even if concealed by the politics of sexual hetero-redemptions. The effects of holiness which come from bodies are affective, political, theological and belong to the economic order. Their combination forms the whole ideology of sanctity, but also disrupts it.

Mary Grey in her book *The Wisdom of Fools?* considers revelation as a community-based experience, to be shared through 'epiphanies of connection' (Grey 1993: 84). The holy effects of bodies need to be connected and experienced in an integral way as part of a militant holiness without areas of exclusion: sanctity is a totality. However, Grey remarks that this requires a different way of knowing and of knowing traditions (Grey 1993: 85). The transmission of tradition needs disruption, but the disruptions come as effects of rebellious bodies. This works in the same way that we have attempted to reflect in a previous chapter on a Queer hermeneutics from a libertine epistemology for reading the Bible. This represented a different sexual position from which Queer readers mixed different bodily experiences with revealed truths. Grey's important theological challenge is this element of connectedness in revelation which brings into focus the neglected theology of the structures of holiness. Much time and attention has been devoted by liberation and Feminist Theologies to the structures of sin, but little consideration has been given to the structures of sanctity. In part this may be due to the inability of Christian heterodoxy (or 'straight' dogma) to deal with the non-identical, or with what defies its logic of sexual and economic sameness. The project of connected or participatory revelation from Grey cannot be thought through without diversity and this has been, to some extent, a fact recognised by many contemporary theologians working on economic issues. For instance, D. Stephen Long opens his book *Divine Economy* with a paragraph on revelation and the historical non-identical repetitions of the 'Christ event' in the church (Long 2000: 1). Let us pause here to consider for a moment first, how non-identical the mode of transmission of tradition could be in the framework of 'an original revelation' in history, and second, how far this non-identity process, if existent, might be taken.

Reflecting on Benjamin and the demonic, Agamben has observed that origins are not geneses, in the sense that origins do not present us with the process by which things come into being, but only tell us about 'what emerges from the process of becoming and disappearing' (Benjamin in Agamben 1999: 156). Therefore, from this perspective, the original Christ event is an irruption which tells us nothing of the process behind such an emergence, for instance, the sexual and economic construction of God behind the interpretation of the event, what Croatto would call the pre-text of the Christ event (Croatto 1984: 9). Historical repetition is then the characteristic of what manifests itself as original (or what Benjamin calls singularity and repetition). Therefore, what Agamben calls the task of criticism or the task of prophecy needs to be present in order to save redemption from retention. This is, by the way, another meaning of Benjamin saying that in 'historical redemption what happens in the end is what never took place. This is what is saved' (Benjamin in Agamben 1999: 158), for what is saved is not the original. The original is not a repetition without creativity. How non-identical then is the transmission mode of the Christ event if God is located as a genesis and not an origin? But this leads us to a further questioning of this idea of non-identical transmission, which some theologians naïvely consider to be events from a process coming from an identical God. For instance, Long indicates that the content of theology may be related to friendship as the 'true end of creation' (Long 2000: 3) but what sort of friendship can be developed with an identical God? Would She lick my fingers? In any case, what love and friendship can be expected with masters? In our world and in the context of any common working environment friendship with God, without involving major identity changes, could be considered illegal because of the disproportion of power involved in the process. It would be like sex and the politician, a case of seduction by power.

This takes us back to a previous discussion on God the Orgy (Trinitarians), because both Grey's concept of revelation in connectedness and Long's idea of friendship with the creator require an additional point made on the genesis of the Christ event, especially in relation to the project of developing a structures of sanctity theology. This is necessary because although to be Queer does not imply to be holy, holiness does imply that a certain queerness is built into the process (and not only in the event) in order to disaffiliate and disrupt imperial transmission modes of redemption and sanctification. To be holy is not to become retentive, but disruptive of the law. Therefore, we need to reflect back on the need to queer God by facilitating what we have called the process of guiding God to stray and to err from the heterodox path and to survive the divine statisticians who are more comfortable with counting up to three than in promoting a coming out of the theological closet.

The whole issue of the kenosis of God, as the coming out of God from a dyadic identity and the relocation of hospitality in the Trinity, is fundamental for a theology struggling with homogeneity. The Christ event cannot come from theological laws of utility, from what we have called the strangers (Queer) at the gates and a genesis which displaces Sexual theological knowledge. The location of power which needs to be distributed in friendship relationships depends on that displaced knowledge. What we proposed in an earlier chapter, 'the exchange of dresses' of power and the habitat of affection, is the first matter that a Queer Theology needs to address when dealing with the revelation of God amongst us. Queer Theology processes tend to be dialogical: God needs not only the revelation that comes from our own Queer communities, but also the processes of redemption and sanctification. That is precisely the point with economic holiness, understood as a theological structure of holiness where the empowering epiphanies of connection in revelation, proposed by Grey (Grey 1993: 92), require a different praxis of friendship as the foundation of a different praxis of exchanges. The connective way to sainthood requires economic praxis too. Let us now reflect on the life and death of some poor children in Argentina and the globalisation of holiness and its consequences for their lives.

Crucifixion in the slums

Politics, law and justice are rooted in embodied Imagining.
(Campbell 2000: 168)

... [people] ... don't know what madness means ...
(El Cali in *Página 12*: 2001)

Wednesday 25 April 2001. Buenos Aires, Argentina. The country is returning to normality after lengthy processions, radios playing only classical (funereal) music and the interminable sequences on TV from the Vatican showing the Pope and groups of nuns. Argentina is recovering from the traditional celebrations of Holy Week. The festival is very much alive, although in recent years it seems to have lost some of its former sinister grandeur. The following is an extract from an article which appeared in *Página 12*, a newspaper published in Buenos Aires:

> First they were tied up, then a cloth was wrapped around their mouths and in the end, when they were defenceless, they were shot, in the middle of the night. Monito [literally 'Little Monkey'] Galván, a fourteen year old boy, got eleven bullets ... Piti Burgos, a sixteen year old boy, got six bullets ... distributed [in his body] in a shocking way, with one bullet in each foot, as if they were nails [in] a Christian crucifixion.
>
> (Alarcón 2001: 1)

Monito Galván and Piti Burgos were two boys from a Buenos Aires slum. They lived at the far side of Bancalari, where the paved streets end and the dirt roads begin. Piti's house was a hut with walls made of discarded pieces of cardboard boxes. The roof consisted of rusty circuit boards and an assortment of old cathode-ray tubes. Monito's father used to earn some money by repairing old black and white TVs and the old circuit boards and tubes were recycled in this way. These were boys accustomed to violence. They belonged to gangs and would go out to steal things to get money for food and for drugs. Piti lived in his house made of discarded parts of black and white TVs, in a slum surrounded by adverts for Benetton and other famous brands. His girlfriend of the same age spent much of her time making a scrap book with pictures of the Backstreet Boys. In their brief lives they already knew poverty, violence and horror. El Cali, another adolescent boy from the area, explained to Cristian Alarcón, the journalist who interviewed him about the death of his friends, that in reality, they were all good kids. They just stole a bit to eat, or for glue. The following is part of the dialogue about his friends and their lives:

> – We used to get some 'flashes' every so often, that's all [*flasheábamos*, meaning by that the effects of inhaling cheap glue] – that's what el Cali told me, with his elusive eyes full of sadness. – Sometimes we went to steal when we were very crazy.
> – Is that the reason why, sometimes, you are so violent [mad]?
> – This is what people say, because they don't know what madness means. When you go to steal, *te rescatás* [literally: you are rescuing/saving yourself]. [You need to act violently] for other people to feel scared of you...
> – When did all of you go out to steal?
> – When we didn't have any more money; when we needed money for food or for drugs and when we didn't have anything at all. But now, I am *recatado* [literally, behaving in a modest way, or with restraint]...
>
> (Alarcón 2001: 3)

The pictures in the newspaper show el Cali, against the background of the slum and wearing a T-shirt with some brand names in English. The selection of words had no specific meaning in Spanish but they conferred a certain value on the humble wearer of the garment. El Cali used English, not only with the brand names on his T-shirt but he also sprinkled his Spanish with words such as 'flashear', a composite term made up by combining an English word (flash) with a Spanish infinitive verbal ending. Two words of similar spelling but different meanings were used all the time by several of the other boys from the slum who spoke to the journalist: *rescatar* (to rescue) and *recatarse* (to act modestly, restrained). *Rescatar* is a synonym of the verb 'to save', or 'to set free' and in a legal sense similar to the verb 'to redeem' (to rescue by buying something back from another). *Rescatar* is the verb used amongst those boys to identify those who have been 'rescued' from sniffing glue (or 'the little bag', *la bolsita*, as they call it) by someone else. After being *rescatado*, one becomes *recatado* (constrained). Also the witnesses of crimes in the area are said to be *recatados*, that is, silent, demure. *Recatado*, by the way, is a word with sexual implications. In the fashion of an older style of speaking in Argentina modest girls were *señoritas recatadas*, who stayed at home and did not entertain conversation with men except in the presence of chaperons. It is interesting to notice how a term, as old-fashioned and distinctively middle class as *recato* has become a favourite slang expression for a form of behaviour born out of the need to become anonymous and quiet, when facing, for instance, death threats arising from drug wars. Apart from the bullets in their bodies distributed like crucifixion nails, they also had plastic bags on their heads, as if mock crowns of thorns had been given to them. It was as if the bags, a symbol of their glue sniffing habit, were saying 'Who did you think you were? Kings of the Glue Sniffing gang? See how powerful you look now'. If we chose still to use that metaphor of the camera obscura, the reversal process of ideology appears quite clearly in this sad example. The myth (or false consciousness) of globalisation relies on a corporatist agenda with the privatisation of security resources such as the police (to avoid the rampant crimewave of poor children, for instance). However, privatisation is also redistributive and in the same way that capital is allocated in the area of central accumulation, Christian beliefs such as the death and resurrection of Christ are redistributed amongst child killers. The Christian crucifixion means nothing and the same can be said about globalisation, if only the myth and not the reality behind it reaches people's lives.

Why are we taking time, in the midst or our reflection about holiness and paths to sainthood, to consider the fate of Monito Galván and Piti Burgos and the observations of their common friend el Cali? Because we are going to reflect on holiness and processes of Queer sainthood as part of economic processes, in a context of structural sanctity in opposition and tension to the sainthood processes of globalisation. The starting point of Queer Theology is Queer lives and Queer relationships.

Consider for instance the following anecdote as told by the Uruguayan popular historian Eduardo Galeano:

> In the neighbourhood of Cerro Norte, a poor suburb of Montevideo, a magician performed in a street festival. Using a magic wand the magician produced a dollar bill from his closed hand or from his hat. When the festival ended the magic wand disappeared, but the following day neighbours saw a barefoot child walking along the street with the magic wand. The child touched various objects which he came across with the wand – and then waited. Like many other children in the neighbourhood, this nine year old used to sniff *Novoprén* from a bag. And sometimes he explained this by saying, 'In this way, I go to another country [*Así, me voy a otro país*].'
>
> (Galeano 2000: 259)

Capitalism, which is much more than a simple economic system (especially in its current expansive mode of globalisation) needs to start to be considered from the perspective of people's lives. When for instance, we contrast Michael Novak's concept of liberty, based on a Christological perspective which seems in his view to become institutionalised in the concept of the market (Novak 1993: 94) with Gustavo Gutiérrez writing on freedom and liberation, then the meaning of 'liberty' must come not from a dictionary but from el Cali's life. When we read the other-wise interesting account on Liberation Theology as an economic theology presented by Long, we sense that it would have been more useful if the dictionary had taken account of the life of the child who went to another country while living in a garbage dump or the life of el Cali, than the approach which has been adopted, that is, attempting to read reality from a dictionary definition. Thus dependency theory may well have been superseded but it has not 'collapsed' as Long implies (Long 2000: 115), because there has never been such a world of complex and mul-tiple dependency as exists today. If previously it could be said that people are born free, but are everywhere in chains, now it might be said that dependency theory is passé, but the South has never been so dependent as it is today. There is a common mistake amongst Western economic theologians who have not heard the words of el Cali – that they do not know what madness means. They hear the words of Michael Novak, who defines madness as not being like the Japanese when he says:

> If Latin Americans shared the ethos, the virtues and the institutions of the Japanese, they would assuredly be among the economic leaders of the world.
>
> (Michael Novak in Long 2000: 45)

Novak continually advocates liberty in forgetfulness of the fact that the economic liberty of his own country has been bought at the price of denying liberty to other countries, more graphically denying liberty to the lives of children such as Monito Galván. That of course makes us suspicious of the Christological ideol-ogy which lies behind Novak and the so called theologians-cum-economists who read people's hunger and frustration as if life should conform to dogma and not vice-versa. Marx's whole understanding of ideology as a method relies on the dis-covery of the reification of life for the sake of the coherence of Christologies.

It is useful to remember this as the background to the fact that the globalisa-tion processes in Latin America comprise of recycled madness in which, as Samir Amin has observed, the rule is always conflict (Amin 2000: 3). We might suspect that the madness of the system is rarely addressed theologically because theology has a moralising instinct. The judgements of 'who are the bad' and 'who are the good' seem to come before the theologian has opened her mouth. This has been at the root of the now discredited discourse of theology and development and it is at the root of any well-intentioned evangelical political theology which considers that the present economic system needs a conversion. This is the assumption that once we correct and re-direct what is wrong, those things that damage people's lives (such as the cancellation of the external debt and its accumulated interest), things can continue as before. This is a moral approach which ignores the fact that the present madness of the system in which we are living is a constitutive part of it (Amin 2000: 13). This point was made to me last year in a conversation with the Cuban theologian Adolfo Abascal-Jaén, editor of COELI, one of the most impor-tant (and authentic) Liberation Theological journals published today. Some of us gathered in conversation were university teachers confronting the increasing alienation of the conditions of theological production under the tentacles of the current globalisation commercial criteria. Abascal-Jaén remarked that the alienation of such academics could be taken as an index of the success of the present economic system. If some academics needed more Prozac, or were drinking more than usual, driven by the despair arising from the alienating conditions of production, that was a desirable and successful outcome – in terms of the consumerism of the market. After all, alcohol and pharmaceuticals are important industries. Adapting Maria Mies, who uses the motto 'Have a happy life' as a formula of resistance, we might adopt that motto 'Fuck the system by simply being happy'.

For Capitalism, poverty, unemployment and exclusion are consistent with the polarisation of the system. Amin has made the point that the logic of the capitalist system is incompatible with development. Capitalism aims for capital expansion and it is independent of otherwise well-intentioned theories of development which, in any case, are ideological in the sense that they depend on other a priori criteria (Amin 2000: 15). To try to espouse development according to the logic of capital expansion creates the same confusion and contradictions as when theology tries to 'incorporate' a gender (not even sexual) balance in its discourse. What is urgently required is not the improvement of a current theology through some addenda such as gender and sexual equality, but a theology with a serious Queer materialist revision of its methods and doctrines. In this way we might be able to act and reflect without a priori or spurious interests which end up reifying and submitting people to theology rather than vice versa. In the theological discourse of 'Christ first' (or Christologies as the starting point of *Christologies*), we forget that it is real people who participate in Christologies and also make them real. The aim of theological and economic reflection should not be a new system of distribution, but a different system of production. This is precisely the point of reflecting on sainthood in the context of the expansion of capitalism and the development of Queer alternatives. This includes also consideration of the cost that such a theology must pay for the radical vision of its production. Sainthood is about bodies and bodies in economic conflicts which are expected to reproduce systems instead of disrupt them. Disruption is the Queer element in sainthood and today this is more true than ever because we are living through a time in which Queers have become the protagonists of resistance. From Seattle to the Carnival against Capitalism, the People's Movement has been growing steadily with what Amin calls the awakening of collective social identifications (Amin 2000: 55). These various resistance groups are not homogeneous but they do respect diversity and it may be this which gives them the different logic by which they have become a new movement. Less flamboyantly, movements such as the Landless (Los Sin Tierra) in South America have come together as a result of many Queer alliances amongst people of different spiritualities, political ideologies and locations of race and class.

However, Queer also brings a sexual dimension to the struggle, not for goals of equality but for the creation of different processes and systems which do not require provision to be made continually for exceptions. As politics and justice are always, in the words of Jan Campbell, in embodied imaginings (Campbell 2000: 168), so heterosexuality cannot love: it reifies what it touches and compels conformity to the reign of the homogeneous. It is at the core of globalisation when it promotes identity systems which distort people's vocations for social holiness.

Monbiot has said that somehow 'in a world where intelligence is banned from public life' we must show our backsides in resistance to the dictatorship of corporations (Monbiot 2001: 15), but also that behind those backsides are complex understandings of where our present world is going. These are somehow the prophetic voices of our times. The Queer carnival dancers of vision and the travelling circus of anarchists can be seen as standing in the tradition of the marginalised Hebrew prophets of resistance who opposed the house prophets of the royal court. Queer Theology is the theology of baring behinds as an act of protest and defiance against ways of thinking which must be dis-authorised and discredited. Holiness is a Queer path of disruption made by curious amatory practices of adding people to communities of solidarity and resistance, in ways that heterosexual Christian theology has never been able to understand. Issues of sainthood and globalisation show us how *un*-queer and marketable is holiness under the expansion of capitalism. The stealing of souls has become complex, and the Logos and the logo are in competition.

The Logos and the logo: the Absolute Christ

People feel touched and there has been conversion in our prayer group of several who looking at this picture of Christ, felt that for the first time, Christ was speaking to their condition ...

(A comment received from a prayer group in Buenos Aires, relating to a postcard advertising Absolut vodka which shows Christ amongst drunkards sleeping rough in the street of a city.)

I sent some friends in Buenos Aires a postcard advertising Absolut vodka because I found interesting (and shocking) the fact that Christ could be so well painted (a 'classic' Christ figure) as one showing compassion towards drunkards and homeless people, while in fact the theme was not about compassion at all, but an advert for a brand of vodka. Moreover, the postcard was printed with soft colours, as if the whole scene was surrounded by mist, thus adding some mystery to the composition and making it more difficult to understand its commercial meaning. It was not clear whether Christ was inviting the homeless for a drink or whether He was dissuading people from drinking. The Christ of the vodka card was ambiguity itself. Only a few bottles of the many depicted in the scene read 'Absolut' and my friends in Buenos Aires, unfamiliar with the brand, only saw in it a contextual image of Christ which moved them deeply because it seemed to be showing the love of God amongst drunkards in the streets, instead of condemning them as the church representatives usually do. My friends finished up framing the picture and using it as a meditation point for their prayer meetings. They should have called it 'The *Absolut* Christ'.

That vodka advert might have converted people to Christianity. Monito Galván died with bullets distributed in his body as if in a simulacrum of a crucifixion and people in the slum who knew him could have thought that Monito died like Christ. The deaths of public figures in Latin America are frequently identified with Christ's crucifixion. Examples of this include the last picture of Ché Guevara which gave rise to the 'San Ernesto de la Higuera' stories. Similarly there are traditions surrounding the death of Evita, who is said to have died at the same age as Christ. It is worth noting that this is not about Christ. It is about brands. This is not about processes of sanctification as we know them, but branding processes in which the church and the economy, once again, show hidden contracts.

Monito Galván, with his T-shirt inscribed with fashionable logos, was no Christ (the Logos) because crucifixion in Bancalari has reverted to what it was in the Roman empire, a form of deadly torture. The simulacrum is in reality more factual than theologies, in the sense that his body showed the reality of death by torture, including the mockery of crowning him 'the king of glue sniffing', with the symbol of the plastic bag wrapped around his head. This was a simulacrum of crucifixion because crucifixion in Christian theology has lost its meaning of torture and death. In that sense, it was a simulacrum of a simulacrum. This may be due to the fact that torture is an accessible, transparent concept, easily understood in Bancalari because it is present in everyday life amongst the poor. At this moment gangs are using instruments of torture such as electric cattle-prods to force people to instantly part with their money. The tremendous violence which permeates the life of people in a city such as Buenos Aires (where it is said that it takes only two hours to buy a gun) is now about torture, because torture represents an identity of power and terror. It is reminiscent of the time of the military juntas, when torturers in concentration camps claimed to be as powerful as gods. Torture bestows an identity based on power. It is criminality with impunity and as such it is a brand recognised by poor people. It saves you (*te rescata*) from impotence, from being a nobody – from anonymity and poverty.

In another way, we could say that the vodka in the postcard of Jesus Christ seems to save, not just because of the contrast between the presence of a bottle and the presence of Christ amongst the poor – this would require the viewer to make a substitution of terms – but because brands are themselves routes to salvation.

The context of this process by which branding steals sanctity is the expansion of capitalism and globalisation, but branding has its own complex theology, similar in important respects to what Stuart refers to as the stealing of souls, in her study of the female theology of sainthood. How does this work? Brands give people a social as well as a spiritual identity. Naomi Klein, in her book *No Logo*, identifies this process as one which requires a continuous imaginative flow, a search for spaces of dissemination. She describes dissemination as in itself a process constituted by extensions (Klein 2001: 5). Branding is a key element in the formation of nationalist identities and has even replaced the traditional role that some religious groups performed, especially for the poor, such as the paths to sainthood among the marginalised, paths which many Pentecostal churches have been providing for decades.

Brands offer identity to poor people, even if it is through nothing more than a free T-shirt with a logo printed on it: it is a way to transcendence in the slums. However, this sanctity process into which the marginalised enter in search of meaning and truth in their lives is in reality the soul of corporations. Naomi Klein quotes Bruce Barton of General Motors who claims that 'the role of advertising is to help corporations to find their soul' (Klein 2001: 7). Is it for the soul of corporations that the marginalised are searching as they seek to establish their identities in what we might call the production of the brand scene? That brand scene is a piece of a promised Kingdom of Heaven. It is variable, always novel and of relatively easy and instant access. The power of the stories of brands (as seen on TV or on posters) is even more powerful than *teleteatros*, the popular TV soap operas of Latin America. These are stories written around themes of salvation from poverty and lack of love: typically the plot features a poor girl who ends up marrying the landowner in whose mansion she used to clean the floors. But brands are about qualities and not just products. Klein, referring to the case of Richard Branson, has considered for instance how from the point of view of marketing, quality and innovation are now more important than specific products (Klein 2001: 24). The whole process is therefore akin to revelations of new qualities and characteristics which confer on us new identities by creating different relationships between ourselves and the world which surrounds us: it sets before us new options for our lives. This recalls also Mary Grey's sense of revelation as connectedness, organising (and imagining) cultural experiences considered to be positive around the process of making the values and attitudes called brands. It is in this way that Novak, for instance, tries to sell a positive view of capitalism as indebted to Christianity, for Novak's capitalism is a brand and the path of holiness could just as well be using a T-shirt, that is, making a connection with something which in this case has supplemented the cultural understanding of life and God. (Clearly I am not a Japanese theologian!) For Novak, as for Stackhouse, corporations have become 'forms of grace' (Long 2000: 51) or Christological images which mediate between humanity and God. For Stackhouse, revelation also needs to be compatible with ideology (Long 2000: 50). As corporations have replaced cultural forms (or culture is changed or discouraged from change to suit corporations) they also seem to want to replace indigenous theologies. The path of sanctification for the marginalised lies in intense political persuasion, which in poor countries means by violence.

In the same way, crime is redeemed and rehearsed by the soul of corporations. In April 1998 in Buenos Aires, an advert for jeans presented the horrific image of eight young people chained to heavy blocks of concrete, lying dead in the depths of the ocean, in the same atrocious way that people were killed by the military dictatorship during the 1970s. The words under the picture said: 'They are not your first jeans, but they could be the last. At least, you will leave a beautiful corpse.' (Galeano 2000: 213). The logo's persuasion is not related to a peaceful art of advertising, but to a criminal one, as was the case some years ago with some mothers from rural Argentina. These poor women unintentionally killed their babies when, unable to buy them powdered milk, they gave them flour mixed with water as a substitute, thinking that it would be good food for the children. Branding also kills by grace, that is, by inspiring in us a complex set of values and attitudes which are desirable for us as human beings. These include the art of forgetting and the desirability of denying the past.

However, the processes of branding as forms of paths to market sanctification are similar in methodology to those followed by the Vatican. As revelation needs to be ideologically contained, the lives of many saints have been retold to exemplify this idea of 'good humanity' (Stuart 1996: 68) from the perspective of patriarchal theology. This manipulation, which ends up by making heroes of saints, succeeds in alienating sainthood from the lives of common people, as Carter Heyward has already observed. Thus she says, referring to this hero-making procedure by the church, 'as our liberators ... heroes have brought us pipe-dreams and smokescreens and everything but salvation. And this ... because we tend to search everywhere except amongst ourselves-in-relation for peace' (Stuart 1996: 39). One of the problems in all this lies in the fact that the saintly discipleship model brought to us by the sponsorship of the church requires us all to become Japanese (by analogy with Novak's claim). We are required to participate in a corporative interested soul-searching process in which theology as culture is replaced by whatever Novak chooses to call being Japanese – which of course need not relate to anything found in Japan. As Carly Stasko asked while contemplating a Barbie doll, 'What came first? The Beauty or the Myth?' (Klein 2001: 290). Queer theologians might care to consider what is the proportional relationship between sainthood and church sponsorship. Should we begin with the life and path of the saint as we seek understanding of, and encouragement to live under, a sense of revelation as connections of disruptions of common orders, or should we begin instead with the message of the sponsor which is geared to preserve the dogma-corporation with all its apparatus of power and privilege?

In all this, Queer Theology has much to say and to contribute to the debate in more ways than one. First of all, by defending the theological space of discussion outside profit, what Klein has called 'unbranded spaces' (Klein 2001: 105) of thinking and acting. Queer Theology should fight for a non-marketable assimilation of radical thinking which the present system devalues as neither tradable nor economically efficient. Second, Queer Theology can help to unmask much deeper mechanisms connecting the global expansion of capitalism and its brand theology with the critical exclusion of sainthood from the lives of the marginalised of the system. Queer holiness may be the only option and real alternative open in a world which has neither options nor alternatives, because it might represent the different (*hagios*) which needs to be manifested in our lives in relation to God's plans of justice. It is that quality of difference in making the world holy by embracing elements of difference and understanding the oddity of Jesus as a Messiah against the normal or common sense, that makes Christian holiness a Queer holiness. Moreover, continuing with our understanding of Queer Theology as a materially based theology, holiness becomes a project, and a strategy of resistance. The Queer God may then show us God's excluded face, which is the face of a non-docile God, a God who is a stranger at the gates of our existent loving and economic order. That might make Queer Theology a utopia, but remembering Ricoeur, we might declare it a 'necessary utopia' (Ricoeur 1984: 29), a utopia which gathers together the aspirations of many communities for an alternative. That alternative can partake neither of capitalism nor of Heterosexual Theology. The theoretical basis of both these systems must be questioned and delegitimised. In the orthopraxis of any alternative theology, which seeks to question the foundation and the theoretical base of Hetero-Theologies and not simply to reform them, the Queer God is the foundation of such an alternative.

9

QUEER HOLINESS
Post-colonial revelations

They contained many idols of baked clay, some with demons' faces, some with women's, and others equally ugly which seemed to represent Indians committing sodomy with one another.

(Díaz 1963: 19)

There exists a relationship between male homosexuality and [Afro-Brazilian] worship, at the level of collective representations and at the level of effective praxis.

(Fry 1977: 106)

Sodomising zemis

If Queer holiness has a characteristic, it may be its un-representability. It is not that we should like to concede victory to the rhetoric of the so-called un-representability of God (which, by the way, has reached peaks of saturation in Heterosexual Theology) but to point rather to the fact that holiness is always the holiness of the Other. From a colonial reading of the strategies of the holy in imperial discourses, re-presenting holiness has been related to processes of duplication which succeed by erasing differences and thus normalising the praxis of the holy. The capacity to reflect on Queer holiness resides precisely in the undoing of the colonial path of duplication. Queer Theology acts as a mirror or as a scene (in the sense of the libertine scenes previously discussed) which allows us to search for the Queer who is entombed in us, pointing us to a different praxis of the holy in our lives.

In Latin America, duplication as a strategy for suppressing the queerness of holiness has a long tradition, albeit a church tradition. Serge Gruzinski, in his book *La Guerra de las Imágenes* (the war of images) has considered for instance how Latin America was religiously and politically constructed according to a logic of duplication (Gruzinski 1995: 15). The colonial process of making the Americas was undertaken in accordance with a logic of transportation of religious and legal images and a praxis of holiness based on the dynamics of superimposition, for instance, the imposition of Spanish and Portuguese language and culture, in a movement of mercantilist expansion (an early phase of capitalism). In order to interpret and understand the continent baptised *América* by the conquistadors, categories such as 'idolatry' and 'the demonic' (terms of exclusion capable of multiple associations) needed to be laid upon the religious universe of Others. The result was domination and a theology based on an incipient branding (or the logo as the soul of a corporation) as in a capitalist expansion such as globalisation. Duplication is the process of the promotion of the identical, in the same way as the promotion of brands, a process of the promotion of values and attitudes which is not as creative as might appear, but on the contrary, relies on fixed capitalist values. These values derive from a restricted repertoire of hegemonic principles and market values based on competition, which at the same time struggle with each other every time a new economic or cultural production appears. Therefore, they inform models of life and behaviour (the praxis of the holy) encouraged by the ethical principle of 'managing the world through the market' (Amin 2000: 17).

At this point, we need to reflect on zemis and their role in the alienation of Queer holiness in Latin America by capitalist colonial expansions. When in October 1492, the mercantilist expansion, known also as the first period in the expansion of capitalism, arrived to the Americas, with cross and sword mutually supporting the enterprise, Columbus noticed the existence of strange cultural objects which puzzled and intrigued him. These were called zemis. Apparently, they were what today could be called cultural devices or 'figurative objects' (Gruzinski 1995: 19). The problem for Columbus was that he became troubled with their function. If zemis were a praxis, then what sort of Queer practice did they facilitate? It is interesting to note that in the records of Columbus himself the question about the use of these zemis frequently recurs. As Gruzinski observes, Columbus did not ask himself about any representative value the zemis might have had, but rather about their function. Already the spirit of profit was appearing in the making of a theology and a holiness discourse, focussing on the mechanisms of theological production. What zemis are was not as important as how they function, what they produce and what benefit or otherwise can be obtained from them. Representing zemis as idols (illegal spiritual helpers, in European categories) was contradicted by the discovery made by Columbus himself that the natives of the Caribbean islands only worshipped 'the celestial numen' (Gruzinski 1995: 19). Even their temples (called by Columbus and the others 'temples of idols') seemed to have functioned more like museums or art exhibitions than locations for worship. Whatever the zemis were they were more complex than the idea of idols. In any case this term relies on an illusory dualistic comparison since the contrasting of the true God versus the idols belonged to Christian and not Caribbean epistemology. However, the idols as helpers versus the true God of the empire challenged the system of monopoly. From this perspective the idols were not the illusions of deluded heathens but real workforces which threatened the spiritual market. What was needed was a co-operative of gods, but the theological mode was mercantilist. Economics shapes the concepts of what is normal in society, how society is organised and how exchanges (including affective ones) are produced. Queer is what has doubts about that normality expressed in capital, understanding capital as referring also to relations (Hunt 1990: 21).

Although the indigenous people also questioned the validity of the pattern of relationship with Christianity, there is no reason to believe that their line of argumentation was developed with respect to the 'God versus idols argument'.[1] In fact, the Caribbean peoples had neither God nor idols and whether or not zemis represented something in between we shall never know, since we know too little about how their society functioned. And it is the functioning of a society which tells us about the function of divinities. As far as we know the only testimonies that we have from the divine among Caribbean people are duplications of a certain central core European Christian belief. In this, we find a similarity with the process we have called branding. The redemption path and the praxis of holiness of the conquistadors' model relied not on differentiation processes but on the duplication of an understanding of Christian faith and an imperial cultural and political universe. Curiously, in globalisation processes, brands also rely on the duplication of the market spirit and although they present the illusion of something mobile and changing through the constant introduction of variety for consumption, the value system which sustains them is in all cases identical. Holiness lost its queerness in the conquest of the Americas.

In the understanding of the zemis there is power to break down religious, political and sexual duplication in theology. The unique characteristic of revelation in history lies in its queerness, that non-normalising, subversive discourse which resists identity's claims to finality and fixity. If we take a metaphor related to the construction of femininity and masculinity, then we can say that a revelation which only changes gender codes cannot succeed except in redistributing the defined normalcy alongside the discourse of faith in society. This is the revelation that justice is equality, but equality with whom? The problem is that revelation might still be participating in the framework of colonial duplication present in Christian theology. Christian theology has difficulty in dealing with non-identical understandings of, for instance, paths to holiness based on the breakthrough provided by revelations of a different nature, or using our example of the divine inexpressible of the Other, the revelations of zemis. Since we are here considering revelation as manifested in history and in the history of human liberation, we should also consider the role of tradition or continuation which is passed on from one generation to another. However, the theological discourse which emphasises this communitarian sense of identity and belonging which tradition provides seldom considers the tradition of zemis. The problem we are confronting here is that the queerness of revelation in history is easily forgotten when assimilated to patterns of duplication. Therefore, in revelation the Queer which is not remembered should probably be considered heretical, that is, a brand which duplicates an identical, unchallengeable spirit, which is not revelatory but is a confirmation of a pre-empted discovery of the presence of the

Sacred amongst a people. Zemis are and were untranslatable, because the spirituality of the Other is usually untranslatable unless within a different referential revelatory system which is accepted as valid. What is being said here at the level of images and representations of revelatory events in the lives of different peoples needs to be extended also to the paths of holiness.

When Cortés tried to persuade Moctezuma to become a Christian he also needed to persuade him of a different path of holiness based on a different understanding of the market, that is, the construction of holiness in profitable relationships. By this we mean that a different understanding of the sacred defines a way to construct intimacy and loving relationships amongst people. Thus, according to Bernal Díaz del Castillo, Cortés urged Moctezuma to abandon the ways of sodomy and robbery in his life: the two concepts were strangely tied together. Cortés followed a well known ideological method of starting with the book of Genesis as an authoritative discourse from the past (or at least, as far as Moctezuma was concerned, from the past of Cortés) and ending with sodomy (which was represented in zemis). The following narrative of the method will sound familiar to many of those excluded from churches today:

> [Cortés] very carefully expounded the creation of the world, how we are all brothers, the children of one mother and father called Adam and Eve; and how such a brother as our great Emperor, grieving for the perdition of so many souls as their idols [e.g. zemis] were leading them to hell, where they burnt in living flame, had sent us to tell him this, so that he might put a stop to it, and so that they might give up the worship of idols and make no more human sacrifices – for all men are brothers – and commit no more robbery or sodomy.
>
> (Díaz 1963: 222)

What Cortés has done is to claim as revelation a tradition which in reality has long since lost whatever revelatory meaning it had originally, to be replaced by a sexual hetero-ideology. The revelatory narrative of Genesis may be that of the expulsion of multiple sexualities from the construction of humanity. In a sense, if the relation between God and man was disrupted by gender difference in paradise, Genesis' subversive message is to embody zemis and to develop holiness as a demonology, that is, a praxis of rebellious spirits. The rebelliousness which is at the core of the praxis of zemis is that of sexual irredemption. Conjugal prohibitions, unless prophetically denounced and subverted, are obstacles to holiness because they may contribute to the dismantling of economic and political trends in the praxis of the holy. As such, conjugal prohibitions provide us with interesting clues in our search for Queer holiness.

Although exclusion has been a constitutive part of the project of sexual dominance which has been the substance of imperial power (Stoler 1997: 15), sexual redemption has been at the core of the political and sexual re-inscription of the Other in the imperial story of Christianity. This applies to different processes of conquest. If Christian redemption were negotiated as a positioning of saved and unsaved, as part of a broad universe of Christian expectations about salvation, colonial theology produced a variety of 'selective redemptions' which in turn provided intimacy with the new order, while sometimes contrasting with the hardness of the sexual and social boundaries created. These were redemptions linked, for instance, to political and racial differentiation, which selectively accepted some people according to services paid to the system, while leaving others outside. Thus, some women became temporarily redeemed from class and sexuality, becoming 'white'. The example of the zemis shows us that homosexuality was a common pattern of intimacy before the *Conquista* and also that the gods were Queer. The zemis were, in a way, the sacred come out of the closet and this must have had implications for relationships in society, supporting as they did a whole cosmology of affective and economic exchanges. Meanwhile, the Christian God was still sleeping rough in the closet and did not commit suicide by leaving it during the *Conquista*.

The implications of our discussion so far lead us to conclude that globalisation processes, working through religious mechanisms such as branding, cannot cope with revelations in the form of Queer revelations. The surprising conclusion is that in the present time revelation needs to be Queer, because it needs to come from a Queer God, manifested in people whose lifestyle and values are not easily assimilated by capitalist spirituality. However, God may have come out of the closet of Christianity in Latin America, because of people's subversive spirituality which has forced Christianity to make alliances with the religions of the Other. This is the equivalent to saying that God could not have come out without the help of the zemis.

If we consider an example provided by the Batuque[2] worship in Brazil, we can see this coming out of the Queer God in Queer relationships through the oppressed people in Latin America. They disorganised Christianity and continued as far as they could their belief in a more Queer God manifested in different relationships amongst people and with the sacred. Somehow, the holiness praxis manifested in the life of the marginalised in Latin America seems to pass through sexual deviance, because it is not until the sexual ordering of human and gods is challenged that the obstacles to receiving sacred revelations as disruption can succeed. For the following reflection I am indebted to the research material provided by Peter Fry of the Universidade Estadual de Campinas, Brazil, and published under the title *Mediunidade e Sexualidade* (Mediumship and Sexuality; Fry 1977).

Holiness in the struggle: the way of Queer spirits

Candomblé was born, partly, for homosexuality.

(Fry 1977: 121)

Batuque worship in Brazil is, according to Marco Aúrelio Luz, the most popular form of African Brazilian spirituality (Fry 1977: 107). Batuque or Macumba are terms which refer originally to the use of drums in worship and to the dynamic of liturgical worship, dances and songs created by their rhythm. Batuque worship comes from the Yoruba religion of the African nations kidnapped and forced into slavery in Brazil. In their struggle for life the slaves produced a synthesis with Roman Catholicism, but without giving up their different cosmology or ways of affective relationships. According to Fry, whose study was based on the Brazilian town of Belém, the *casas de culto* (literally, 'worship houses') of Belém have facilitated the expression of not only a relationship with the sacred but also non-heterosexual identities. It is interesting to note further that this research, undertaken at the University of Campinas, refers to the most popular forms of worship which include Umbanda and Candomblé. Although they originate in the religious systems brought from West Africa to Brazil they became a diasporic religion expressed in many forms of displacements. For instance, while Umbanda can be considered as a religion of middle-class people in Brazil, Macumba has remained much more defiant and non-conformist. That understanding rules out the assumption by any theological discourse that the spirituality of the poorest of the poor is either submissive or liberative, but in necessary agreement with, for instance, Roman Catholicism or Pentecostalism. Homosexuality and lesbianism seem to have been common in the Batuque worship of the poor in Belém and the originality of the Batuque worship according to Douglas seems to be related to the place of non-heterosexuality in the religious system (Fry 1977: 106). It was thought right and proper that people at the margins of the heterosexual system should have a greater say in Batuque religion than heterosexuals. This was due to the fact that Batuque worshippers considered themselves to be marginalised by church and state alike and therefore needed to be represented by people with genuine experience (secular and sacred) of living at the margins of society. Thus Douglas says that in Batuque worship, 'to be at the margins, means to have a contract with the dangerous, witnessed by a source of power' (Fry 1977: 106). If it is true that, according to this research, Belém is a town where sexual classificatory systems are more flexible than in other places, it may be that the true relationship between a lesbian priest, her God and her community needs to be understood in terms of difference in spiritual representation and even in liturgical manifestation. Fry considers that the context in which Umbanda, Candomblé and the Batuque worship developed should not be emphasised more than their original African or European spiritual sources. In that sense, we might say that sexuality was also part of the Batuque context which required some appropriation of the most traditional forms of sexual control present not only in Roman Catholicism but also in Umbanda worship. Apparently, the worshippers have a developed form of interconnections and a communication network based on gossip and exchange of information (Fry 1977: 107) which tends to disclose who is who, sexually speaking. In the worship houses of Umbanda, for instance, issues of homosexuality may well be seen by some *pai-de-santo* or *mãe-de-santo* (priests and priestesses of Umbanda) as not conforming to the standard of religion as inherited by a homophobic Roman Catholic theology. However, in Belém and amongst the Batuque worshippers, homosexuality has become a constitutive part of the worship. There is even a common saying that a *vida no santo ñao tem nada a ver com a vida do medium* (the life of the gods does not have anything in common with the life of the medium). The point is not simply that Belém has a less strict sexual ordering of society than other towns, thus providing worshipful acts with a sort of sexual indifference, especially in relation to the sexual orientation of the priests. Rather the point is what homosexuality can give to the Batuque worship to enhance it, for instance in the splendour of the liturgy which is so important and the transvestite aesthetics in spiritual incorporation (especially of goddesses). In addition they provide a network of solidarity for other homosexuals who experience problems in their families or neighbourhoods (Fry 1977: 116). Batuque worship allows homosexuals to develop themselves as religious professionals, if they so wish, in a context of respect and support and without hiding their true sexual identity. At the same time they can provide a sense of family to those who have been rejected by their own relatives. However, what is important in the sense of religious power is precisely the power conferred by marginalisation from society. *Mãe* and *pai-de-santos* have the experience of being 'double (or triple) outsiders'. They are outsiders first, as Batuque worshippers: a religion originating in West Africa is considered socially inferior to Christianity which came via Europe. Second, as poor worshippers: even the worship houses are geographically located in the poor areas outside of the towns. Third, they are sexual outsiders, outside heterosexuality. That sense of triple marginality is interpreted by Batuque devotees as being both powerful and unique. They believe that outside the established religious system (e.g. Roman Catholicism) there is a source of mystical powers available only to people at the margins. Holiness then becomes a category of the marginalised, when we consider that the saint is meant to be an outsider to society, not in the sense of failing to participate actively in the political life of her community, but due to her dissenting role. It is participation in the transformation of the structures of society which marks the distance from the centres of order and power. That is Queer dissent, and divine dissent, as in prophetic or other models surrounding the idea of Holy women and men in popular spirituality. In the case of the worshippers of Batuque it is not only homosexuality but sexual deviance (prostitution, promiscuity, sexual liaisons) which also prevail. As one *pai-de-santo* has said,

> If you look carefully at the whole of Brazil, you will have difficulty in finding a *pai-de-santo* or a *mãe-de-santo* who is absolutely correct from a sexual point of view. They always have sexual affairs. Candomblé was born, partly, for homosexuality.

(Fry 1977: 121)

The point is that although religions are made for, or around, clear sexual classificatory patterns, sexuality limits or opens up the horizon of religious systems. The subversiveness of revelation is a disruption of common orders (the orders of ideology) and the paths of sanctity are the ones which tend to privilege marginal locations, in the sense of being located sites of struggle and non-conformity. From Queer Theology we might receive insights of the Queer God who manifests Godself through Batuque worships as part of a manifestation of different forms of relationship, which also includes relationships with God. What is revealed here might also disturb us, when the sainthood of the Other gives rise to stories which Christian theology cannot hear without modifying or editing.

Where have all the Queers gone in Christian theology? Why don't we have our Holy Week of the Queers, or a Batuque of self-marginalisation from central definitions of sexual classificatory systems in church and theology? We do not have them because in Christian theology we encounter difficulties in the dynamics of understanding, what Gramsci would call the inner motivations of religious systems (Gramsci 1974: 70). As any understanding of a mythical or mystical nature struggles against a Christian understanding, it is people, as the subject of the religion of the Other, who suffer exile in the process. If the religion of the Other is Batuque, it is the body of the poor and its sensuality which is excluded from a dialogue with Christianity. At this point Christianity could learn much about its own pervading capitalist thinking. Jaci Maraschin, reflecting on issues related to Christianity and sexuality, has made the point that Christianity is one of the most materialist of all religious systems (Maraschin 1985: 206) and it is precisely that materialism which has so much to give to the present world economic order. This is not because we need to go back to what Amin has called the moralist trend, affirming that the good principles of love and compassion present in Christianity, once incorporated into the present order, would act as a corrective to usury and financial speculation. As we have already discussed, that would be the equivalent of theological developmentalism, the logic of which is improvement and not radical change. However, it is good to remember that if in capitalism poverty and unemployment are necessary components of world polarisation (Amin 2000: 16), in theology sexual margins are not just part of a moral injustice or a lack of equality in the praxis of the church. The margins of sexuality in theology are constitutive parts of the polarisation of the logic of salvation and the disruption of real, dissident holy praxis in the church. Although a Queer Theology can only be seen as a process rather than a final result, its contribution to solving the present crisis is precisely that of providing an end to the docetism and current de-materialisation of theology, not by suggesting a new reformation, but rather a radical change in Christianity.

For Maraschin, capitalism is the ideology of de-incarnation and a theology of docetism. The processes of reification and the ideological method of globalisation make abstractions of human realities and produce a theological aesthetics of surplus value. Christian theology needs to consider how, by stopping the systematic calumny against hedonist love (non-profitable love), the monopolistic thinking of the churches can give way to a real materialist body theology de-linking revelation from the logic of global brands, and thus liberating holiness. That is, to reject the view that every impression of change and movement is illusory, because class, race and sexual contracts promote a religion of de-incarnation and productive reifications. Meanwhile, the religions of the poor, such as the Batuques and Macumbas of Brazil, resist the Christian attack on sexuality and the de-incarnation of life. It is there that we should look for a positive ecumenical dialogue in which the well known saying about 'listening to the poor' could become a key element for changing theological and economic attitudes. The Batuque people are wise to claim that it is only at the margins of the central administration of religion that power from a real relationship with God comes. It is even wiser, from this Queer ecclesiological perspective, to make people at the margins the people of God, those who are at the leading edge and not simply those who are at the receiving end of a central institution. From affective relationships at the margins to a sacred understanding of God and God's people as marginalised, comes also an appropriation of joy and beauty in life and the empowerment of dissent, the Queer dissent.

Sites of holiness: the end of the monopoly–fidelity game

We must not commit any kind of sexual immorality.

(Küng 1996: 11)

In an interview published in the *Third Way* magazine of February 2001, Hans Küng spoke at some length about the idea of the global ethic project, as well as giving his own views on the globalisation process. He describes himself as 'reformist': a man in the middle of extremes in thinking about globalisation 'with the accent on reform' (Küng 2001: 18). It is evident that he does not understand globalisation as a process of capitalist expansion. Küng says: 'When I went to UNESCO to speak about the global ethic, I met a French socialist for whom "globalisation" was just another name for Capitalism and he was fighting against it in a rather stupid way ... As I told him, even those who are against globalisation are debating it on the internet' (Küng 2001: 18).

What then is globalisation for Hans Küng? In his own words, it is something that is happening which has both positive and negative aspects and which can be particularly identified with one of the several monopolistic empires of capitalist expansion (the media). Globalisation is also an inevitable process which, according to Küng, requires to be subjected to a process of consensus on ethical standards. For instance, Küng refers to globalisation in the context of democracy and the need for ethical standards as a substratum to any democratic process. This happens because Küng has not yet realised that local, independent democracies are a thing of the past and that local governments are completely disempowered, not least while searching for transnational corporations and neo-colonial alliances to help them in the deep crisis into which many countries are submerged. There may be other theologians who seem to think that globalisation is a kind of force (*fuerza* in Spanish; curiously also a metaphor for Spirit) that can be positive, if only it can be used to teach people respect for basic religious principles, such as not to lie or have sex with their neighbours. The path of holiness here may look innocent enough but can lead us to known horrors which require from us domestication and obedience to capitalist expansion instead of resistance. Küng's path to holiness has nothing to do with George Monbiot's analysis of the Anarchist Travelling Circus against globalisation, nor their favourite gesture of defiance, that is, showing their backsides to the G8.

This situation makes us wonder just how far Christian theology today is suffering from the influence of the corporation spirit, when trying to seek an alternative to the current situation of polarisation of wealth and resources, which is excluding millions of people in our world from their right to life. Can a theology and a church whose own practices of exclusion have become fixed traditions contribute to a credible critique of globalisation? Which alternative path to social holiness can churches share with people suffering from exclusion, when from high councils to humble committees the churches cannot even understand the most simple issues of gender analysis? The problem is that Küng's 'Golden rule' of global ethics, defined by him as 'simple standards' (Küng 2001: 19) such as: do not lie, do not steal, etc, seems to ignore what happens at the level of structural sin, and capitalist sin to be more precise. For instance, he speaks as a free man for whom truthfulness is not a right but something that arises from his own human dignity and responsibility. However, some of us come from political systems in which capitalism had much to say, such as the dictatorial regimes during the 1970s in Latin America, where to be truthful was a right and a human right, to be more precise, denied by the system. The late Paulo Freire, in a private conversation, once told me that when he was detained by police in Brazil and tortured, he was asked to confirm the names of political activists. Freire told me that he knew them all; they were his friends, yet he denied under torture that he knew them. And Freire reflected how by lying to his torturers, he was being truthful. The political and sexual closets in which people live are sometimes not optional. The interesting point is that heterosexuality, that matrix of hierarchical thinking, discrimination, persecution and oppression, is never mentioned in Küng's global ethic project. One would think that heterosexual normativity has much to do with oppressive and discriminatory thinking, yet, when I asked Küng about the position of the global ethic project on sexuality, I received a curious answer. According to him, since the world religions didn't have any agreement on issues of sexuality and gender, it was better to ignore them. Interesting reply, indeed! One could argue that the problem is precisely the contrary, since all religions seems to have a heterosexual epistemology behind them. As for leaving sexuality aside because there was no consensus, that seems a contradiction of his claims that only Jesus, and not Bishop's conferences (that is, dogmatism), should guide us (Küng 2001: 21). We will not advance on ethical principles if we don't challenge structures of sin accepted without questioning.

In the global ethic project globalisation is supposedly to be controlled by a consensual religious ethic which, by the way, was not born out of consensus at all. A consensus such as the so-called Ten Commandments reflects an elite perspective of life and a particular understanding of the relationship between law and justice. It is the consensus of property owners and people in control. This is the perspective of benign patriarchs and mono-loving acts of faith, but mono-loving acts exclude a multitude of loves in our lives and demand that we sacrifice some friendships and the solidarity of ex-lovers. The problem is that the good principles which could be found behind the commandments seem to work (or to be used) as aid agencies of Christian principles in the sense that they work in harmony with the prevailing system because of their reformist (and not subversive) standings. Once again in recent times, developmentalism has made its nest in a curious global ethics where colonial theological modes, developmental frameworks and euro-theological centrism prevail. What we need is to rethink the geography of holiness which the expansion of capitalism has scrambled and sent back to colonial moods. In a materialist Queer reflection on holiness, where affective and economic relationships matter, holiness is spatial and its locations can be subverted or re-distributed in history.

In Roman Catholic theology, limbo is the space where the holy innocent live after death. Because it is the space of those who are neither saved nor lost, we might consider that the concept of limbo has a post-colonialist critique of paths of holiness which come from imperial theologies. Global capitalism, as Peter Hitchcock has pointed out, has a 'de-incarnation' policy (Hitchcock 1999: 144). This non-corporeal way of thinking results in the disappearances of bodies. The worker's body disappears from the global capitalist's analysis. The body of the environment and the bodies of women (through the traditional Christian association of nature and women) disappear too. But as Hitchcock points out, the 'shades' (or ghosts) of the disappeared are continually trying to be re-corporealised. Holiness, as a social practice, may also be under threat of disappearance, unless we find new theological locations for reflection on options, salvation and the right to dissent. In this demonology that we are proposing as part of a Queer path to holiness, what Giorgio Agamben calls a need for radical objection to redemption (or capitalist redemption) may open a new path for reflection (Agamben 1998: 7). When Agamben reflects on this subject he considers the punishment of the souls in limbo, that is, their deprivation of the sight of God, and points out how futile that punishment is. If the innocent souls who had neither sinned nor known salvation are somehow occupying a space where God has forgotten them, because they did not know God in the first place, the result is natural joy, instead of pain (Agamben 1998: 6). He calls the state of these souls one of divine abandon, where God's forgetfulness seems impotent simply because they have already forgotten God and ignored that created need for salvation in the first place. This is the point of the radical objection to redemption and their neutrality towards salvation. This becomes an interesting point for us to reflect on because in reality what we are facing here is a dislocation of imperial strategies in holiness and the path of a de-colonisation of souls.

Let us consider this point in detail for our discussion on Queer holiness and global capitalist tactics of de-corporealisation. When some years ago I was reading with some students the poem on the conversion of the Cacique Nicaragua in

Ernesto Cardenal's *The Doubtful Strait* (Cardenal 1995: 30) someone asked a crucial question. Why was Nicaragua converted? From what sin did he need to repent? What structures of grace were imported into Central America to make Nicaragua a sinner, while according to his own beliefs and cosmology he might well have been a just man? Christianity as a Sexual Theology has exported to the so-called new world a whole structure of holiness which was ideologically grounded in a situation of imperial occupation, but which was not necessarily salvific for the oppressed nations. In fact, Nicaragua probably did not need a conversion but, on the contrary, he needed a radical objection to this offer of redemption. Nicaragua was in a space of Queer holiness, or limbo, because he was ignorant of the structures of holiness devised for purposes of oppression. At the same time he was living according to his own praxis of holiness amongst his people. He presented what Agamben calls a neutrality against salvation (Agamben 1998: 7) which is in itself a de-colonisation tactic, claiming space for a strange God amongst strange people. So Agamben says that the immoral is not present in indifference as much as in lack of particularity and sexual particularity. The natives defy grace by claiming their own particularity. The libertine does the same. This is the limbo space of the particularity of the Queer nation, which is neither an indifferent community, nor does it 'know' goodness in the terms used by the heterosexual ideological path of holiness in common with global capitalism. The paths of holiness outside the decent orders of imperial Christianity are meant to suffer the absence of God. That is their interpretation of the space of limbo in our lives. Queer Christians seem to be condemned to be outside the gates of the church and away from the presence of God, while in reality they know by their own lives of suffering and commitment to integral justice that they can claim not victim-hood but agency in their praxis. Queer dissidents in search of paths of holiness through social practices of justice in sexual, religious and political areas of their lives might well be reducing the hetero-God and church to impotency. It is not the church which has forgotten us: the truth is that we do not know that church. We do not give authority or recognition to sinful structures calling from that very sinfulness. In this sense, Queer spirituality is an affirmation of agency and a de-colonisation process in itself. It can claim that God the Stranger amongst our community of strangers may have declared us, made us, irredeemably lost in the eyes of the church and Christian ethics, yet it is not we who are lost. As in every colonial process, the space of limbo depends on this oscillatory tension between a God who forgets the 'non-saved' and a people who do not know that they need to be saved. This is particularly so when what is required is, generally speaking, sexual conversion to heterosexual ideology and to patterns of thought translated into a discourse of the sacred. But the point is that holiness is then dependent on suffering. Not being in the presence of the imperial God must create suffering. However, that is not the case. Sexual and political dissidents have been around longer than that particular conception of God. Reconstituting the agency of Queer holiness, that is, its corporeality, defiance and critical thinking in relation to God, is to reclaim a theology of limbo as a theology of uniqueness and identity in struggle. Limbo is not a colonial place where God as the *Unicum* (Agamben 1999: 49) imposes unicity, but a space of joy and happiness grounded in a spirituality which refuses to acknowledge, or to know, the God of the colonial power. In this refusal, that God fades away, for that God was more dependent on the souls deliberately deprived of God's presence than they were on Him, just as colonial powers depend more on the poor countries they oppress than vice versa. Re-corporealising holiness means to come out with the issues of real bodies in theology and with the Queer restlessness of our hearts. We are called to object radically to redemption on colonial terms. Therefore, claiming our right to limbo means to claim our right to Queer holy lives and innocence and by doing that we end up destabilising many powers and principalities by simply refusing to acknowledge their authority in our lives. Queer holiness is a path of freeing our lives from the control of authorities, when those authorities justify their position on false claims which cannot be found in a path of justice. As such, Queer saints are a menace and a subversive force by the sheer act of living in integrity and defiance.

Queering hell: holiness and ethical options

Images of limbo provide us with material for reflecting on holiness as a negation of the status quo and the destabilisation of power through holiness as the de-legitimisation of (hetero) church praxis and theology. Hell confronts us with the difficult issue of Christian ethical discourse on options. Are heaven and hell optional spaces or totalitarian realities? How can the space of hell be conceived so that it opens rather than closes the path of dissent and transgression in Christian theology? For this reflection, we shall refer to the work of the late Uruguayan Liberation Theologian, Juan Luis Segundo, in his book *El Infierno* (Hell) (Segundo 1997).

Segundo was a very radical thinker whose creativity led him to reflect on why certain themes have been excluded from theology in the last few years. For instance, hell as a theological theme seems to have disappeared. Among fundamentalist Christians it has appeared sporadically when they have sought to use the imaginary of ultimate punishment for their own pedagogy of terror. What Segundo wanted was a serious reflection on hell as a space related to holiness and condemnation. In Segundo's own thought, limbo and hell are two theological categories located outside divine grace and as such they may present us with alternatives to salvation in the present world (dis)order (Segundo 1997: 15). We are told that under the current expansion of capitalism there are no alternatives left, politically or otherwise. We are now called upon to seek salvation by the logo and transcendence via the soul of the corporations. Therefore, queering holiness and its spaces such as limbo and hell may be considered a dangerous thing to do, especially if we bear in mind Segundo's contention that hell (and limbo) are spaces contained within us, capable of being challenged in our daily lives. These embodied spaces of perdition (like the act of losing sight of God) may also be considered spaces of economic and even sexual subversion.

Hell and spaces of disbelieving

Hell needs to be seen as the space where we may actively produce a praxis of disbelieving, or distancing ourselves ideologically from what may be called the soul of corporations. Hell as a site of disobedience is the space where we not only find those who reject goodness but those who refuse to continue to be interpolated by the goodness of the capitalist system in which we live and its current values. In this sense we occupy the space of hell when we refuse to believe in ideological constructions but also when we disbelieve in the Straight God. We wait for the sexual kenosis of the Trinity to disclose the heterosexual construction of religious reality which excludes people and sacralises ideology in theology.

A refusal to conversion

A characteristic of this act of disbelief is that the rebellious subject refuses to form a new (imposed) identity. She does not convert but remains stubbornly firm in what she is or has become, independently of any theological colonial claim upon her soul. Therefore, Queer people may commit a capital (or capitalist?) sin of refusing to join the market of salvation by remaining in a state of disbelieving heterosexual claims upon her identity or converting to the gospel of corporations. Conversion has been a colonial and neo-colonial enterprise in which globalisation still partakes. Religious conversion when imposing an absolute does not give space for options. That option, according to Segundo, is the space of hell.

Outside salvation

Hell is not limbo, but it does have one feature in common, already discussed: in neither of these spaces do people require salvation. God is notoriously absent from both, but if it is true that in limbo no one misses God (since the innocents there do not know God anyway) and in hell God is not missed as an option, then these spaces share the commonality of independence from salvation. Therefore, both in limbo as in hell we are confronted with alternatives to salvation. Salvation, in the *imaginaire* of limbo, challenges colonial holiness by embracing distanciation and autonomy over sameness and dependence from neo-colonial models of grace. Hell becomes a radical option against the grace of the system, especially against the body-grace of the heterosexual system which pervades church and theology. Salvation becomes a Queer space of grace when it includes options, responsibilities and dialogue.

The point is that the imaginary of hell is part of a sophisticated body theology related to the dynamics of inclusion and exclusion of bodies by the designation of bodies as proper or improper (Segundo 1997: 26). The corporal signs of punishment in the construction of hell are unmistakable. Teeth clenching denotes anguish, fear, coldness and also tears (Matthew 13:40–42). Also the way people present their bodies may exclude or include them into this *imaginaire* of hell. For instance, how people dress in the parable of the wedding (Matthew 22:13) is indicative of the possibility of the exclusion of bodies from grace. While Christianity may claim that there will not be sex in heaven, thus presenting us with the idea of the disembodied imaginary of holiness, in hell by comparison everything is related to bodies. There may be no-body in heaven, but there will certainly be some-body in hell. How can we provide the common understanding of hell with an alternative reading, based on eschatology and ideology which includes the possibility of a mature dissent from what is metaphorically represented here, that is, a theology of body-exclusion? We may recall at this point a dialogue on holiness between Dietrich Bonhoeffer and a young pastor. In a letter which Bonhoeffer sent to his friend, Eberhard Bethge (Tamayo Acosta 2001), he records that while the pastor claimed that his greatest desire in life was to become a saint, Bonhoeffer replied that for his part he wanted to learn to believe, adding that only by living life to the full would an outcome be achieved. However, learning to believe also requires an active dialogue with the imaginary of hell by confronting and creating dissent, by contradicting the political and sexual ideologies pervading Christian discourse. Hell becomes an option and a Queer one at that when it is a deliberate option for refusing to participate in the divine theodicy of a patriarchal God within the law, but outside justice.

What we need to realise is that the imaginary of hell conforms to a judicial and political type of thought which defines holiness by default. In this we may find an echo of Sade's novels, because Sadean literature has much more to do with the tyranny of laws and the role of institutions than with just sexuality (Del Campo 2001: 2). Queer holiness constitutes holiness by a process of decolonisation of sexual thought in theology and also challenges understandings of law and society, including ecclesiology. The interesting thing is that from libertine epistemologies such as that of Sade, we can consider Queer holiness to be a privileged space for the envisioning of a new ecclesiology; it is the space where the decolonisation and unmasking of ideology happens.

Sade and holiness

Tyrants are seldom born in anarchism; one can only see them standing up at the shadows of the law, or basing themselves in the law. This constitutes the essence of Sadean thought: its hate for tyrants ...
(Deleuze 1969: 78)

Yet another effort, Frenchmen, if you would become republicans.
(Sade 1991: 296)

... From Cain to Christ, it is then the same sign ending with a Man on a cross, 'without sexual love, without property, without country, without complaining, without a job, dying voluntarily and personifying the idea of humanity.'

(Deleuze 2001: 14)

In his study on Sade, Deleuze focusses on a point which is important for our discussion, the crucial anti-language of Sade which transgresses the symbolics of tyranny. Emiliano del Campo, in an article on Masoch and Sade, emphasises how abhorrent 'the shadows of law' are for Sadean characters (Del Campo 2001: 2). This is part of the moral Sadean way of thinking, constructed like mirrors which reflect the magnitude of the oppression of the law by portraying the magnitude of the transgression necessary to eliminate it. It is precisely the imposing magnitude of the force of the law which keeps Sade attempting in vain to perform the ultimate, definitive transgression which will put an end to the moral legitimacy of a tyrant God and a tyrant state. As Deleuze points out, without this understanding we cannot comprehend the principle of the Sadean negation, which is the process of total destruction and disorder necessary to start a new order (Del Campo 2001: 8). There is Queer irony and humour in Sade and a desire to remove the yoke of the law which is unlimited. For Sade, the expression of passions is contained and limited while the law is the opposite. However, to destroy the law (in this Queer search for Sadean justice, where law and justice are somehow indistinguishable) Sade needs to go radically outside the nature of the law and that leads him to the path of 'absolute' transgression. The point for us is to reflect theologically on how 'Queer' represents precisely the transgression of the law and how this is related to holiness. In reality Queer people live lives which are as innocent, more or less, as any other person in this world, but by a process of heterosexual fencing and displacement they have been subjected to a high body theology of transgression. As women's bodies have historically represented virtues (such as the Statue of Liberty, Christian faith or the portrayal of nations and their freedom), Queers embody the ultimate trespass in theology. Therefore Queer lives, lived in justice even if outside the law, function as a Sadean mirror by denouncing the inflexibility and the injustice of the heterosexual divine law in the church by the excess of the exclusion suffered. However, Queer holiness does not live in the shadow of the law, but on the contrary, is independent of it. Queer holiness has a pedagogic role to play in church and in society. In an article published in a Buenos Aires newspaper, Dr Armando Bauleo, writing about the mothers of Plaza de Mayo, uses the concept of *Contrainstitución* (counter-institution) (Del Campo 2001: 2). Such a counter-institution (here the mothers in their fight for justice against the disappearances in Argentina during the 1970s) has a function in the systematic denunciation and examination of the issues arising from the ideology of normality in society. Queer just people also function as a counter-institution of holiness, denouncing the legal (hetero)theological ethos of sainthood and the need to transgress the body/soul split in

theology by the same Sadean Queer devices in fictional literature. At this point
we need to remember that Sadean literature is also religious literature, even if in
a highly transgressive mode. As Deleuze says, there is a power higher than the
law for Sade (Deleuze 1969: 77). That higher or superior power which Sade
struggles to unveil by the systematic destruction and disordering of clericalism
and the law in his writing is a material, Queer foundation. That foundation is as
follows. For Sade, the law is reversed in its Platonism by finding a new superior
principle which does not partake of the ideal of the law. This is, by the way, a
sophisticated post-colonial way of thinking which radically departs from the
roots or foundation of an idea which has pervaded the life of institutions by theological assumptions. This is the equivalent of saying that, for instance,
non-violence as a concept still partakes of a conceptual framework of understanding violence, because of the dependence of the negative form on that which
is to be negated. Therefore Sade's bisexual way of thinking also constitutes a
break with thinking in terms of a superior power or foundation above the law.
Sade does this through a path of high, shocking transgression because, literally
speaking, it may be the only way to convey the reversal of the law. Now it is a
materiality which imposes itself over Platonism and also a reversal and disorder of
unjust laws (or, in a Kantian expression, The Law) (Deleuze 1969: 75).

Del Campo further elaborates upon this dramatic disorder pattern of reflection in Sade (following Deleuze) by saying that the 'Sadean pure negation' desire
is an impossible utopia. Sadean ethics searches for a foundation outside any legal
system and that is the reason why negative processes are portrayed by Sade in
reverse, as positive ones. That is also what materialist and liberationist theologies
do when they claim that holiness is made by actions of social justice in our lives,
or what feminists do when Feminist Theologies refuse to give more theological
credit to the soul than to the body. In a sense that way of total negation and
impossible utopias is already amongst us and does not constitute a novelty.
However, Queer Theologies might carry this even further by saying that Queer
holiness is based upon the ultimate negation of heterosexual thought (and its
vast implications) and therefore that it shares the Sadean desire to find the Queer
God in the ultimate act of God's self transgression in Christ, or in a kenosis of
Christ from heterosexual closets. Thus the Deleuze quotation on Christ dying
without sexual love and property and by his own will provides us with hints of
the act of total negation of God in Christ. All the laws are negated, including the
law of contractual sexuality, that is, marriage, and therefore Jesus died without a
recognised or publicly 'out' sexual love. Christ's crucifixion is Queer and as such
a divine gesture of a Queer God.

The Queer way of holiness implies colonial mobilisations such as in the
movement of ultimate negation, anticipated somehow by the theology of limbo
and re-appropriated in a queer reading of hell as a space of options. It also partakes of Queer strategies of social holiness, manifested through irony and
humour, good examples of which are the Sisters of Perpetual Indulgence
Worldwide or the camp creativity in the political demonstrations of lesbi-gay,

bisexual and transgender communities. I have seen people in Edinburgh demonstrating with badges saying 'Bisexuals for Biodiversity' and 'Transsexuals against Transnationals'. Through their humour and irony, they demonstrate a kind of way of transcendence of the just Queers, which is one of high political and sexual dissent: it also comes from a love of pleasure. There are many forms of political and theological aspiration written from the body of the excluded. Amongst Christians, Queer metaphors like these may express the truth of searching for a Bi/Christ as a Christ for diversity, for instance, or a Transsexual Christ who might also be opposed to transnational corporations. But what we have here in essence is how Queer holiness finds God, as a stranger at the gates of Hegemonic Theology, amongst loving expressions of relationships at the margins of the defined decent and proper in Christianity. Indecent love becomes pedagogic because it teaches the difference between the church as a heterosexual colony (or neo-colony) and the church as the Queer *Kingdom* where the love which exceeds institutions (as God exceeds Godself in Christ and in the Trinity) knows more and knows better about alternative projects for justice and peace.

And the beauty of this is that the Queer God, calling us towards a life of Queer holiness, has been coming out for a long time, in bisexual towns of Latin America, in the *Soq'a* theology of sexual affairs and also amongst the social excluded living in the slums of Buenos Aires. From the love/knowledge of transvestites gathering in economic solidarity in boarding houses of Argentina to the Sisters of Perpetual Indulgence and their camp high calling to sainthood through actions of compassion, the Queer God – fluid and unstable as ourselves, but also laughing and taking pleasure while pursuing a divine destiny of the kind of transgressive justice which disorders the law – comes in glory and in resurrection. The Queer nation of the world represents in this way the second coming of God the Stranger. Curiously, it seems that we can know God better through a radical negation of the way of closeted knowing found in the tradition of the church and theology. This is the Queer, stranger God who in our time and age is showing God's face amongst people who are God's lovers – and Queer lovers at that.

NOTES

INTRODUCTION

1 See Kathy Acker's *Great Expectations* (New York: Grove, 1982) and *My Death My Life* by Pier Paolo Pasolini in *Literal Madness: Three Novels* (New York: Grove, 1989).

1 KNEELING

1 In this context I am using the term 'Indecent Theology' to refer to a Queer Theology whose hermeneutical circle is informed by Latin American Liberation Theology and therefore is based on a political praxis of liberation. I use the concept of 'indecency' because the axis of decency/indecency is constitutive of the regulation of the order of society in my own country, Argentina, and especially for women.

2 For theological reflections on the environment and the responsibility that patriarchal Christian theology carries for nature's destruction see for instance Lynn White's influential article 'The Historical Roots of our Ecological Crisis' (White 1967). White's thesis is that human ecology is deeply dependent of our religious worldview, and in the case of Christianity, an androcentric worldview has created hierachical thought, dominion of women and nature and selfish attitudes towards the environment.

3 Robert Goss refers to theological Queer reflections in term of 'accessorising' theology. That is, adding elements while leaving others temporarily aside to reflect the contextuality of Queer theologies (Goss 2002).

4 In this book we will refer sometimes to T-Theology as theology as ideology, that is, a totalitarian construction of what is considered as 'The One and Only Theology' which does not admit discussion or challenges from different perspectives, especially in the area of sexual identity and its close relationship with political and racial issues. It represents the Law of the Father-without-a-body of Lacan in theology (Marini 1992: 173). The use of terms such as North Atlantic Theologies or Third World Theologies lack accuracy, and the same can be said of terms such as Feminist Theologies or Political Theologies because they all may be repeating the Law of the Father in their theological reflection, even if using political or postcolonial or even gender analysis, by not disarticulating the relation between the construction of sexuality and systematic theology in depth.

5 The work done by theologians such as Elizabeth Stuart in *Just Good Friends* (1995); *Spitting at Dragons* (1996); Mark Jordan, *The Invention of Sodomy in Christian Theology* (1997) or Ken Stone on Queer hermeneutics in his *Queer Commentary and the Hebrew Bible* (2001) are good examples of the work being done in queering church traditions.

6 For these reflections I am following M. E. Wiesner-Hanks's insightful study on sexuality in Latin America after the conquest in the fifteenth century (Wiesner-Hanks 2000).

7 A few years ago, during a trip to Buenos Aires, I witnessed the discussions generated by the Roman Catholic Church's acceptance of people receiving the Eucharist standing up, instead of kneeling at the altar. A small street demonstration was organised and posters were pasted on walls and lamp-posts, urging people not to accept the Eucharist unless kneeling in front of the priest, under the risk of committing sacrilege.

8 People who were forced to leave their country under political persecution usually feel their exile as an interruption of their lives. It is common amongst exiled people to tell each other stories, as confessions of their past lives, in an attempt to reintegrate their lives. A confessional form of speech is not only common amongst the exiled but also amongst non-heterosexuals and heterosexuals out of the closet. These are confessions of pain and perplexity and they are part of the process and discourses of 'coming out'.

2 QUEERING HERMENEUTICS

1 'Sexual story-telling' is a part of the methodology of Sexual Theologies. For an undestanding of how it works see for instance my book *Indecent Theology* (Althaus-Reid 2000) especially the chapter 'The Theology of Sexual Stories'. For other examples see Robert Goss's theological reflection in *Queering Christ: Beyond Jesus Acted Up* (Goss 2002), Lisa Isherwood's *Liberating Christ* (Isherwood 1999) and Elizabeth Stuart's *Gay and Lesbian Theologies* (Stuart 2002) for critical assessments of the method.

2 For a comment on Lacoste's kenotical project see Graham Ward's article 'Kenosis and Naming' in Paul Heelas *Religion, Modernity and Postmodernity* (Ward 1998).

3 The concept of 'dirty' is also related to class ideology and issues of marginalisation. The metaphors of 'dirty work' have many debts to early industrial capitalism, where 'dirt' became a category related to the undervaluation of the body, manifested for instance in the sweat and smells of the body of the worker (Law 1994: 216).

4 I am using the concept of 'per/version' in the sense of choosing different (and not necessarily approved) methodological 'versions' or options in the way one does theology.

3 QUEERING GOD IN RELATIONSHIPS

1 Graham Ward considers that the kenosis discussion is at the centre of different forms of postmodern theologies (see Ward 1998: 233–58). For other Queer reflections on the Trinity see, for instance, Elizabeth Stuart's *Just Good Friends* (1995) where the Trinity is understood in terms of friendship and community.

2 For this point see for instance my article 'Grace and the Other: A Postcolonial Reflection on Ideology and Doctrinal Systems' (Althaus-Reid 2000a: 63–73).

3 I am referring here to the processes of codifications and de-codifications which are part of the conscientisation work pioneered in Latin America by the late Paulo Freire (Freire 1993).

4 *Amigovios* is a term used in Argentina for non-exclusive friendships which may include sexual relationships (Althaus-Reid 2000: 144).

4 LIBERTINE DISCLOSURES

1 Numerous articles have been written on the influence of Emmanuel Levinas in Liberation Theology, especially in the development of the category of the culturally and politically marginalised or 'ultimate others' of the continent. Amongst the Latin American liberationists who have been inspired by Levinas we need to mention Juan Scannone, Daniel Guillot and Enrique Dussel. These three coincide by critically assessing the work of Levinas as de-contextualised and lacking concreteness. Dussel and Guillot, for instance, accuse Levinas of not being able to see the Other as a poor Latin American or African person. For Dussel, the poor in Levinas does not rebel or

articulate a political position of liberation, and lacks agency. This is in a sense an ide-alised Other, condemmed to remain outside history (Dussel and Guillot 1975: 8). In the developing of the Queer Other, it is important to use concrete categories of exclusion, including sexual categories.

2   For this point and an attempt to produce a counter argument, see Daphne Hampson's 'On Autonomy and Heteronomy' (Hampson 1996: 5–6).

3   For an interesting discussion on lesbian thought and heterosexual authoritarian pat-terns in some understandings of lesbianism, see for instance Tamsin Wilton's argument in *Finger-Licking Good: The Ins and Outs of Lesbian Sex* (Wilton 1996). Wilton challenges what she calls the mentality of sex policing in lesbian communities and the politics of who is really a good lesbian or not, while arguing for unity between the Queer and the lesbian community around issues of sexual and social justice.

4   Leonardo Boff in his work on the Trinity mentions the symbolic but perhaps unnec-essary function of the number three; he carries this argument especially when arguing about the presence of the Virgin Mary in the Trinity (Boff 1988: 103). Also, although in a different line of argumentation, Nicolas Lash has asked what sort of three are included in the Trinitarian discussions (for instance, persons or relation-ships?) (Cunningham 1998: 28–9).

5 PERMUTATIONS

1   For this point concerning the Hebrew roots related to the concept of oppression see for instance Thomas Hanks, *God so Loved the Third World: The Bible, The Reformation and Liberation Theologies* (Hanks 1984: 31).

2   For a discussion on the differences between identity and behaviour see Jeffrey Weeks *Invented Moralities* (1995: 29–34).

3   Hood and Crowley, in their introduction to *Marquis de Sade for Beginners* (1995: 3), mention the fact that Sade's novels are still catalogued in the British Library on the 'special category' shelves. That means that any reader who would like to read any novel from Sade in the British Library will be assigned a seat in a certain part of the library, under the vigilance of a member of the staff.

4   According to Quell and Stauffer (1949) several words conveying the meaning of 'love' in the Hebrew Scriptures are suggestive of passionate relationships. So they claim that the word for love in the Scriptures is rooted 'in sex life' and that 'love means such a strong expression of personal life that even when the word is used in connection with things there is a suggestion of passion …' (p.3). The meaning of love from the New Testament, as Agape, revolves around fraternal love and mutual respect and sympathy in relation to the call to become a Christian and be saved (p.65). From that perspective, love in the Hebrew Scriptures remains somehow a more promiscu-ous category which in the New Testament is under the law of salvation and therefore more discriminatory.

6 THE ECONOMY OF GOD'S EXCHANGE RATE MECHANISM

1   During the military dictatorship in Argentina, political women and dissidents such as the mothers of Plaza de Mayo were called 'the mad women of Plaza de Mayo' (*las locas de Plaza de Mayo*).

2   See David Foster *Sexual Textualities: Essays on Queer/ing Latin American Writing* (Foster 1997: 50). I also consider 'No Brilliance Whatsoever' as a more proper ren-dering of the title of Hilst's book *Rútilo Nada* (Hilst 1993).

3   On *Madame Edwarda*, see my article 'Indecent Exposures: Excessive Sex and the Crisis of Theological Representation' in L. Isherwood (ed.) *The Good News of the Body* (Althaus-Reid 2000b).

4   For this point on bartering theology, see my article 'Grace and the Other' in *Concilium* (Althaus-Reid 2000a).

5   Quell and Stauffer mention the relation between the noun *rehem* (womb) and its abstract plural *rah^amin* (sympathy towards those in need and a way to express the love of God) as obscure, although the word Rahum in the Scriptures (merciful) applies exclusively to God (Quell and Stauffer 1949: 1).

6   The words 'lord' and 'mister' are translated in Spanish with the same word *señor*. *Señor* is the respectful way to address a man, irrespective of his social status. In Castilian Spanish, Lords or peasants receive the same address as *señores*.

7 POPULAR ANTI-THEOLOGIES OF LOVE

1   *Ayllus* are the ancient, traditional communities of the Incas. They were based on a co-operative system in which people had a common territory and were linked by familial, religious, linguistic and geographical links. It is calculated that an *Ayllu* comprises around 300 people. The Andean people have fought for centuries for their right to keep them and there are still around 5,000 *ayllus* in Perú today.

8 DEMONOLOGY

1   See for instance J. Comblin *The Church and the National Security State* (Comblin 1979). Frank Graziano's book *Divine Violence* (Graziano 1992) provides a very detailed and sophisticated analysis of the links between sexuality, Christianity and political persecution in Argentina.

2   Post-colonial theology has already considered the complex relations organised around Christianity in continents at the receiving end of the missions. Sugirtharajah claims that biblical hermeneutics was negotiated between colonisers and colonised in a way which blurred divisions. In that sense, the boundaries of redeemers and redemptors was also blurred. See for instance Sugirtharajah 2001.

9 QUEER HOLINESS

1   Moctezuma replied to Cortés's demands on believing the Christian creed and the Scriptural account of Creation with the following words:

> My lord Malinche ... I understand what you said to my ambassadors on the sandhills about the three gods and the cross, also what you preached in the various towns through which you passed. We have given you no answer, since we have worshipped our own gods here from the beginning and know them to be good. No doubt yours are good also, but do not trouble to tell us any-more about them at present. Regarding the creation of the world, we have held the same belief for many ages ...
>
> (Díaz 1963: 222–3)

2   Batuque or Macumba refer to the samba rhythm provided by the use of drums in Umbanda and Candomblé worship and to the dynamic of liturgical worship, dances and songs created by their rhythm.

BIBLIOGRAPHY

Acker, K. (1982) *Great Expectations*, New York: Grove Press.
—— (1988) *Empire of the Senseless*, New York: Grove Press.
—— (1989) *Literal Madness: Three Novels*, New York: Grove Press
Agamben, G. (1998) *The Coming Community*, trans. M. Hardt, Minneapolis: University of Minnesota Press.
—— (1999) *Potentialities. Collected Essays in Philosophy*, Stanford: Stanford University Press.
Alarcón, C. (2001) 'Informe Especial: El Asesinato de Chicos Rateros' in *Página 12*, published online <http://www.pagina12.com.ar/2001/01-05-06/pag19.html>
Allison, D., Roberts, M. and Weiss, A. (1995) (eds) *Sade and the Narrative of Transgression*, Cambridge: Cambridge University Press.
Althaus-Reid, M. M. (1998) 'The Hermeneutics of Transgression: Time and the Children of the Streets in Buenos Aires' in G. de Schijver (ed.) *Liberation Theologies on Shifting Grounds: A Clash of Socio-Economic and Cultural Paradigms*, Leuven: Leuven University Press.
—— (2000) *Indecent Theology. Theological Perversions in Sex, Gender and Politics*, London: Routledge.
—— (2000a) 'Grace and the Other: A Postcolonial Reflection on Ideology and Doctrinal Systems, *Concilium*, 4, 63–73.
—— (2000b) 'Indecent Exposures: Excessive Sex and the Crisis of Theological Representation' in L. Isherwood (ed.) *The Good News of the Body. Sexual Theology and Feminism*, Sheffield: Sheffield Academic Press.
Amin, S. (2000) *Capitalism in the Age of Globalization*, London: Zed.
Andahazi, F. (1999) *The Anatomist*, London: Anchor.
Azcarate, A. (1960) *Misal Diario para América*, Buenos Aires: Editorial Guadalupe.
Barthes, R. (1971) *Sade/Fourier/Loyola*, Berkeley: University of California Press.
Bataille, G. (1967) *La Part Maudite*, Paris: Editions de Minuit.
—— (1971) *Ouvres Complètes*, vol. 3, Thadeé Klossowski (ed.), Paris: Gallimard.
—— (1987) *Eroticism*, London: Marion Boyars.
——(1995) *My Mother, Madame Edwarda, The Dead Man*, New York: Marion Boyars.
—— (1995a) 'The Use Value of D. A. F. Sade (An open letter to my current comrades)' in D. Allison, M. Roberts and A. Weiss (1995) (eds) *Sade and the Narrative of Transgression*, Cambridge: Cambridge University Press.
Baudrillard, J. (1996) 'The Map Precedes the Territory' in W. Anderson (ed.) *The Fontana Post-Modernism Reader*, London: Fontana Press.
Bennington, G. (1995) 'Introduction to Economy I' in C. Gil (ed.) *Bataille. Writing the Sacred*, London: Routledge.
Bernstein, C. and Politi, M. (1996) *His Holiness. John Paul II and the Hidden History of Our Time*, London: Bantam Books.

Berry, P. (1998) 'Kristeva's Feminist Refiguring of the Gift' in P. Blond (ed.) *Post-Secular Philosophy: Between Philosophy and Theology*, London: Routledge.

Bloch, M. and Guggenheim, S. (1981) 'Compadrazgo, Baptism and the Symbolism of a Second Birth', *Man* (NS) 16: 376–86.

Blond, P. (ed.) (1998) *Post-Secular Philosophy: Between Philosophy and Theology*, London: Routledge.

Boff, L. (1988) *Trinity and Society*, New York: Orbis.

Bogue, R. (1989) *Deleuze and Guattari*, London: Routledge.

Bohache, T. (2000), ' "To Cut or not to Cut?" Is Compulsory Heterosexuality a Prerequisite for Christianity?' in R. Goss and M. West (eds) *Take Back the Word: A Queer Reading of the Bible*, Cleveland: The Pilgrim Press.

Bordieu, P. (1997) 'Marginalia- Some Additional Notes on the Gift' in A. Schrift (ed.) *The Logic of the Gift: Toward an Ethic of Generosity*, London: Routledge.

Bristow, J. and Wilson, A. (eds) (1993) *Activating Theory: Lesbian, Gay, Bisexual Politics*, London: Lawrence and Wishart.

Bryden, M. (ed.) (2001) *Deleuze and Religion*, London: Routledge.

Buchanan, I. (2000) 'Introduction' in G. Ward (ed.) *The Certeau Reader*, London: Blackwell.

Butler, J. (1990) *Gender Trouble: Feminism and the Subversion of Identity*, London: Routledge.

——(1993) *Bodies that Matter: On the Discursive Limits of 'Sex'*, London: Routledge.

Califia, P. and Campbell, D. (1997) (eds) *Bitch Goddess: The Spiritual Path of the Dominant Woman*, San Francisco: Greenery Press.

Campbell, J. (2000) *Arguing with the Phallus: Feminist, Queer and Postcolonial Theory. A Psychoanalitic Contribution*, London: Zed.

Camps Cruell, C. (1994) 'Las Dimensiones del Espíritu y los Diseños de Nuestra Creatividad', *Cristianismo y Sociedad*, no. 120: 37–51.

Cano, G., Neufeldt, K., Schulze, H. *et al.* (1981) *Los Nuevos Conquistadores. El Instituto Lingüístico de Verano en América Latina*, Quito: CEDIS/FENOC.

Caputo, J. (1997) *Deconstruction in a Nutshell: A Conversation with Jacques Derrida*, New York: Fordham.

Cardenal, E. (1995) *The Doubtful Strait/El Estrecho Dudoso*, trans. J. Lyons, Bloomington and Indianapolis: Indiana University Press.

Carrette, J. (2000) *Foucault and Religion: Spiritual Corporality and Political Spirituality*, London: Routledge.

Carter Heyward, I. (1989) *Touching Our Strength: The Erotic as Power and the Love of God*, San Francisco: Harper and Row.

——(1995) *Staying Power: Reflections on Gender, Justice and Compassion*, Cleveland: The Pilgrim Press.

Cixous, H. (1981) 'The Laugh of the Medusa' in E. Marks and I. de Courtivron (eds) *New French Feminism: An Anthology*, Brighton: Harvester.

—— (1994) 'Extreme Fidelity' in S. Sellers (ed) *The Hélène Cixous Reader*, London: Routledge.

Cixous, H. (1997) 'Sorties: Out and Out: Attacks: Ways Out: Forays' in A. Schrift (ed.) *The Logic of the Gift: Toward an Ethic of Generosity*, London: Routledge.

Cixous, H. and Clément, C. (1994) 'The Newly Born Woman' in S. Sellers (ed.) *The Hélène Cixous Reader*, London: Routledge.

Clarkson, J., Edwards, J., Kelly, W. and Welch, J. (eds) (1973) 'Encyclical Miserentissimus Redemptor' in *The Church Teaches: Documents of the Church in English Translation*, Rockford: Tan Books and Publishers Inc.

Coakley, S. (1996) 'Kenosis: A Subversion' in D. Hampson (ed.) *Swallowing a Fish Bone? Feminist Theologians Debate Christianity*, London: SPCK.

Collier, R. (1999) 'Men, Heterosexuality and the Changing Family (re) Constructing Fatherhood in Law and Social Policy' in G. Jagger and C. Wright (eds) *Changing Family Values*, London: Routledge.

Comblin, J. (1979) *The Church and the National Security State*, New York: Orbis.

Croatto, J. S. (1984) *Hermenéutica Bíblica*, Buenos Aires: La Aurora.

Crocker, W. (1974) 'Extramarital Sexual Practices of the Ramkokamekra-Canela Indians: an Analysis of Socio-Cultural factors' in P. Lyon (ed.) *Native South Americans: Ethnology of the Least Known Continent*, Boston: Little, Brown and Co.

Cunningham, D. S. (1998) *These Three are One. The Practice of Trinitarian Theology*, London: Blackwell.

de Certeau, M. (2000) 'Walking in the City' in G. Ward *The Certeau Reader*, London: Blackwell.

Del Campo, E. (2001) 'Deleuze: Presentación de Masoch con Sade', published online <http://www.acheronta.org/acheronta12/deleuze.html>

Deleuze, G. (1969) *Sacher Masoch and Sade*, Córdoba: Editorial Universitaria de Córdoba.

—— (1989) *Masochism: Coldness and Cruelty: Venus in Furs*, New York: Zone Books.

—— (1994) *Difference and Repetition*, London: The Athlone Press.

—— (1997) *Essays Critical and Clinical*, Minneapolis: The University of Minnesota Press.

—— (2001) *The Logic of Sense*, London: The Athlone Press.

Deleuze, G. and Guattari, F. (1976) *Rhizome: Introduction*, Paris: Minuit.

—— (1987) *A Thousand Plateaus: Capitalism and Schizophrenia*, Minneapolis: University of Minnesota Press.

—— (1990) *Anti-Oedipus. Capitalism and Schizophrenia*, London: The Athlone Press.

—— (1994) *What is Philosophy?* New York: Verso.

Derrida, J. (1977) *Of Grammatology*, Baltimore/London: The John Hopkins University Press.

—— (1981) *Disseminations*, Chicago: University of Chicago Press.

—— (1998) *Monolingualism of the Other or The Prosthesis of Origin*, Stanford: Stanford University Press.

—— (2002) 'Force of Law. The 'Mystical Foundation of Authority' in J. Derrida *Acts of Religion* (ed. and with an introduction by G. Anidjar), London: Routledge.

Díaz, B. del Castillo (1963) *The Conquest of New Spain*, London: Penguin Books.

Diprose, R. (1994) *The Bodies of Women: Ethics, Embodiment and Sexual Difference*, London: Routledge.

Dolar, M. (1994) 'La Femme-Machine', *Lacan and Love*, New Formations, 23, Summer 1994: 43–55.

Dowell, S. (1990) *They Two Shall Be One: Monogamy in History and Religion*, London: Collins Flame.

Drucker, P. (1996) 'In the Tropics There is no Sin. Sexuality and Gay-Lesbian Movements in the Third World', *New Left Review*, 218: 75–102.

Dussel, E. (1988) *Ethics and Community*, New York: Orbis.

Dussel, E. and Guillot, D. (1975) *Liberación Latinoamericana y Emmanuel Levinas*, Buenos Aires: La Aurora.

Eadie, J. (1993) 'Activating Bisexuality: Towards a Bi/Sexual Politics' in J. Bristow and A. Wilson (eds) *Activating Theory: Lesbian, Gay, Bisexual Politics*, London: Lawrence and Wishart.

Fioravanti, A. (1973) 'Reciprocidad y Economía de Mercado', *Allpanchis* v: 121–31.

Flores Ochoa, J. (1973) 'La Viuda y el Hijo del Soq'a Machu', *Allpanchis*, v: 45–57.

Foster, D. W. (1997) *Sexual Textualities: Essays on Queer/ing Latin American Writing*, Austin: University of Texas Press.

Foucault, M. (1970) *The Archaeology of Knowledge*, New York: Pantheon.

—— (1973) *The Birth of the Clinic: An Archaeology of Medical Perception*, New York: Vintage Books.

—— (1980) *Power/Knowledge: Selected Interviews and other Writings 1972–1977*, Sussex: Harvester.

Freire, P. (1979) *Pedagogía del Oprimido*, Montevideo: Tierra Nueva.

—— (1993) *Pedagogy of the Oppressed*, London: Penguin.

Freire, P. and Shor, I. (1987) *A Pedagogy of Liberation: Dialogues on Transforming Education*, Basingstoke: Macmillan.

Fry, P. (1977) 'Mediunidade e Sexualidade', *Religião e Sociedade*, May, no. 1: 105–25.

Galeano, E. (2000) *Patas Arriba: La Escuela del Mundo al Revés*, Madrid: Siglo Veintiuno.

Gibbs, R. (2000) *Why Ethics? Signs of Responsibilities*, Princeton: Princeton University Press.

Gibson, W. (1995) *Neuromancer*, London: Voyager.

Gill, C. B. (1995) *Bataille: Writing the Sacred*, London: Routledge.

Godelier, M. (1971) 'Q'est-ce que définir une "formation économique et sociale": L'example des Incas', *La Pensée*, no. 159, October.

Goodchild, P. (2001) 'Why is Philosophy so Compromised with God?' in M. Bryden *Deleuze and Religion*, London: Routledge.

Goss, R. (1993) *Jesus Acted Up: A Gay and Lesbian Manifesto*, New York: Harper Collins.

—— (2002) *Queering Christ: Beyond Jesus Acted Up*, Cleveland: Pilgrim.

Gramsci, A. (1970) *Antología*, Mexico: Siglo XXI.

—— (1974) *Obras Escolhidas*, vol. I, Lisboa: Estampa.

Graziano, F. (1992) *Divine Violence: Spectacle, Psychosexuality and Radical Christianity in the Argentine 'Dirty War'*, Oxford: Westview Press.

Grey, M (1993) *The Wisdom of Fools? Seeking Revelation Today*, London: SPCK.

Gruzinski, S. (1995) *La Guerra de las Imágenes: De Cristóbal Colón a 'Blade Runner'* (1492–2019), Mexico: Fondo de Cultura Económica.

Guattari, F. (1995) *Chaosophy*, New York: Semiotext(e).

Gutiérrez, G. (1987) *On Job: God-talk and the Suffering of the Innocent*, New York: Orbis.

Hampson, D. (1996) 'On Autonomy and Heteronomy' in D. Hampson (ed.) *Swallowing a Fishbone? Feminist Theologians debate Christianity*, London: SPCK.

Hanks, T. (1984) *God so Loved the Third World: The Bible, The Reformation and Liberation Theologies*, New York: Maryknoll.

Hénaff, M. (1999) *Sade: The Invention of the Libertine Body*, Minneapolis: The University of Minnesota Press.

Henkin, W. and Holiday, S. (1996) *Consensual Sadomasochism*, San Francisco: Daedalus.

Herzfeld, M. (1997) *Cultural Intimacy: Social Poetics in the Nation-State*, London: Routledge.

Hilst, H. (2001) 'Poem', published online. <http://angelfire.com/ri/casadoso/hhilst.html>

—— (1993) *Rútilo Nada: A Obscena Senhora D. Qadós*, Campinhas: Pontes.

Hitchcock, P. (1999) *Oscillate Wildly: Space, Body and Spirit of Millennial Materialism*, Minneapolis: University of Minnesota Press.

Hood, S. and Crowley, G. (1995) *Marquis de Sade for Beginners*, Cambridge: Icon Books.

Hunt, E. K. (1990) *Property and Prophets: The Evolution of Economic Institutions and Ideologies*, New York: Harper & Row.

Irigaray, L. (1980) 'This Sex Which is not One' in E. Marks and I. de Courtivron (eds) *New French Feminisms,* Brighton: Harvester.

—— (1997) 'Women on the Market' in A. Schrift (ed.) *The Logic of the Gift: Toward an Ethic of Generosity*, London: Routledge.

Isherwood, L. (1999) *Liberating Christ: Exploring the Christologies of Contemporary Liberation Movements*, Cleveland: Pilgrim Press.

Jordan, M. (1997) *The Invention of Sodomy in Christian Theology*, Chicago: Chicago University Press.

Jagose, A. (1996) *Queer Theory: An Introduction*, New York: New York University Press.

Judit (1994) 'Border Conflict' in J. Ramos, *Compañeras: Latina Lesbians*, New York: Routledge.

Kairos Central America (1988), New York: Circus.

Katz, J. (1983) *Gay/Lesbian Almanac: A New Documentary*, New York: Harper & Row.

Klein, N. (2001) *No Logo*, London: Flamingo.

Klossowski, P. (1989) *Roberte Ce Soir and The Revocation of the Edict of Nantes: Two Novels*, trans. A. Wainhouse, New York: Marion Boyars.

179

—— (1995) 'Sade, or the Philosopher-Villain' in D. Allison, M. Roberts and A.Weiss (eds) *Sade and the Narrative of Transgression*, Cambridge: Cambridge University Press.

Küng, H. (ed.) (1996) *Yes to a Global Ethic*, London: SCM.

—— (2001) 'Thinking Big. R. McCloughry talks to Professor Hans Küng', *Third Way Magazine*, vol. 24, no. 1:18–21.

Lacoste, J.-Y. (1994) *Expérience et Absolu*, Paris: Presses Universitaires de France.

Lala, M. C. (1995) 'The Hatred of Poetry in Georges Bataille's Writing and Thought' in C. Gill (ed.) *Bataille: Writing the Sacred*, London: Routledge.

Lancaster, R. and di Leonardo, M. (eds) (1997) *The Gender Sexuality Reader*, London: Routledge.

Land, N. (1992) *The Thirst for Annihilation: Georges Bataille and Virulent Nihilism*, London: Routledge.

Lara, J. (1960) *Poesía Popular Quechua*, Cochabamba: Canata.

Law, G. (1994) 'Confessions of a Complete Scopophiliac' in P. Gibson and R.Gibson (eds) *Dirty Looks: Women, Pornography and Power*, London: Routledge.

Lerner, G. (1986) *The Creation of Patriarchy*, Oxford: Oxford University Press.

Long, D. Stephen (2000) *Divine Economy*, London: Routledge.

Lukács, G. (1972) *Tactics and Ethics*, trans. M. McColgan, New York: Harper & Row.

Lyotard, J.-F. (1997) *The Postmodern Condition: A Report on Knowledge*, Manchester: Manchester University Press.

MacCannell, J. F. (1994) 'Love Outside the Limits of the Law', *Lacan and Love: New Formations*, 23, Summer: 25–43.

Maraschin, J. (1985) Fragmentos das Harmonias e das Dissonâncias do Corpo' (1985), *Estudos de Religião,* 1, March: 193–213.

—— (1986) 'Os Corpos do Povo Pobre', *Estudos de Religião*, 3, March: 27–42.

Marini, M. (1992) *Jacques Lacan: The French Context*, New Brunswick, New Jersey: Rutgers.

Meier, S. (1998) *Alpha Centauri*, Redwood City: Electronic Arts Inc.

Mendoza, P., Montaner, C. and Vargas Llosa, A. (1999) *Fabricantes de Miseria: Las Verdaderas Causas de la Pobreza en el Tercer Mundo*, Barcelona: Plaza & Janés.

Mies, M. (1997) 'Colonization and Housewification' in R. Henessy and C. Ingarham (eds) *Materialist Feminism*, New York: Routledge.

Mitchell, J. (1975) *Psychoanalysis and Feminism*, New York: Vintage.

Moi, T. (1985) *Sexual/Textual Politics: Feminist Literary Theory*, London: Routledge.

Monbiot, G. (2001) 'Stealing Europe', *Guardian*, June 20.

Morris, P. (1993) *Literature and Feminism*, Oxford: Basil Blackwell.

—— (1994) (ed.) *The Bakhtin Reader: Selected Writings of Bakhtin, Medvedev, Voloshinov*, London: Edward Arnold.

Mouffe, C. (ed.) (1996) *Deconstruction and Pragmatism*, London: Routledge.

Mowry LaCugna, C. (1991) *God for Us: The Trinity and Christian Life*, San Francisco: Harper Collins.

Namaste, K. (1996) 'From Performativity to Interpretation: Toward a Social Semiotic Account of Bisexuality' in D. Hall and M. Pramaggiore (eds) *Re Presenting BiSexualities: Subjects and Cultures of Fluid Desires*, New York: New York University Press.

Nin, A. (1977) *Delta of Venus: Erotica*. New York: Harcourt Brace Jovanovich.

Novak, M. (1993) *The Catholic Ethic and the Spirit of Capitalism*, New York: The Free Press.

Nuñez del Prado, B. (1974) 'The Supernatural World of the Quechua of Southern Peru as seen from the Community of Qotobamba' in P. Lyon (ed.) *Native South Americans. Ethnology of the Least Known Continent*, Boston: Little, Brown and Co.

Ortiz, A. (1982) 'Moya: Espacio, Tiempo y Sexo en un Pueblo Andino', *Allpanchis*, vol. xvii, no. 20: 189–208.

Patton, C. and Sánchez-Eppler, B. (2000) (eds) *Queer Diasporas*, Durham and London: Duke University Press.

Péguy, C. (1961) *Oeuvres en Prose*, vol. II, Paris: La Plèiade.

Pérez Aguirre L. (1994) *La Iglesia Increíble: Materias Pendientes para su Tercer Milenio*, Buenos Aires: Lumen.

Pizarnik A. (1965) *Los Trabajos y las Noches*, Buenos Aires: Sudamericana.

—— (1968). *Extracción de la Piedra de la Locura*, Buenos Aires: Sudamericana.

—— (1971) *La Condesa Sangrienta*, Buenos Aires: Acuarius.

—— (1985) *Textos de Sombra y Ultimos Poemas*, Buenos Aires: Sudamericana.

Prior, M. (1997) *Bible and Colonialism: A Moral Critique*, Sheffield: Sheffield Academic Press.

Probyn, E. (1990) 'Travels in the Postmodern: Making Sense of the Local' in L. Nicholson (ed.) *Feminism/Postmodernism*, London: Routledge.

—— (1996) *Outside Belongings*, London: Routledge.

Protevi, J. (2001) 'The Organism as a Judgement of God: Aristotle, Kant and Deleuze on Nature (that is, on biology, theology and politics)' in M. Bryden (ed.) *Deleuze and Religion*, London: Routledge.

Punday, D. (1998) 'Theories of Materiality and Location: Moving Through Kathy Acker's Empire of the Senseless', *Genders 27*, published online <http://www.genders.org>

Quell, G. and Stauffer, F. (1949) *Love*, London: Adam and Charles Black.

Quicaña, F. (1994) 'The Gospel and the Andean Culture' in G. Cook (ed.) *The Changing Face of the Church in Latin America*, Maryknoll: Orbis.

Radford Ruether, R. (1983) *Sexism and God-Talk*, London: SCM.

Ricoeur, P. (1984) 'Paul Ricoeur' in R. Kerney *Dialogues with Contemporary Continental Thinkers: The Phenomenological Heritage*, Manchester: Manchester University Press.

—— (1991) *From Text to Action: Essays in Hermeneutics II*, London: The Athlone Press.

Rivera Cusicanqui, S. (1990) 'Indigenous Women and Community Resistance: History and Memory' in E. Jelin (ed.) *Women and Social Change in Latin America*, London: Zed.

Sade, M. de (1990) Compiled and trans. A. Wainhouse and R. Seaver, *The One Hundred and Twenty Days of Sodom and Other Writings*, London: Arrow Books.

—— (1991) *Three Complete Novels: Justine, Philosophy in the Bedroom, Eugénie De Franval and Other Writings*. A. Wainhouse and R. Seaver (eds), London: Arrows Books.

Sarlo, B. (1994) *Escenas de la Vida Posmoderna: Intelectuales, Arte y Videocultura en la Argentina*, Buenos Aires: Ariel.

Savigliano, M. (1995) *Tango and the Political Economy of Passion*, Oxford: Westview Press.

Sebreli, J. J. (1990) *Buenos Aires, Vida Cotidiana y Alienación*, Buenos Aires: Siglo Veinte.

Sedgwick, E. Kosofsky (1994) *Tendencies*, London: Routledge.

Segundo, J. L. (1997). *El Infierno: Un Diálogo con Karl Rahner*, Buenos Aires: Trilce.

Sobrino, J. (1992) *Reflecciones sobre la Decisión de Leonardo Boff*, Santander: Sal Terrae.

Spivak, G. (1996) 'Explanation and Culture: Marginalia' in D. Landry and G. MacLean (eds) *The Spivak Reader*, London: Routledge.

Stoekl, A. (1995) 'Recognition in Madame Edwarda' in C.B. Gill (ed.) *Bataille: Writing the Sacred*, London: Routledge.

Stoler, A. (1997) 'Carnal Knowledge and Imperial Power' in R. Lancaster and M. di Leonardo (eds) *The Gender Sexuality Reader*, London: Routledge.

Stone, K. (ed.) (2001) *Queer Commentary and the Hebrew Bible*, Sheffield: Sheffield Academic Press.

Stuart, E. (1995) *Just Good Friends: Towards a Lesbian and Gay Theology of Friendship*, London: Mowbray.

—— (1996) *Spitting at Dragons: Towards a Feminist Theology of Sainthood*, London: Mowbray.

—— (2002) *Gay and Lesbian Theologies: Repetitions with Critical Difference*, London: Ashgate.

Sugirtharajah, R. S. (2001) *The Bible in the Third World: Pre-colonial, Colonial and Postcolonial Encounters*, Cambridge: Cambridge University Press.

Symons, A. (ed.) (1898) *The Confessions of St Augustine*, London and Newcastle-On-Tyne: The Walter Scott Publishing Co.

Tamayo Acosta, J. J. (2001) '*¿Hay Razones para Creer?*', published online <http://www.uca.edu.ni/koinonia/logos/logos077.htm>

Tolbert, M. A. (2000) 'Foreword' in R. Goss and M. West (eds) *Take Back the Word: A Queer Reading of the Bible*, Cleveland: the Pilgrim Press.

Trible, P. (1987) *God and the Rhetoric of Sexuality*, Philadelphia: Fortress Press.

Vargas, C. (2000) 'Chavela Vargas. No Tengo de qué Avergonzarme' por Rosa Pereda, *El Pais*, 5 November: 14–27.

Vargas Llosa, M. (1996) *La Utopía Arcaica: José María Arguedas y las Ficciones del Indigenismo*, Mexico: Fondo de Cultura Económica.

Vega, B. (1994) '¿Adónde está la Salsa en SalsaSoul?' in J. Ramos (ed.) *Compañeras: Latina Lesbians*, New York: Routledge.

Ward, G. (1998) 'Kenosis and Naming: Beyond Analogy and Towards Allegoria Amoris' in P. Heelas (ed.) *Religion, Modernity and Postmodernity*, Oxford: Blackwell.

Weeks, J. (1995) *Invented Moralities: Sexual Values in an Age of Uncertainty*, New York: University of Columbia Press.

White, L. (1967) 'The Historical Roots of our Ecological Crisis', *Science*, 10 March: 1203–7.

Whitten, N. (1976) *Sacha Runa: Ethnicity and Adaptation of Ecuatorian Jungle Quichuas*, Urbana: University of Illinois Press.

Wiesner-Hanks, M. (2000) *Christianity and Sexuality in the Early Modern World: Regulating Desire, Reforming Practice*, London: Routledge.

Wilson, E. (1993) 'Is Transgression Transgressive?' in J. Bristow and A. Wilson (eds) *Activating Theory: Lesbian, Gay, Bisexual Poilitics,* London: Lawrence and Wishart.

Wilton, T. (1996) *Finger-Licking Good: The Ins and Outs of Lesbian Sex*, London: Cassells.

Winterson, J. (1990) *Oranges are not the Only Fruit*, London: Vintage.

Wisley, B. (1973) 'Interpretaciones Populares de "Espíritu Santo"', *Allpanchis*, v: 167–185.

Žižek, S. (1994) 'Otto Weininger, or, 'Woman Doesn't Exist' in *Lacan and Love. New Formations*, 23, Summer 1994: 97–115.

INDEX

colonialism, theology of 36, 46–7, 104, 106, 123, 133–4, 167, 175*n*2; *see also* Latin America: European conquest
Columbus, Christopher 155
Cone, James 43
confession 12–14; age/gender issues 10–11; alternative views of/approaches to 23; symbolic significance 18–19
consensus 163–4
Corinne, Tee 34
Cortés, Hernán 157, 175*n*1
cross-dressing 9–10, 26
Cunningham, David 76

Daly, Mary 43, 49
dance *see* song/dance
de Certeau, Michel 73–4, 79, 80
de-incarnation 164–6
deconstructionist analysis 80
del Campo, Emiliano 169, 170
Deleuze, Gilles 22, 71–2, 73, 79, 90, 142; collaborations with F. Guattari 48, 52, 60–1, 71; (with Guattari) on 'Lobster God' 65, 66–7, 68; on Sade 169–70
Derrida, Jacques 28, 78, 80, 137
di Leonardo, M. 135
Díaz del Castillo, Bernal 157
Dickens, Charles 3
Diprose, R. 21
disaffiliation 43
Doctrine of National Security 136
Dolar, Mladen 75
Douglas, Mary 159
Dowell, Susan 113
Drucker, Peter 116–17
Dussel, Enrique 173*n*1
dyad, role in religious ritual/thought 12–14, 62, 80; alternatives to 14–17, 59

Eadie, Jo 66, 90
ecology 172*n*2
'El Cali' 145–7
Engels, Friedrich 77
epistemology 25–6
exile 173*n*8

faith, nature of 58
Flores Ochoa, Jorge 125–7
Fortescue, Adrian 136
Foucault, Michel 14, 18–19, 21, 62, 82, 87, 90, 100; *The Birth of the Clinic* 41
Freire, Paulo 18–19, 56–7, 163
friendship 48, 141–2
Fry, Peter 158, 159

Galeano, Eduardo 146
Galván, Monito 144–6, 147, 150
Genesis (Book of) 31, 82–3, 157; patriarchal teachings 7–8; Queer readings 8, 27, 84–5, 91–2, 104; *see also* Rahab; Sodom

Gibson, William, *Neuromancer* 83, 89
globalisation 4, 110, 147–8, 156, 162–5, 167; opposition to 4, 170–1
God(s): attributes of 36–8, 53, 126; as destroyer 91–2, 97; (de)territorialisation 60–2; gender-identity 75–6; as 'Lobster' 65–7, 68; omnipotence/omnipresence 51–3, 56; as 'simulator' 79; as 'Sodomite' 86–8, 98, 108–9; as 'voyeur' 38, 39–40, 42–3, 53; as 'whore' 94–5, 98–101
Goethe, Johann Wolfgang von: *Elective Affinities* 134
Goretti, Maria, Saint 141
Gospels *see* Jesus: biblical narratives
Goss, Robert 81, 93, 98, 172*n*3
Gramsci, Antonio 115
Greer, Germaine 113
Grey, Mary 17, 144, 151; *The Wisdom of Fools?* 142
Gruzinsky, Serge 154
Guattari, Félix 49–50, 53; *see also* Deleuze, Gilles
Guevara, Ché 140, 150
Guggenheim, S. 136
Guillot, Daniel 173*n*1
Gutiérrez, Gustavo 146–7

habit, role in human behaviour 50–1
Hagar (biblical character) 95, 99–100, 108
Hampson, Daphne 43
Hanks, Tom (theologian) 98, 174*n*1
Heidegger, Martin 135
hell, conceptions of 18–19, 52, 166–8
Hénaff, Marcel 26, 27, 29, 34, 35, 47–8, 85–6, 87
hermeneutics 3, 31–3; biblical 79, 80–3, 109, 142, 175*n*2; Sadean readings 26–30
Heyward, Carter 74, 141, 152
Hilst, Hilda 3, 30, 34, 97; *Rútilo Nada* 97, 105
Hitchcock, Peter 30, 52, 164
Hjelmsev, Louis 67
Holiday, Sybil: *Consensual Sadomasochism* 35
holiness 134, 141–2, 160, 164–6, 168, 170–1
Holy Spirit 124, 127; and sexuality 3
homosexuality: in indigenous cultures 158, 159–60; 'straight' attitudes to 20
Hunt, Mary 98

icons/idols *see* zemis
imperialism *see* colonialism
Irigaray, Luce 70–1, 106
irony 61
Isherwood, Lisa 17

Jagose, A. 81
Jehovah's Witnesses: persecution 32
Jesuit missions 9

.